THE MAKING OF A PARATROOPER

Airborne Training and Combat in World War II

KURT GABEL

Edited and with an Introduction
and Epilogue by WILLIAM C. MITCHELL
Foreword by THEODORE A. WILSON

UNIVERSITY PRESS OF KANSAS

Modern War Studies

Series Editors
Raymond A. Callahan
J. Garry Clifford
Jacob W. Kipp
Jay Luvaas
Theodore A. Wilson

© 1990 by the University Press of Kansas
All rights reserved

Map on page 256 © Putnam Publishing

Maps on pages 258, 259, 261, and 267 are reprinted with permission of Charles Scribner's Sons, an imprint of Macmillan Publishing Company, from *Airborne at War*, by Napier Crookenden. Copyright © 1978 Napier Crookenden.

Published by the University Press of Kansas (Lawrence, Kansas 66045), which was organized by the Kansas Board of Regents and is operated and funded by Emporia State University, Fort Hays State University, Kansas State University, Pittsburg State University, the University of Kansas, and Wichita State University

Library of Congress Cataloging-in-Publication Data

Gabel, Kurt, d. 1978.
  The making of a paratrooper.
  (Modern War Studies)
  Includes bibliographical references.
  1. World War, 1939-1945—Aerial operations, American. 2. United States. Army—Parachute troops—History—World War, 1939-1945. I. Mitchell, William C. II. Title. III. Series.
  D769.347.G33 1990   940.54'4973   89-24907
  ISBN 0-7006-0409-X (alk. paper)

British Library Cataloguing in Publication Data is available.

Printed in the United States of America
10 9 8 7 6 5 4 3 2 1

The paper used in this publication meets the minimum requirements of the American National Standard for Permanence of Paper for Printed Library Materials Z39.48-1984.

To the Officers and Men
of the
513th Parachute Infantry Regiment
Activated 1943
Deactivated 1945

Contents

Illustrations and Maps *ix*

Foreword, *Theodore A. Wilson* *xi*

Acknowledgments *xv*

Introduction, *William C. Mitchell* *xix*

Part One. Training

1 Hollywood, 1943 *3*

2 Initiation *18*

3 Fort Benning: The Frying Pan *35*

4 Parachute Basic Training I *46*

5 Parachute Basic Training II *63*

6 Jump Training: B Stage *79*

7 Jump Training: C Stage *98*

8 Jump Training: D Stage *110*

9 England *134*

Part Two. Combat

10 France and Belgium, December 1944–January 1945 *153*

11 Mande St. Etienne (Bastogne) *169*

12 Bois de Fragette *189*

13 Toward the Our River *202*

14 To Niederwiltz, Luxembourg *219*

15 Niederwiltz *234*

16 Châlons-sur-Marne, February 1945   *248*

Epilogue. One Last Great Jump: Operation Varsity,
    William C. Mitchell   *254*

Appendixes, *William C. Mitchell*

  A. The Honors of War   *273*

  B. Some Costs of War   *274*

Index   *277*

Illustrations and Maps

Photographs

1 Kurt Gabel circa 1944   *ii*

2 The Chattahoochee ferry   *47*

3 Capt. John Spears, 1946   *50*

4 A forty-foot mock-up tower   *84*

5 Learning proper exit from a C-47   *114*

6 A trooper glides down during a practice jump at Camp Mackall, 1943   *117*

7 Troopers of the 513th PIR in a mass practice jump in the Sandhills area of North Carolina   *130*

8 1st Sgt. Joe Carter   *139*

9 Sgt. J. C. Dalton, 1944   *139*

10 Joe Cooley   *143*

11 Lt. Samuel Calhoun   *174*

12 Lt. Col. A. C. Miller II   *182*

13 Getting ready for the jump across the Rhine River, 1945   *262*

14 A few hours after the jump across the Rhine River   *265*

15 A fate that befell many British gliderists and Horsa gliders   *269*

Maps

1 Situation, March 28, 1945   *256*

2 German Defensive Localities and Gun Positions, March 24, 1945   *258*

3 Operation Varsity Routes   *259*

4 British and American Dropping and Landing Zones   *261*

5 Final Positions of British and American Airborne Units, March 24, 1945   *267*

Foreword

Even before the echoes of the last round died away and the ink dried on the Japanese surrender document signed on the deck of the USS *Missouri*, the process of celebrating and dissecting America's participation in World War II began. During the fifty years since Hitler's attack on Poland plunged Europe into war, the barrage of memoirs, novels, films (and now television miniseries), documentary collections, technical treatises, popularly written histories of battles and campaigns, and scholarly studies has rarely slackened. Far more is known about this conflict—the debates over grand strategy and alliance politics, the details of theater operations and small unit actions, the attitudes and outlooks of individuals as disparate as General George S. Patton, Eleanor Roosevelt, Private Slovik, and "Rosie the Riveter," and the characteristics and performance in combat of every item of equipment employed by the armed forces of the United States—than about any other era in America's history with the possible exception of the Civil War.

When a work such as Kurt Gabel's autobiographical account of his wartime experiences comes along, nearly five decades after these events, the shock of encountering something new, of obtaining fresh and important insights, is thus intensified. This is the story of a young man inducted into the U.S. Army in 1943 and what he experienced in the barracks, on the rifle range, on the parade ground, and in the mess hall. It is the story of how Gabel became first a soldier and then a paratrooper. It would thus seem familiar, another of the many fascinating personal chronicles of combat during World War II.

But Kurt Gabel's narrative differs in two respects from most autobiographies and "told-to tales." First is its focus on the cycle of training—the stages by which Gabel was transformed from raw if eager inductee to proficient combat infantryman/paratrooper and how the unit to which he ultimately won assignment (A Company, 1st Battalion, 513th Parachute Infantry Regiment) metamorphosed from an agglomeration of young recruits, unfamiliar with each other and with their own capabilities, into a finely honed, confident, cohesive military organization. Surprisingly few of the flood of personal narratives of World War II military service give much attention to the phenomena of basic training, specialized training courses, and the efforts to prepare squads, platoons, companies, battalions, and regiments to enter combat. Aside from observations—enshrined by postwar films as platitudes—about first encounters with other GIs with odd accents, the tough-but-kindhearted drill sergeant, the bad food, the obstacle course, and the first weekend pass, these accounts typically hurry to embarkation, the subject's baptism by fire, and the hurly-burly of battle. This is understandable because the authors were in almost all cases civilians for whom the one uniquely memorable aspect of military life was combat. What came before or after the experience of "seeing the elephant" was to them of little enduring importance.

Reinforcing the idea of combat as a singular experience and one essentially unrelated to individual or unit training was the typical U.S. battalion, regimental, or divisional history. Rushing through the organizational and training phases, these histories—mostly published in the years immediately after World War II—emphasized a detailed chronological narrative of the unit's participation in battle. Notably, among the first of the Green Books (the U.S. Army's official history of World War II) to appear were two compilations based on wartime studies: *The Organization of Ground Combat Troops* (1947), by Kent Roberts Greenfield and Robert R. Palmer, and *The Procurement and Training of Ground Combat Troops* (1948), by Robert R. Palmer, Bell I. Wiley, and William R. Keast. These works focused on the vital importance of recruitment, personnel selection, organization, and training, logistical support, troop deployment, and replacement and unit reconstitution policies, especially for a force built from the ground up as was the U.S. Army in World War II. But the lessons these works offered were not followed either by historians or by the army establishment, principally, it appears, because their implementation would have been costly and politically awkward. Only in the past decade have the direct links between individual and unit training, personnel turbulence (with consequent effects on morale and unit cohesion), and combat performance come to the fore with the publication of such works as Martin Van Creveld's *Fighting Power: German and U.S. Army Performance, 1939–1945* (1982), William P. Leinbaugh and John D. Campbell's *The Men of Company K* (1985), and John Sloan Brown's *Draftee Division: A Study of the 88th Infantry Division, First All-Selective Service Division into Combat in World War II* (1985). In its special way Kurt Gabel's memoir contributes to this reawakening of interest in how and why some Americans performed superbly during combat.

The second crucial difference between the great majority of World War II memoirs and Gabel's account is his perspective. This comes in part from his having written his recollections some thirty years after the events he describes. But he also wrote about his World War II experiences for an unusual reason: with the deliberate aim, as William C. Mitchell notes, of "discovering and explaining what makes a soldier and, perhaps more important, what produces a first-rate combat unit such as he knew during World War II." Gabel wanted to know why his unit turned out as well as it did. Although never referring directly to S. L. A. Marshall's classic study of the American soldier's behavior during combat in World War II, *Men against Fire* (1947), Gabel clearly was familiar with its principal argument: that the American combat infantryman who "actually fired at enemy positions or at personnel with rifles, carbines, grenades, BARS, or machine guns during the course of an entire engagement" was a rare bird indeed. Marshall's assertion—now being subjected to serious challenge on methodological grounds—that only a minority (variously estimated at between 15 and 25 percent) of the troops in any unit actually did the fighting reflected basic assumptions about the training and employment of American combat troops that had guided U.S. personnel selection, training, and replacement policies during and after World War II. As had many other combat veterans, Gabel refused to accept these judgments about the lack of initiative and self-confidence, poor fighting qualities, and low unit morale supposedly characteristic of American troops. His own experience taught him otherwise, and it is testimony deserving of careful attention. The Kurt Gabel who admitted in an interview for John Toland's *Battle: The Story of the Bulge* (1959) that during his first exposure to combat in the Ardennes he had no desire to fire his rifle was convinced by his own subsequent experience that Americans, properly trained, highly motivated, and skillfully led, would fight and fight superbly.

The soldiers whose fighting qualities Kurt Gabel extolled represented, of course, elite troops. From their inception the paratroops obtained a disproportionate share of the physically and intellectually best-qualified recruits available to the Army Ground Forces. Precisely how significant the composition of such units was to their success is a matter for debate. But because of the special skills and training requirements associated with the paratroops, units such as the 513th Parachute Infantry Regiment did not undergo the constant personnel changes that beset most U.S. infantry units organized during the middle of the war. Gabel and his buddies experienced stability and continuity; therefore it is not surprising that he finds leadership and unit esprit to be the primary ingredients of outstanding performance in battle. That seems to be a matter upon which Gabel and the U.S. Army today agree.

Theodore A. Wilson

Acknowledgments

Those who live in the past not only miss out on an exciting present but also run the risk of boring if not annoying others, especially those who cannot possibly relate to that bygone time. Many friends, colleagues, and others have surely had their patience taxed as I took off time from my normal academic pursuits to work on this book. Their understanding will, I believe, be amply rewarded by reading this wonderful military memoir, a memoir not only of its author, Kurt Gabel, but of all who served with him in the 513th Parachute Infantry Regiment.

In preparing Kurt Gabel's manuscript for publication, I had the good fortune of renewing old military friendships as well as acquiring new friends. Each one has been helpful, often at personal cost. I want to express my appreciation to some of them without at the same time discounting what others have contributed to my work, morale, and memories of distant places and unbelievable events.

Among those who knew Kurt Gabel and shared their memories, I especially wish to thank Joe Carter (1st sergeant, Headquarters, 1st Battalion). His knowledge of the 513th Parachute Infantry Regiment is without equal, as has been his generosity in providing information, photographs, personal impressions, and so on. Col. John Spears, Kurt's first company commander, has been a fountainhead of 513th history and lore. Spears, who went on to a long and distinguished career in the airborne and the Green Berets and fought in three wars, to this day believes that the height of his career was achieved as CO of Company A. That such a man who has served his nation so admirably should offer me constant encouragement is one of my fondest treasures. Other members of Company A and 1st Battalion Headquarters who served with Kurt have also aided and encouraged my efforts to celebrate their comrade. Robert L. MacDonald (A Company) of Texas shared his remembrances as well as supplying important information. J. R. Cooley (Headquarters, 1st Battalion) also knew Kurt well enough to appear in these pages. Not only did he offer memories and photographs, he also became a friend. Jake Dalton (sergeant, Headquarters, 1st Battalion), lent important materials for my use. And Ben Scherer (A Company) gave his materials and enthusiasm to the project. Although Maj. Samuel Calhoun, Ret. (platoon leader in F Company), who led the bayonet attack depicted in this book was asked to comment on the episode, he volunteered, as he has so often in other matters for the 17th Airborne Association, his rich recollections of service with both the 513th Regiment and the 101st Airborne Division. I am most indebted to Sam and now count him as a friend. Lt. Col. Kenneth L. Booth of California, former CO of the 466th Parachute Field Artillery Battalion, has also been most helpful. Although not a member of the 1st Battalion, my fellow Eugenean and esteemed friend Ernie Rosen (E Company) and his wife, Phyllis, have been staunch supporters of my work. I owe much to them, not the least of which is their proximity.

In my quest to learn about Kurt's civilian career during the 1970s, I had the good fortune of meeting Caroline Anderson and Robert Slimmon, Kurt's coworker and supervisor, respectively, of the Planning Department of Monterey County, California. Because both worked closely with Kurt for several years and knew him well, they were able and disposed to answer my inquiries. Kurt was blessed indeed to have labored with such thoughtful, competent, and friendly associates.

Although I have been enriched by all who have aided me, I am especially indebted to two people, one of whom figures prominently in these pages; I refer to Col. Allen C. Miller II and his wife, Jean. Because I served as an enlisted man in the 1st Battalion and "Ace" was commanding officer of the 2d Battalion, I did not get to know him; I only saw him from a distance and knew of him. In fact, I did not meet the Millers until September 1987. Since that time, however, we have become fast friends. The colonel and Jean represent all that is best in our military tradition. That a nation should produce, let alone deserve, such able and dedicated servants is among the more remarkable fortunes bestowed upon us. I was honored to be in the same regiment with Ace during the war—today I am confounded that this splendid gentleman and former fighting man and his wife are my friends.

Thanks must go to Larry Malley of Duke University Press for putting me in contact with the University Press of Kansas. The press staff's editorial requirements were matched only by their dedication in producing a book worthy of Kurt's memory. I also want to express my appreciation to Professor Theodore A. Wilson for his highly perceptive foreword to this book.

This book was originally typed by Kurt Gabel, who, although, not a professional typist, did an excellent job. The final copy was produced on a word processor by Cheryl Looney. Cheryl's patience, good humor, and kindness are every bit equal to her considerable professional skills. When asked whether she was having problems with the manuscript, Cheryl unwittingly paid Kurt his highest compliment: She said the typing was going slowly neither because the manuscript was difficult to follow nor because it contained so many unfamiliar German names, quotation marks, and so on but because it was one of the few manuscripts she had typed that she actually read as she went along. What more can I say?

William C. Mitchell

Introduction

Kurt Gabel died May 5, 1978, leaving an unfinished manuscript detailing his three years (1943-1945) as an enlisted man in the paratroops. This memoir pertains to Kurt's service both in A Company, First Battalion, and in Battalion Headquarters Company, 513th Parachute Infantry Regiment (PIR), of the 17th Airborne Division. The 17th was one of five airborne divisions (the others include the 11th, 13th, 82d, and 101st) organized during the war; all but one (the 13th) saw intensive and often prolonged combat. The battle record established by these divisions is unparalleled and provides some of the truly legendary chapters in American military history.

More than twenty-five years after his World War II airborne experiences and after a distinguished military career, Major Gabel retired in 1969 and became a civil servant employed by Monterey County in California. As an investigator for the Planning Department, he was authorized to examine alleged violations of zoning ordinances and prepare files and cases for adjudication. Gabel's associates and supervisor were all highly impressed by his diligent and meticulous investigations and sensible, fair-minded resolution of differences among interested parties. Kurt was as dedicated and able a civil servant as he was a military man.

Despite having lived in this country since 1939 and served in its armed forces for twenty-five years, Kurt's Old World background exerted itself in his civilian work and home life. As some of his former colleagues observed, Kurt projected an aura of European civility, quiet deference, and privacy. He was, apparently, the only member of his office to wear a coat and tie every day. He was unfailing in his attention to the courtesies of daily life, something hard to imagine given the informalities of a Californian existence. He was also a highly private man for whom family meant a great deal. And, although not wealthy, he managed to live well in the affluent residential area of Pebble Beach.

In 1975, a few years after he began his civilian employment, Gabel became a "weekend writer," intent upon discovering and explaining what makes a soldier and, perhaps more important, what produces a first-rate combat unit such as he knew during World War II. He gave expression to his concern in a letter to a potential publisher:

> If I may, I'd like to explain why I am attempting this book. Subsequent to the events described I remained in the Army. During the Korean conflict I became an officer and was assigned to the 187th Airborne Regimental Combat Team as a rifle platoon leader and later as the S-2 of its 1st Battalion. As Battalion S-2 I noticed certain misconceptions about troop motivation on the part of many officers who had not served as enlisted infantrymen which sometimes resulted in avoidable morale problems.
>
> In post-combat assignments, particularly at HQ Seventh Army in Germany, this deficiency in assessment of the individual enlisted man continued to bother me.
>
> By the mid sixties, when the quality of the Army was allowed to deteriorate, I thought it might be a good idea for someone to write an illustrative account about the motivation of the individual rifleman and of the requisite ingredients for a superior line unit like the 513th Parachute Infantry Regiment described in my narrative. (Since its deactivation in 1945, I have not seen another organization remotely like it, including Special Forces in which I served on my terminal assignment.)

Kurt approached his tasks not as a military sociologist, philosopher, or military historian but as an experienced soldier who had fought in two wars, including his experiences as an airborne officer in the Korean War. Although he drew upon his extensive background as both an enlisted man and an officer, his World War II regiment served as his model.

Kurt answered his questions with a narrative or memoir recounting the history of the regiment from his perspective. It is a unique document because Kurt was as highly conscious of his intellectual mission as of his vivid personal experiences. Despite having written this memoir long after the actual events, Kurt displayed an extraordinarily accurate memory for striking, crucial, and even seemingly unimportant detail; indeed, one might easily claim that he had a photographic memory. That memory had room for both technical detail and social interaction whether in training or combat. Despite this rare talent, Kurt honored the historian's discipline by a minute and painstaking checking of names, places, dates, and so on. And we who shared his experiences can readily testify to the overall authenticity of the records he composed.

But this memoir is more than an accurate depiction of long-ago wartime events; it constitutes a moving testament to the valor of the airborne regiments, to their gut-wrenching courage in facing the extreme demands of service—ever-present fear, exhaustion, injury, and all-too-frequent death. Kurt understood fully and valued these paratroopers' sense of community, esprit de corps and élan because he had been a highly impressionistic, idealistic youth whose only aspiration was to be one of them. He fully appreciated the means employed by the Jump School and the Regiments to mold such eagerness into a dedicated and well-honed unit.

That Kurt idealized the military comes as no surprise to those who knew him. As a German-Jewish émigré in 1939, he was always keenly aware of the sharp contrasts between the country of his birth and that of his citizenship. Given his background (detailed in Chapter 1), it is understandable that he was close to his mother, his regiment, and the profession of arms. Like all idealists, Kurt was most disturbed by the failures of those he most admired. Although he enjoyed a notable and satisfying military career, it seems that its pinnacle was reached at its beginning, a summit never again to be achieved, not even with the famed 187th paratroops during the Korean War nor with the Green Berets later.

We should not dwell too much on the speculative because Kurt was not a philosopher. He was, however, a thoughtful man and above all a masterly writer. Even though—or perhaps because—English was not his native language, he acquired a thorough mastery of both written and spoken English. His ability to recapture the exact, colorful lingo of the airborne is just superb. His exposition is always direct, lucid, and compelling and never forced, didactic, or even grammatically incorrect—a major achievement for one whose first language was German! Kurt's death has deprived us of a first-rate writer, one who might well have gone on to achieve major status on matters both military and otherwise.

After a generation or more of cynical war novels, memoirs, and movies replete with gore and sex and antiheroes, Gabel's views may seem simple and naive. His sole intent was to become a first-rate soldier and, more particularly, a paratrooper. His was an odyssey of wonderment, a renewal of faith in what young men can accomplish if only they have the heart. Gabel set out to discover the wellsprings of airborne commitment and achievement on the battlefield. And, although his innocence could have produced clichés and moralizing, he never succumbed to the temptation. Given the direct narrative style, his literary achievement is all the more remarkable. His answers emerge without the self-conscious preaching or pretentious yet banal philosophizing of most who seek meaning in war. Gabel never intrudes on the narrative; there is no egotism, no "look at me." Nor is there an endless repertoire of war stories by a garrulous old vet. Instead we have the superb story of a proud regiment preparing for war and then its immersion in the unrelenting demands of combat. One need not have been a member of the 513th Parachute Infantry Regiment or of the paratroops in general to understand and prize the trials and tribulations of which Kurt writes; they are universal experiences for all who fought in World War II or any other war. And yet they will be fascinating to those too young to have personally known the tragedies and triumphs of such endeavors.

Gabel did not live long enough to complete his book. He intended to write a chapter on the last battle fought by the 17th Airborne, a battle and jump in which Kurt participated but as a member of Division Headquarters rather than with his beloved 513th. He had been transferred to the counterintelligence unit of Division Headquarters after the Battle of the Bulge, no doubt because of his linguistic skills as well as superior knowledge of the Germans. In any event, I have assumed responsibility for "completing" the book by providing an account of Operation Varsity entitled "One Last Great Jump," a heading I firmly believe would have won Kurt's approval.

Rather than mimic Kurt's style—something I neither wish nor could in any way do—I have written an impersonal account of the operation, explaining why it came about, how it was conducted, and, most important, its consequences in terms of costs and gains. I do not provide intimate, detailed accounts of small units and individual paratroopers because they would be based not on Kurt's experiences and memory but on mine. Nevertheless, I hope I have provided important knowledge about a major airborne operation of which Kurt was justifiably proud and about which he would have sung our praises.

Readers should also be informed of my role as editor. I have resisted the constant temptation to insert editor's comments and limited myself to correcting errors—factual and grammatical—that Kurt would have, sooner or later, caught as he prepared the manuscript for publication. I have also assumed responsibility for eliminating the opening chapter in the original manuscript. It recalled a somewhat painful event in Captain Gabel's service as a briefing officer in the Civil Affairs Section of the American Military Government (7th Army) serving in occupied Germany during the mid-1950s. After World War II and before his return to the airborne during the Korean War, Gabel served in Germany in the Criminal Investigation Division of the army. During these two tours of duty in Germany, Gabel began to worry about the quality of the U.S. military, a concern that focused on the role of the officer corps and its misunderstanding of the enlisted men who do the fighting. He felt that by writing his memoir of the 513th Parachute Infantry Regiment he could somehow teach the next generation of officers what it means to become a soldier. Although Gabel's goal was laudable and the chapter did have an integrity of its own, it added little to the subsequent narrative and could easily be eliminated. It is entirely possible that Kurt would have agreed.

I have also taken the liberty of attaching two appendixes containing useful information about the 17th Airborne and the 513th Parachute Infantry Regiment; various maps that should supply a more graphic setting for my chapter; and a number of photographs, including three of Kurt Gabel during World War II.

I close by noting that I am deeply honored that I was once a member of Kurt's battalion and regiment. My fondest wish is that I could have known him—we were so close in space and, above all, in spirit.

William C. Mitchell

Part One
Training

1
Hollywood, 1943

"Greetings." From the way people talked about it, I had imagined the word in Gothic letters dominating a parchment. Actually, it was only the second largest word in the middle of a plain sheet of paper headed "Order to Report for Induction." A stamp in the upper left corner identified the local draft board in Los Angeles County to which the president of the United States directed me to report on the eighteenth day of May in 1943.

Unlike a great many men greeted in this manner, I was delighted with my induction order. When I was still in high school, I had tried to enlist but was turned down. The problem was that I had been born in Germany of German parents on October 8, 1923; since coming to the United States with my mother and stepfather in 1938, I hadn't applied for naturalization. So I was not only an alien but an enemy alien. An enemy alien could not enlist, I was told. But he could be drafted, and he could volunteer for induction; so I had volunteered.

There were other things an enemy alien could not do. He could not join the Navy or the Marine Corps, and he could not become a pilot. Pilots of the Army Air Corps were commissioned officers, and an enemy alien could not be an officer. Only the Army would have me. And the Army, at least to my contemporaries at Hollywood High School in the glamour capital of the world, consisted of the unglamorous pool of rejects who were not fit for anything else. Indeed, the word "Army" conjured up visions of drab, dusty lines of stupidly plodding infantry—and what could be more unglamorous than that? Was Clark Gable in the infantry? Was Jimmie Stewart? Was Robert Taylor? Not that we cared about these and other celebrities who started their military careers as captains and majors and colonels. Only the girls thought of Gable as a real Air Corps captain and of Taylor as a real naval lieutenant. The girls! Christ Almighty, what can you expect from a species that would scream with hysterical delight when emaciated Frank Sinatra in his floppy tuxedo moaned into his microphone?

Ah, the girls of Hollywood High! Perhaps they did it just to annoy us robust boys. Surely most of them were simply teasing. Still, no varsity letterman would want to tell his girl or his friends that he was going into the infantry. That would be almost as bad as saying he would wait until he was drafted or that he had been classified 4-F. No. Just as you couldn't very well stay home during this war, you couldn't join the wrong service. Varsity went into the Navy V-12 or into the Air Corps or into the Marines. The Army was for draftees and rejects from the other services.

By the middle of 1942, however, there appeared within the Army a hero-figure closely approximating the stature of a fighter pilot: the paratrooper. He was my salvation. I could not become a fighter pilot, but I would become a paratrooper.

When I announced to my classmates that spring in 1942 that I had volunteered for induction, I quickly added that I would go into the paratroops. My status was secure.

But my orders to report did not come for almost a year.

School became unbearable. Each week someone left for boot camp at San Diego or flight training in Texas or wherever else their enlistments took them. Their goodbyes were expressions of benign superiority as they reassured the rest of us that our turn would also come sooner or later. Week after week the cream of the junior and senior classes was skimmed off by the war. And still no induction orders for me.

My mother had thought I should attend high school to rid myself of a not-too-heavy foreign accent. By 1942 I was bilingual in German and English; I wanted something other than education to pass the time until I could jump out of airplanes (I had never been on an airplane). So I left school and found a job.

It was an ideal job and I was afraid that I might not get it when I informed my prospective boss that I was waiting to be inducted. I was to work as a "clearing house rider" for the California Bank at its headquarters on Spring Street in downtown Los Angeles. My very title rang with a wild-west connotation that instantly intrigued me; it was just the type of experience I needed to prepare me to be an American paratrooper. I was to be one of six motorcycle riders who picked up checks at branch offices and delivered them to the clearing house downtown.

The motorcycle was an imposing machine that worried me momentarily. It was a Harley-Davidson "80," the type used by the Los Angeles police in the 1940s. (It finally went out of production and was replaced as the heaviest machine on the road by the Harley "74.") For someone five feet seven inches high, weighing one hundred eighteen pounds, riding it seemed akin to riding an elephant. Luckily I had owned an old Indian Scout "45" that I bought after my Model A Ford died. It rarely ran, but I was always working on it and it maintained my status as a "hot-rodder" without the considerable expense of keeping a Model A in dual carburetors, milled heads, and high-lift cams. Though it was only half as big as the Harley, I could at least say that I had riding experience.

My first ride on the big Harley was from the underground garage up a circular ramp into heavy Spring Street traffic. I had no idea in advance how powerful the machine was; it was nothing short of miraculous that I roared up, out, and over and came to a safe though abrupt stop at the Eighth and Hill traffic light. The head rider who was supposed to check me out came alongside. "OK, you've made your point," he growled. "But there ain't gonna be no hot-roddin' on *this* job. Now just go back in nice and easy, and no more goddamn stunt riding." After only a couple of days, the machine and I had become one.

No motorcyclist is worthy of the name unless he wears a black leather jacket and a visored cap. It took me hours to select and purchase these vital items. Back home I put them on and while trying out various nonchalant and lethal attitudes before my bedroom mirror, my bliss was interrupted by my mother's voice behind me: "What's all this?" Those damn carpets and the not-quite-closed door to my room had given her this embarrassing edge.

I turned red and blurted, "Just trying these on. I got a job as a motorcycle rider for the California Bank and I'm moving out of this house Saturday. Leni has rented me a room." I turned away from the mirror, took off cap and jacket, and faced my mother.

"Motorcycle rider?" she said incredulously. I was sure her dismay was not so much over the potential danger of riding a motorcycle in Los Angeles traffic as over the image of her son in such a plebeian street-job not unlike that of a truck driver or letter carrier. There she stood, handsome and trim in an expensive beige suit, just back from afternoon coffee with the "girls" at the Farmers Market; her carefully plucked eyebrows over large, green eyes were arched in an expression of utter disapproval. She knew that I had been invited for an interview at the California Bank but had had no idea for what job.

At the time of her marriage to my stepfather, she had for some time been executive secretary to the governing board of the Export Bank Warburg in Hamburg. It was a job tailor-made for her, requiring a good-looking woman of good family who could speak French and English and blend into the Berlin-Paris-Brussels-London café society. Her constant travels for the bank were the prime reason I lived with my grandparents. Naturally, a bank interview for her son conjured up visions of a golden-tanned young executive in a white dinner jacket standing on some terrace of the Côte d'Azur after having accomplished a grand international financial coup. The leather-jacket show here in her Hollywood apartment was therefore simply grotesque.

"Motorcycle rider?" she repeated furiously. "The little time you have left before they call you into the Army you want to squander like that? The least you can do is to learn something decent so that you have a head start after the war!" Neither her fury nor her arguments touched me. The furthest I could see into the future was the day I would be earning my parachutist wings in the Army. Meanwhile I would be working and living independently, as an embryonic paratrooper should.

My mother recognized that she was confronted with an accomplished fact, that the end of an era had arrived, and that further discussion was pointless. The next practical step would be to help me move my things and so to make the best of a situation she could not control.

Since there had been constant traffic between my new landlady's house and our apartment—she here for tea, my mother there for bridge, both constantly thrown together at parties and at that most popular of all Hollywood hangouts, the coffee-and-cake patios of the Farmers Market—the transition of my move to Leni's house was nearly painless. After my clothes had been hung in the closet and my new bed made, my mother surveyed the room and said to her friend, "I'll check on him tomorrow. If you need anything, call." She was talking as though she expected Leni to be an extension of herself.

I slept the sleep of the righteous that night and was the first one up the next morning. Black breeches tucked neatly into shiny boots, wearing my gray turtleneck sweater, I sat at the family breakfast table with Leni, her husband, John, and two-year-old Peter, their son. "Enter the master race," Leni had said as I walked in. Her husband had added, "You'll be a POW before you get to work." After breakfast I put on my leather jacket and cap, experimented with a few more attitudes before the mirror, and clattered out into the cool Los Angeles morning—to the *bus* stop at Fairfax and Beverly. But my Harley was waiting.

What a friendly send-off that had been! I remembered my unhappy mornings shortly after arriving in the United States when I left our house at 4:00 A.M., leaving everybody asleep. At my mother's insistence, in most un-American leather shorts I was pursuing that most American of occupation—delivering newspapers. The aim was to acclimatize me to a new way of life. But I utterly failed at the monthly endeavor of asking adults for money. To each customer I would make my little deprecating German bow and with my head lowered would mention something about the date, absolutely consumed with embarrassment. If the customer didn't realize what I was trying to get at, I would slink back to my bicycle and take off, dreading to face the next subscriber. At the end of such an early morning's effort, I would find myself in an emotional shambles, knowing that the next day I would have to repeat the performance for two customers who had not understood my tactful hints and for five who had not been at home. After a few months my mother said I didn't have to deliver papers any more.

Meanwhile she'd heard about the Boy Scouts of America and had found a troop that met near where we lived. She explained to me that the Boy Scouts were the national equivalent of the *Hitler Jugend* and that I might make some friends among the members. In Hamburg at age nine or so I'd seen the older boys of the Hitler Youth, perfectly drilled, marching in parades. I couldn't join them until I was fourteen. Well, I joined the scout troop in Los Angeles and was appalled. They couldn't march. They sang songs but not marching songs. And they goofed off. The leader would say a pleading "Hey, fellas," instead of a commanding and enforcing *"Ach-tung!"* So I unjoined the Boy Scouts.

Now I was to get *paid* for riding a Harley!

At the bank an hour later, when I swung into the saddle of Number Four, Joe's wink in my direction told me that all was well, including my uniform.

It took four days to learn the office and maintenance routine and my traveling routes. The latter were ideal. The Hollywood–Beverly Hills was by far the most glamorous of all the runs Calbank had to offer, one that had a special allure for me because Ruth Walton worked on that route.

Ruth had been in my class in Hollywood High. She was now a senior and worked after school as a cashier in the Egyptian Theater, a movie theater of the "Grauman" variety on Hollywood Boulevard, a U-turn away from the Calbank branch at Highland Avenue.

Ruth was a slender, graceful, almost delicate girl with long, golden hair and gentle, blue eyes. But she was the best student in our class. She was my not-so-secret love of the moment, and I was absolutely petrified whenever I had the nerve to talk to her, which had not been often. Once at school for current events, I had given a talk on the evolution of the German Army from the *Reichswehr* to the *Wehrmacht*, much embellished by vignettes of the garrison training of the Seventy-Sixth Infantry Regiment, the Hamburg regiment in which both my father and grandfather had served. My accent had pretty much disappeared, I think. My classmates had been spellbound. I had thought, "If I've got *them*, I must have got *her*, too." But how would I know?

Well, in the yard during recess, Ruth came up to the group of boys I was standing with and said, "Kurt, may I ask you something?" My knees went weak as I left the security of the group of boys and croaked, "Of course." We, just the two of us, walked to a bench and sat down. "What was school like in Germany?" I spent the remaining recess time talking.

I told her about my troubles with math even in elementary school, and how my mother had engaged an absolutely petrifying tutoress for me. My knees knocked as in abject misery I approached the steep steps to her high, narrow dwelling after school. It became clear quite early that I was not the type to enter law, medicine, engineering, scholarship—in short, I sadly lacked the intellectual endowments of a professional man. The only things I was enthusiastic about were the Hitler Youth and my grandfather's horses, huge dray animals that he kept for use with his imported cheese business. So when my mother married, and I found it all but impossible to adjust to life with parents rather than with grandparents, four aunts (who vied for the privilege of playing with me throughout my childhood), and two uncles, I was sent to what would probably be called a trade school in the United States. The subject was agriculture. I lived for some years at that school in Hanover, not too far from Hamburg to preclude spending vacations there but staying most of the year behind a high red-brick wall that shielded the shady grounds from the street.

Talking to Ruth about these matters came easily, but I felt I was staring at her and tried not to, which only made matters worse. I silently cursed the blood that went to my head. When the bell rang and we got up, Ruth said, "Thank you, Kurt. I'd like to hear more sometime, OK?"

"Any time, Ruth," I said and hurried away on winged feet. As I rejoined my little group on the way back to class, I endured with total equanimity the "Well, *finally* . . . . Casanova made it. . . . Hey, you didn't even faint. . . . She *loves* you" jeers of my so-called friends.

I was too shy to ask Ruth to the junior prom and took one of her girlfriends instead. It was a miserable evening. I didn't know how to dance, and I couldn't keep my eyes off Ruth waltzing in the arms of a musclebound varsity letterman. I told my date several times that it was fun to be with her, but I'm sure I said it too often and too absentmindedly for her to believe me, and I never dared ask her out again.

And now I walked out of the California Bank branch at Hollywood Boulevard and Highland Avenue, a small bank sack full of canceled checks in my hand. I stowed the sack in one of the Harley saddlebags, cranked the machine up, and made a screeching U-turn. In front of the Egyptian, I swung the motorcycle perpendicular to the curb, gunned the engine once, and shut it off. Casually in leather I walked over to the cashier's window from which Ruth had been solemnly watching me. "Hi, Ruth," I said, leaning on the ticket counter without any idea as to what to say next. But I didn't care. Here I was in black leather, and behind me stood that great machine ready to take me thundering back into Hollywood traffic—so damn the torpedoes!

"Kurt! What in the name of sanity is *this*?" asked Ruth, her steady eyes disapprovingly going from me to the Harley and back.

"My new job," I said jauntily. "Riding for the California Bank. There's one right across the street and so I thought I'd see how the world is treating you."

"Well, this is great, this job. I don't suppose I'll ever be discovered for a starlet, but it's probably just as well not to get any closer to the movie business than this, anyway."

"Before you do get discovered," I said recklessly, "would you go to the Palladium with me Saturday? They've got Benny Goodman and a good dinner."

Ruth smiled her gentle smile and said, "I'd like to very much. Are we going on that?" she pointed to the motorcycle.

"Oh . . ." I said and turned red. "God Almighty. On *that*? Un, no, of course not. Got a car I can borrow. Well, un, pick you up at seven?"

"Swell. Do you know where I live?"

Did I know where she lived! I could have walked to her house blindfolded from anywhere within the greater Los Angeles area. "Yep. See you Saturday." I waved, swaggered back to the Harley, kicked it into a roar, and was off in a cloud of lilac blossoms.

The branch at Vine Street was my next stop. I was secretly smug about being a member of this community, about being on the periphery of the movie world. Practically all my classmates at Hollywood High had, in one way or another, been touched by this world. A very few, like Richard Jaeckel, had entered it, soaring beyond our ken. Some, like Bob Falkenberg, were "related" to it but managed to remain human. Others were like Bob's brother Tom, who, dressed like a cross between a great white hunter and a cowboy, would take a leopard cub for a walk along Hollywood Boulevard of a Saturday noon. Many had parents working in the technical or creative support fields of the movie industry, and most had at least one friend or acquaintance somewhere in that industry.

And on Saturday nights we, the "locals," would cruise the glamour stretch of the Boulevard between Highland Avenue and Vine Street, six of us packed into a "chopped" Model A to sneer at the tourists, superior in our knowledge that we belonged and they would have to go back to Podunk. But we didn't feel superior to the servicemen crowding Hollywood Boulevard at night. They were safe from our sneers. On foot and up close, these visitors in OD or khaki or dress blues could very well have been sneering at *us*. Once before my motorcycle experience, when I briefly held an after-school job as a telegraph messenger and was required to wear the Western Union uniform, I was stopped by a group of four soldiers reeling out of the Brown Derby. "Hey, buddy," one of them had called drunkenly as he grabbed my arm. "What outfit you with?" It went straight to the intestines and stayed there for weeks. I quit my job the next day and deserted the Hollywood streets for quite a while.

But those experiences were forgotten, or at least safely tucked away, as I clicked the ignition off, put the kickstand down, and dismounted from the machine at the Crossroads of the World. I walked into the bank toward the head cashier's desk, secure in my niche of this unique part of the universe, and wondering if Ruth would ever be a star.

But I was nervous on Saturday. I had managed to get Palladium tickets through one of my "in" friends, a remarkable feat even when one reserved such tickets weeks in advance and nearly impossible on short notice. My landlord, an émigré from Nazi Germany like most of my mother's friends, whom I always addressed as "Herr Guttmann" (unlike his considerably younger wife, Leni, whom I called by her first name), had agreed to lend me the family car after hearing of this most important date. He had offered the car without my even asking for it, which reinforced my friendly feelings for the man.

He was in his late fifties and, I thought, ill-suited to be the husband of the blond Berlin girl only about ten years my senior. Nor was the name "Guttmann" his any longer. First it had been Americanized to "Goodman." Then, through the machinations of my young landlady, her son, Peter, had at the age of ten months been given the role of "baby" in the film "Brother Rat," a Hollywood version of cadet life at the Virginia Military Institute. The studio had given Peter the middle initial "B" and had coyly shortened his last name to "Good." *"Pappi"* Guttmann, as he was called in Hollywood émigré circles, had resignedly accepted the new name and Leni became known as the mother of Peter B. Good, friend of movie stars, and the source of delectable inside-studio information. Not that she had an "exclusive"; members of her crowd did, after all, have such acquaintances as Peter Lorre, Conrad Veidt, and Hedy Lamarr (who, as Hedwig Kiessler, had briefly been a classmate of my mother's in Hamburg, I was told). But Leni was directly connected with the largest studio in Hollywood and would at the drop of an olive into a martini glass tell the girls all the news that was not fit to print, and nobody was ever in a position to dispute her stories.

John Good, formerly Hans Guttmann, was of a different breed. He was a banker, a quiet, gentle man of considerable intelligence with a sense of humor that was almost British. He insisted unself-consciously on good form in his house. Dinner was invariably served in the dining room. Napkins were of linen and rolled into silver napkin rings. Expensive flatware was arranged next to the plates in the European manner. The form was no different from what I had felt so uncomfortable with in the house of my stepfather, but here there was a touch of "family" vaguely reminiscent of my grandparents' house. I felt at home and somehow allied with this man as he made devastating, hilarious remarks during the infrequent pauses in Leni's Farmers-Market-and-studio outpourings. Often Leni's stories were demolished in gales of laughter, both hers and mine, while *Pappi* sat quietly with his gentle smile, sipping his wine. And not for a moment did *Pappi* think there was anything outlandish in riding a motorcycle for a living or in wanting to be a paratrooper.

It was time to get dressed. I had just finished my shower and had reluctantly admitted to myself that I did not need a shave for at least another three days. Deciding what to wear was uncomplicated enough. I had only two suits and four ties; the rest of my wardrobe, except for a sports jacket and slacks combination, was mostly motorcycle related. I took out my gray flannel double-breasted suit, a conservative blue and red tie, and one of my three white shirts. The only pair of purely "civilian" shoes I had were polished to a high gloss. All dressed, I stepped out and walked into the *Herrenzimmer*, the paneled, leathery smoking room-cum-library peculiar to the German household.

I warmly remembered my grandfather's *Herrenzimmer*. He was a member of the prestigious Senate of Hamburg and would hold committee meetings in his own room of his own home on the Alster. The *Herrenzimmer* was his invariable retreat after dinner, with or without committee meetings, which neither his wife nor any of his many daughters dared enter, even on the most pressing business. But one evening when I was four or five years old, I took my courage in both hands and timidly, experimentally, walked into the sanctum sanctorum, closing the door behind me, seating myself in a stuffed leather chair, and sniffing as silently as possible the smoke of his fine cigar. He looked at me over his newspaper and nodded! I nodded back and breathed more freely as he returned to his paper. I sat motionless, masculine, and adult for at least five minutes before standing up, exchanging nods again, and leaving as quietly as I had entered. This became a nightly, highly satisfying ritual.

Leni had joined *Pappi* in his *Herrenzimmer* for a predinner cocktail while listening to Bach, *Pappi*'s favorite German.

"How do I look?" I asked, clicking my heels and bowing in the German manner.

Leni rolled her eyes and chuckled, "Devastating. Absolutely wasted on that silly high school girl. *Pappi*, I think I should take our little Kurti out myself, don't you?"

I was just old enough to be flustered by innuendos like this, which had not been the first Leni had made. *Pappi* laughed softly and said, "You really should. And you could take Peter along." We all laughed and *Pappi* handed me the car keys. "Here. Go before Leni gets dressed and leaves me." His kindly smile was mostly in his eyes; the thick mustache that made him look like a benign walrus crossed with an owl effectively hid both his lips.

"Many thanks, Herr Guttmann," I said and shook his hand. Then I bent over Leni and kissed her on the cheek. "Better luck next time, Leni," I said suavely.

Leni made a barking noise and said, *"Teufel!"*

The Guttmann car, a staid four-door Pontiac, was immaculate, just like the Guttmann's house. I had sense enough to handle it carefully. At precisely seven o'clock I rolled up in front of the white two-story house I knew so well from the outside. A tall, friendly looking man with graying, close-cropped hair opened the front door, saying, "I guess you *are* German. Right smack on the dot." He stuck out his hand and said, "I'm the father. C'mon in."

"How do you do, sir," I said, feeling a bit safer. From a pleasant, silver-gray tapestried hall I was shown into a rather large living room, generally of the same hue, with a raised fireplace at the far end. Ruth was sitting on one of the hearth pillows, much to my surprise. I had expected to be interviewed first, with Ruth coming down the stairway, "looking lovely in her silky white gown," like Ann Rutherford meeting Mickey Rooney, a respectable few minutes after the conclusion of parental screening.

Ruth cocked her head, came over to me, said "hi," took my hand, and led me to one of two overstuffed white chairs flanking an enormous white couch. It was all very unceremonious and, in spite of the luxurious aspect of the silver-and-white living room, somehow easy and homespun.

Her mother, slender and almost as good-looking as my own, got up from her chair against all precepts of European etiquette and held out her hand. "This is Kurt Gabel," Ruth said as I shook her mother's hand.

"Mrs. Walton?" I asked, suddenly overcome with an unaccountable self-confidence. She arched her eyebrows questioningly and kept a grip on my hand. "Well, I wasn't sure whether Ruth had an older sister. . . ."

She turned to Ruth, still holding my hand. "German, you said? Sounds more like blarney," and turning to me again, she said, "Sit for a moment." She had a nice, easy laugh. "Think we ought to trust him?" she queried her husband.

He grinned at me and asked, "What else have you got up your sleeve?"

"Well," I replied, still full of that warm, secure feeling, "this sort of thing works wonders with *my* mother; and besides, it seems appropriate."

"Oh, get out of here, the both of you!" laughed Mrs. Walton, springing out of her chair again. I said my goodbyes accompanied by that barely perceptible clicking of heels and the slight bow from the waist that I could never quite shake. They smiled warmly, perhaps because of the German bow, and watched us as we walked toward the car. Ruth *was* wearing a white gown.

"They like you," she said as I closed the car door on her side.

"Wait till they get to know me," I replied and slowly, sedately, still under the friendly eyes of the Waltons, eased the car away from the curb.

The nearer we approached the Palladium, the heavier the Saturday night traffic grew. Luckily the Hollywood division of the Los Angeles Police Department was at hand, and a traffic officer directed a steady stream of automobiles into the large parking lot of the Palladium. With a sense of fraternal approbation, I surveyed the gleaming black-and-white police Harley at the curb before rolling to a stop. My admiration did not escape Ruth, who said, "I think you look awful on one of those things. You look like a German stormtrooper and so do they," indicating the traffic officer with a nod of her head. To me, that was the highest of compliments. Not only was I being compared with Los Angeles's finest; I was also being compared to Himmler's select few whom, less than four years ago, I had admired in awe-stricken silence each Sunday morning when they marched in battalion formation, preceded by their band, down Rothenbaumchaussee toward the Moorweide.

The entire Nazi movement and anything remotely connected with it had been anathema to my family. Hitler was referred to only as "the corporal," "*Schweinehund*," or "bandit." No one knew that I had participated in flag-raising ceremonies at my school, standing at attention in the schoolyard, saluting the swastika with outstretched right arm while singing the first stanzas of the "Deutschlandlied" and the "Horst-Wessel-Lied." No one knew that I spent Wednesday evenings at the local Jungvolk Fähnlein meetings. And later, when we moved to my stepfather's house on Rothenbaumchaussee, which was located directly across the street from the Curiohaus, convention center as well as headquarters for the *Hamburg SS Standarte*, no one knew that I reverently read the SS newspaper, *Der Schwarze Korps*, which was in a display case next to the streetcar stop at the Curiohaus entrance.

Once, as I was waiting for the streetcar on my way to school and standing as usual before the display case, I felt a hand grip the back of my neck, shaking it slightly. I turned around and looked up at a tall SS man wearing the black uniform of the Allgemeine SS and those highly polished black boots that never failed to fascinate Germans of any age. He had a current edition of *Der Schwarze Korps* in his hand to exchange for the old one. "Mach Platz, Buttje," he said with a smile. "Du willst doch das neueste lesen, oder?"

I turned red, thinking the German equivalent of "Wow, he talks to me as though we're buddies" and said, "Natürlich."

After he posted the new paper and closed the display case, he turned to me and grinned, "Viel Vergnügen in der Schule," then turned to go.

I slammed my heels together, flung up my right arm in a regulation salute, and shouted, "Heil Hitler!"

The SS man started at this correction of his deportment, turned back to me, and raised his right arm. "Heil Hitler!" he responded with a sheepish grin, shook his head ever so slightly, and returned into the Curiohaus.

Had my mother been watching this scene, she would have slapped the daylights out of me, right in front of the SS Headquarters.

But when Ruth compared me to an SS trooper, I thought she was making a grudging female admission of respect for the dominating warrior in me and that kept me going until we had settled down at our table.

It wasn't the best table in the house, but then I wouldn't have known or cared. The Palladium was a huge, semicircular ballroom, the two arcs of the circle touching a raised bandstand and enclosing a very large dance floor. From the dance floor outward and two steps up was a carpeted section with the dinner tables separated by aisles leading down to the dance floor. On each table was a candle-lit lamp, and spotlights illuminated the stage. A large chandelier directly over the center of the dance floor and surrounded by six smaller ones dimly lit the dancers. It was, I thought, utterly romantic in spite of its size.

We were seated at a table for two near the dance floor. The waiter asked, "Dinner, sir?" I said, "Please," and he sidled into the haze. Ruth smiled a smile that seemed to say, "He did not, did he, ask whether we would like a cocktail?" My warrior self-image began to fade.

Ruth didn't help matters. She remarked, "What you need is at least some fuzz on your cheeks." Her smile was annoyingly sympathetic.

"For your information, I shaved before I left home," I said with an edge of indignation.

"On what day?" she laughed. And then I was saved by the sound of Benny Goodman's clarinet and Ruth hopped from her chair. Eyes shining, she commanded, "All aboard for 'Tuxedo Junction.' Come on, Kurt!"

For the first time since asking Ruth for this date, I remembered that I couldn't dance. What a rash, stupid thing to have done—ask a girl, particularly *this* one, to go to the most famous ballroom in the land and not know how to dance! "Well, the soup is about to be served . . ." I stalled.

"*Soup*?" Ruth asked with devastating incredulity.

"If there's anything I can't stand, it's cold soup," I said weakly.

Ruth drew herself fully erect. "Enough!" she commented, holding out her right hand. Slowly I wound myself out of my chair and took her hand. Like a ship being pulled from its berth by a tugboat, I clumsily followed in her wake down that busy channel toward the dance floor, mingling on the way with a multitude of other tugboats towing other clumsy vessels.

"There's no room!" I cried triumphantly, trying to turn away as we reached the packed floor.

"There *is*!" Ruth replied firmly and grabbed a bit of padding on my left shoulder.

We danced. Or rather we stood, packed like sardines, and swayed or bounced a little, depending on the rhythm coming from that faraway bandstand. The pressure of the crowd forced our bodies close together and every part of Ruth seemed to register on me. The resulting incipient biological manifestation was immediately arrested when a tall RAF pilot bumped into us and said, "Sorry, chap." With a pang I became conscious only of my civilian clothes.

In the course of the evening my grey flannel suit became more and more embarrassing as my concentration shifted from Ruth to the sea of uniforms: Army officers in "pinks and greens," naval officers in dress whites, soldiers, sailors, marines . . . and here and there a civilian italicized my status as a leper . . . a war out there from which these uni-

16   Training

formed men took a well-earned respite while I took the space away from another of them waiting in line outside.

I managed to get through the evening without coming right out and saying, "Let's go home," but it was my last date of the war in civilian clothes.

And, finally, on a warm evening in May 1943, my young landlady handed me that white envelope the moment I got home from the bank. And there was my "Order to Report for Induction." The document told me when and where to report and stated that transportation would be furnished to the induction station. The small print went on to say, "You will there be examined, and, if accepted for training and service, you will then be inducted. . . . Persons reporting to the induction station in some instances may be rejected for physical or other reasons." That seemed so much out of the question that it shouldn't have been included; I resented it. After reading that I should notify my employer, I let Leni read it. "Better call your mother," she said.

"Not until I get back from the induction station," I responded, suddenly conscious again of those surely inapplicable words, "if accepted for training and service, . . ."

Having "notified my employer," I found that my routes seemed to exist only for the delightful purpose of notifying each bank branch of my impending service. May 18, only a week off, seemed as if it would never come. But come it did, and I reported to the Los Angeles Armed Forces Induction Station No. 2 in the ugly, glass-fronted San Fernando Building on South Main Street.

With hundreds of young men like me, I was fed into the system that day from desks in the lobby to booths, was moved naked through the long lines at the medical stations, on through test batteries to the room where at last, fully clothed again, I stood at attention with my right hand raised and proudly swore to defend the Constitution of the United States. I was given a mimeographed sheet that made me Private Kurt Gabel 39573603 (eleven other privates were on the same orders) and directed me to proceed from Los Angeles, California, to the Reception Center, Arlington, California, reporting upon arrival there to the commanding officer for duty. More mundanely, the orders directed me to be at the downtown Grayhound bus terminal, Sixth and Main Street, on May 25 at 9:15 A.M.

The next six days were heady ones. I made the rounds of all my friends from Hollywood High. I even went to the houses of friends who were already in one of the services to say goodbye to their parents, knowing that the latter would pass the information on. Now I could look everyone in the eye. Just let some soldier ask, "What outfit you with?" And I could reply, "Don't know yet. Ask me next week!"

The last person on my goodbye rounds was Ruth. I had after much cogitation determined that I would not part from her at the Egyptian Theater; I would say my fine farewells to her at her home. So one evening, for the first time since the disastrous Palladium experience, I rang her doorbell. She answered it herself, as I'd hoped she might. I made my bow. "Finally made it," I announced. "You see before you a soldier!"

"Oh, no . . . ," she breathed and towed me into the house. "Mother, Kurt has received his call to the colors."

Mrs. Walton suddenly materialized from the depths of the house. She looked at me and for a moment seemed older than she was. Suddenly she kissed me. Then, I suppose to hide her emotion, she turned abruptly away. "Come on into the kitchen. We're having a cocktail party tonight. Try out my hors d'oeuvres."

It turned out that the cocktail party was for a group of servicemen whom neither she nor Ruth had met. The Waltons had asked for and received from the Hollywood Canteen a list of lonely military men. I knew the list would consist of the usual naval commanders, Marine majors, Air Corps colonels, and a smattering of British flying officers, all considered "suitable" to upper-middle-class households who wanted to do their patriotic duty. Mrs. Walton urged me to stay on for the gathering, but I knew that even though I now was entitled to wear a uniform, I would feel out of place.

When I took my leave, she kissed me again in the kitchen, this time with unmistakable tears in her eyes. Ruth took me to the door; what a tactful mother she had! "After I become a paratrooper," I said, "and when I come home on furlough, I'd like to reserve a date."

"Done!" said Ruth, with a slight quiver of her lower lip.

"After I get my wings," I continued, "I'm also going to ask you for your picture." By now Ruth was crying, much to my delight. I instantly forgave her the naval commanders, Marine majors, Air Corps colonels, and assorted British flying officers. We kissed a long kiss, and I felt Ruth's tears on my face. Then I turned and walked away, head high, arms swinging, and silently counting cadence to be sure that Ruth knew she was watching a soldier.

2
Initiation

The Reception Center at Arlington, California, was a barracks complex of the greenish, temporary, two-storied wooden structures typical of World War II that we were to encounter all over America from this day forward. The relatively small camp was entirely surrounded by a high, meshed-wire cyclone fence topped by a two-foot barbed wire security apron. To our innocent eyes, the compound looked like a prison camp.

Our bus stopped at the entrance gate where a guard checked the manifest, gave us the same look we used to give the tourists in Hollywood, and waved the bus on. We went past a theater, a PX, and a service club, came to a circular drive, and halted in front of a headquarters building. The door of the Greyhound hissed open and someone yelled, "All right; everybody out!" There was a scramble for our overnight bags and nervous shoving as we followed the voice of command and as quickly as we could left the safety of our bus.

A corporal with a clipboard stood by the bus door and said, pointing, "OK, just move over there, put your things down, and wait till your name is called." We moved to the side of the bus and waited awkwardly, some of the men looking longingly at the blue and white bus as it slowly pulled away from us like a luxury liner abandoning its passengers at sea. A sergeant materialized in front of the headquarters building and shouted, "OK, you men; give me your attention!" We stared at him anxiously—a beacon, of little comfort to passengers abandoned at sea, but a beacon nevertheless. "When your name is called, you fall in right in front of me where I show you. Answer 'here' as I call your name." He looked at his clipboard and shouted, "Adams, James S."

"Here," shrieked Adams and bolted to the spot pointed out by the sergeant.

"Armond, William B."

"Here."

"Barth, Alexander."

By the time he got to the Gs, two lines had taken shape in front of him. "Gabel, Kurt." There was something electrifying in hearing my name for the first time at an Army camp. The sergeant pronounced it American fashion to rhyme with "table."

"Here!" I shouted, trying to make my voice deep, and trotted to my place. There I stood, in beige corduroy pants, brown polo shirt, and a dark blue windbreaker, at my first military formation. I involuntarily came to attention but quickly realized the incongruity of that position, or perhaps the presumption of assuming that position without being in uniform, and tried to look like the other men. Most of them superimposed on their obvious nervousness a swagger, or a Joe College type of fraternity initiation attitude, or a good-humored American contempt for anything military. The older ones were clearly depressed and didn't try to hide their anxiety. I put my hands in my pockets in simulation of the swaggerers.

The sergeant paused in the roll call, fixed me with a brief stare, and snapped, "Take your hands out of your pockets, soldier!" I turned beet red and yanked my hands from my pockets as if they had been bitten by a pair of rattlesnakes. In my utter embarrassment, I barely noticed that I had just been addressed as "soldier." The formation shifted perceptibly. One of their number had been taken to task for simply having had his hands in his pockets—a dark portent indeed.

When the roll call was completed, the sergeant put his clipboard under his arm and addressed us, it seemed to me, as a military body. "Gentlemen, as the song goes, you're in the Army now, and so I'm going to move you to your barracks in a military manner. I will call you to attention, give you a right face, and march you on your way. All right." He seemed to brace himself. I thought that, for a military man with as much experience as that sergeant seemed to have, commanding people who weren't even in uniform must be a terrible chore. "Detail—*Attenshun!*" I pretended to have heard "Achtung!" and snapped my heels together, bringing my hands flat against my upper thighs, elbows slightly bent in the best Prussian manner. Alas, this was not a formation of the Hitler Youth. I sheepishly adjusted my bearing to that of the high school lettermen on either side of me. They had scraped their feet together and stood a little straighter than before, perhaps as they might stand when singing the National Anthem. Somewhere between hands-in-pockets and German Army drill, I would have to find an acceptable middle for a while.

"Right—*Face!*" commanded the sergeant. Taking two or three steps to turn in that direction with mumbled remarks and some giggling, our group finally faced right. "Forward—*March!*" I stepped off briskly and bumped into the man in front of me. "Sorry," I said. He turned around, grinned, and said, "My fault." The man in back of me stepped on my right heel, then quickly placed a hand on my shoulder and said, "Hey, pardon me all to hell," and I assured him, "No problem." We lurched on, men bumping their neighbors with overnight bags, stepping on the heels of the man in front, giggling and apologizing until the sergeant commanded, "Detail—*Halt!*" We halted like a long freight train, bumping into people and being bumped into. One man actually fell down and was pulled to his feet by the man next to him. There was more apologizing, more giggling, and here and there a "for Christ's sake."

"Left—*Face!*" the sergeant said without conviction; after we had turned in that direction, he said, quite superfluously, "At ease." We looked at our new home, the first of the two-story wooden barracks we were to experience at close hand. "OK," said the sergeant with what appeared to be a small sigh, "The first squad—line of you men—will go upstairs all the way to the end of the bay. You will take the beds on your *right*. First man takes the first bed, second man takes the second bed, and so on. Then the second squad—line—goes upstairs and takes the beds on the *left* in the same manner. Any questions so far?"

"Yeah, OK to get next to a friend of mine?" asked one of the lettermen.

"Later. We'll try to adjust once you're all in. All right, first squad—that's *you* guys—get going." The "squad" disappeared into the barracks and clomped upstairs. "Second squad, go on." Now there were two lines of us left. "OK," the sergeant said, again with his small sigh, "you men are downstairs." He pointed to what was now the first squad and said, "Same thing. Beds on the *right*. First man, first bed. Get going." That was us. We walked up the porch steps into the barracks, glanced curiously at the washroom-latrine to our right, and made a left turn into the lower bay.

The scrubbed wooden floor, the dark-brown, unfinished wooden walls with clean, curtainless windows evenly spaced on both sides of the long room, steel cots with green blankets standing under each window and two steel wall lockers occupying the wall space between each bed greeted us and slowed our walk. I had seen worse, but there was a momentary shock as I recalled the stark white and yellow dormitory of the German prep school in Hanover that I had been condemned to not many years ago.

The fifth cot on the right was mine and I sat down on it, placing my overnight bag on the floor. I bounced once or twice, testing the creaking springs of the bunk, and let my hand glide over the rough Army blanket. Exploring under the blanket, I found a pillow without a pillowcase. There weren't any sheets, either. Above me, the wooden support beams and the rough floor of the bay upstairs was our ceiling. Six naked bulbs fixed to crossbeams overhead rounded out the decor. I sat, a little pile of unhappiness as my great enthusiasm for the military life drained from every pore. "Ugh," someone grunted. "Home, sweet home," groaned another.

Our other squad came scraping into the dismal room and took its assigned beds with the same stunned resignation. The mood of self-pity was intensified by the voice of our mentor, who shouted, "All right! You men stand by your bunks until we get your bunk assignments firmed up. You saw where the latrine is. You'll draw bedding later."

Later we were marched through the reception company area to a small supply room that seemed to hold only bedding and barracks cleaning equipment. Each of us received two sheets and a pillow case, and back to our barracks we marched. A corporal was waiting for us. "First lesson in the army," he gloated, "is how to make your bunk. Gather round this bed." We gathered.

He went through the procedure, talking as he demonstrated how to fold, where to fold, how to tuck in the sheets and blanket, and how to fold and tuck the second blanket at the head of the bed. "This is the Army way to make a bed. There is no other way. Nothing else is acceptable. Blankets are *tight*, see? If a dime won't bounce on it, your bunk will be torn up and you'll do it over!" He was enjoying his lecture-demonstration immensely. We went to work. My bunk was torn up only once, and after the second try I was permitted to sit—not on the bed but on the floor beside it to watch the rest of the proceedings.

My fellows went through the routine of bunk-making in sullen resignation. The corporal embodied authority of a kind we were unfamiliar with. It was not that of the policeman, nor of the father or mother, nor of any other kind we had ever dealt with—or circumvented as necessary. It seemed best to do as we were told, keeping our thoughts to ourselves. Most of the others evinced some bewilderment, but I understood that the nature of this authority was military. I had acquired this understanding by osmosis as a Prussian in Prussia for the first fourteen years of my life. The military is the ultimate authority, the final enforcer. I knew that and would have no real problem adjusting to the American Army.

From my vantage point on the floor, I quietly watched those who did have problems!

There was the young man my age who had never been away from home except for summer camp. Last night he had been in his familiar room, in his own home. Now suddenly all that was gone. He was making up a coarse, olive-drab bunk in a coarse, olive-drab barracks full of strangers. Tears welled up in his eyes.

Then there was the thirty-year-old married man. For the past few years, he had worked for an insurance company, had lived his uneventful, comfortable life in a nice, little apartment in Pasadena, had listened to the alarm clock in the morning, and had stretched and yawned while his wife got up to make breakfast. While he was at the office, the beds would be made, the apartment would be cleaned, supper would be prepared—by someone else. And now this! And for how long? His face was drawn and worried.

Another young man had started his first year of college. The scion of a Beverly Hills family, he was going to study law; he was destined for great things—to take over dad's law firm, or become a judge, or go into politics. And now an absurd little man in a silly uniform was teaching him to make up a crummy bed! His face mirrored loathing and contempt; he worked in silence.

The man on my immediate left had his bunk torn up for the third time. He too was about my age, tall and thin with sandy hair and good-natured blue eyes. He had a heavy Oklahoma accent and was instantly dubbed "Oakie" by the corporal. "Ah ain't never gonna do it raaht," he drawled, shaking his head as he tucked and stretched the blanket at the head of the bed. Each time it was tight, the other blanket would wrinkle. Secretly I held the side of the blanket nearest me while he struggled with the other side. "Now, eer' day ah do this t'home with not no trouble," he explained. "Course ah got me one blanket and it don't have to get tucked in. But this-yere thing shore does foul me up." The corporal finally gave up on him and told him to sit down.

Slowly the bunk-making exercise came to an end; more and more men were sitting on the floor or on the green wooden footlockers at the foot of each bed, reading or talking softly. "All right," came the crowing voice of our corporal again. "Now for the wall lockers and footlockers. Gather around me at this bunk here." Again we gathered. Using the clothes of the man by whose bunk we stood, the corporal taught us how the Army wanted us to hang our coats and stow our underwear. Clothes on the hanger were hung in the wall locker with the left sleeve facing out, the hook of the hanger facing in. The one shelf of the wall locker could be used for nonmilitary items such as books, magazines, wallets, and other personal things that would be neatly arranged in a military manner. The footlocker would contain underwear and shirts folded as follows. Shaving and other toilet equipment would go on the left side of the tray. "All right, you men. Get your clothes in order. Tomorrow, when your uniforms are issued, we'll go over all this again and then you get inspected. When you're squared away here, stand by for chow."

Those who had barely recovered from the bunkmaking lesson now went sadly about the task of unpacking the Army way. Gone were the spacious closets with the cedar floors, gone the Ethan Allen chests with English drawers, gone the wives and mothers who unpacked and folded and hung coats and murmured, "Dinner as soon as I get this done for you, dear."

And then we were marched, more or less, past other two-storied barracks to a large mess hall and the next trauma. Grab a tray, walk through the line, sit at that table, eat, get out, and, of course, wait in front of the mess hall to be taken back to the barracks.

Tired, dejected, disgusted, worried, sad, we stood in our scraggly formation in front of our barracks in the dusk of our first Army day after a supper of meat loaf, metallic-tasting spinach, rubbery mashed potatoes, and unidentifiable cake, listening to our corporal. "First call at six tomorrow. That's when you get up. You can go straight to the mess hall for breakfast; you all know where it is now. You will be back in the barracks at seven and make your bunks. Inspection of bunks at seven-thirty. Next you will be issued uniforms and duffel and barracks bags; then you can mail your civilian clothes home and write letters. After lunch you'll get an orientation about how long you'll be here and what you do while you're at this reception center. Wall locker and footlocker inspection is at three. Then we'll have close-order drill. That's how you stand at attention and turn and march and all that. All right . . . ," he took a breath, "you guys may walk around this immediate area and use that day room over there or read or listen to the radio. You're in barracks at eight, lights out at nine. Dismissed."

I walked around the barracks area designated as our limits, carefully keeping to myself, and peered into the dusk at the buildings beyond our confines. They looked exactly like ours, but the people moving between them and another small day room were in uniform. That cheered me up a bit because it reminded me that I was in an Army camp and not in some kind of a detention or concentration camp. I realized that my gloom had its source in the recollection of a concentration camp I had once seen in Fuhlsbüttel near Hamburg on a school field trip.

We had been required to write an essay on our special area of interest for our civics class. About ten of us were interested in the judicial system and law enforcement. For two days our group was let loose on its research targets, the group leader with a letter of explanation from the school administration. They were a glorious, though a bit frightening, two days for us. One of our stops was KL Fuhlsbuettel where we stood at the iron entrance gate with its wrought-iron legend *"Arbeit macht Frei"* (Freedom through Work) overhead. Our group leader presented his letter to the SS man on guard and bravely requested that our group be given a guided tour of the facility. The guard frowned, then grinned and said, not unkindly, "You boys must be crazy. Get out of here before someone decides to accommodate you with a few *months* inside." We saluted and left but walked around the camp perimeter, stopping occasionally to stare inside. There were one-story wooden barracks and small structures that could have been day rooms. Here and there were small groups of inmates being marched to a mess hall or work area. Finally a perimeter patrol that must have been alerted by a tower guard stopped us, questioned us, and then escorted us away from what was undoubtedly a restricted area with the warning that *"next* time . . . ."

Except that the Arlington Reception Center had the customary two-story barracks, it could have been KL Fuhlsbuettel; it seemed no place for soldiers. But once I had identified my apprehension for what it was, I felt better. Even the comparison of the interior of our barracks to the German prep school dormitory had been mitigated by the sight of soldiers in the adjoining company street. By the time I was in bed at the prescribed hour, I was at peace.

My hands propped under my head, I looked from my bed at my neighbors for most of whom this was their first experience with institutional living. Except for Oakie, who seemed perfectly happy, their anxieties, sadness, loneliness, and disgust had deepened on their faces. Some read but most simply stared and made an occasional remark indicating that they were thinking of yesterday or last week.

"Lights out. No more talking!" With that, our corporal switched off the glaring, naked bulbs. The effect was a softening of the contours of the room as the light from the adjoining day room filtered in. I thought of tomorrow's uniform issue, of basic training, of becoming a paratrooper. And I thought of Ruth. When I fell asleep on this, my first day in the Army, I slept well and without dreams.

The "first call" whistle shrilled through the barracks and the naked bulbs were turned on. After the corporal with the whistle had gone elsewhere, there were remarks like "Good morning to you, *too,* you son-of-a-bitch" and "Hell, it's the middle of the night" and "What the hell's the rush?" So some of the men at least were feeling a little better already.

I got out of bed, took my towel and shaving gear, and went to the washroom-latrine. Through its open door, steam was wafting over the lower landing of the wooden steps leading to the upper floor of the barracks. I took two steps down and stood on the washroom's concrete floor, undecided whether to shower first or shave.

The steam was coming from the extreme left of the room where five showerheads protruded from the top of a milky-white shower curtain. They all seemed to be engaged. On the same side were three toilets, two occupied by very uncomfortable and embarrassed young men whose bowels would in all probability not perform at all. Directly across from the toilets were four urinals, one of which I decided to try out before doing anything else. Then I found one free washbasin of five lined up along the same wall. I put my shaving gear on a small metal ledge beneath a steamed-up mirror, wiped the mirror clear with my towel, and started my ablutions.

As I applied my brushless shaving cream, I carefully looked at my neighbors and nodded a "good morning" when they looked back. On my right, one of them approached the window and said to no one in particular, "Mind if I open this? Mirror keeps steaming up?" There was a general shaking of heads. No one talked. The only sounds came from the showers, from the flushing toilets, and from water running in the washbowls. In my mirror I saw other men entering the washroom, some reluctantly walking toward the toilets, others quietly standing behind us at the washbowls, waiting their turn. The space on my right was vacated and another man stepped to the basin.

It was a man I had not noticed before. He seemed very old to me, probably almost thirty-five, with a shock of mouse-brown hair already showing streaks of gray on the sides. He was slightly taller than I but quite stout, with a pronounced paunch that bounced like an inner tube against the rim of the washbowl. His face was the most lugubrious I had yet seen. Like a man who is very sick, he seemed not to care how he looked or what went on around him. I felt instantly and deeply sorry for him and wondered what on earth the Army could possibly want with him. He glanced toward me. I smiled and said, "Good morning." He looked at me without interest and mumbled, "Wish it were." Then he lathered his hanging jowls while straining toward the mirror.

I felt good, and the sight of this poor creature made me feel superior and therefore obliged to lighten his burden, so I said, "It's a new day and you won't be here long. Cheer up."

"Won't be here long," he mumbled through his lathered face. "Be further away from home next time."

My cheerfulness seemed to compound his sadness and I fell silent. I had not really intended to engage him in conversation and was glad to get back into my comfortable shell. I allowed as how, if I were as old as that poor creature, I would probably not be looking forward to being a soldier either.

"Hey, Clark," I heard somebody say from my left and turned to see Oakie taking the washbowl just vacated.

"Little late, ain't cha?" I replied. "Thought you farm boys got up real early."

Oakie laughed hugely. "Well, now that ah don't have to work no more, ah'm gonna sleep in."

It occurred to me that I had been talking more than anyone else in the latrine and I hurried my shaving and toothbrushing with a slight feeling of guilt at being less depressed than most of my fellow draftees. "See you at breakfast," I said to Oakie when I was through, and left the washbowl to the man behind me. I gave up the idea of taking a shower at the sight of the line and went back to my bunk, which already seemed a little like home, to dress.

By the time I reached the mess hall, the line that had formed already had a small tail outside the entrance, but the line moved right along. Some people were in uniform—rumpled OD shirt and pants with two round U.S. insignia on the shirt collar as the sole mark of their new status. Garrison caps without braid were stuck awkwardly on their heads or carried in their hands. Most men, however, were still in civilian clothes and seemed to look upon the men in uniform as veterans to be deferred to.

We moved into the large, squat wooden structure. Inside it looked like the third-class waiting room of a German railway station or as I imagined a Salvation Army feeding post in New York's Bowery would look. Everything was a dull brown, clean and sterile. The sight did nothing to improve anyone's morale, and the men continued moving toward the serving line only because they were hungry. Last night there had been too many shocks to assimilate, and the mess hall had not been the worst of them. But at dawn on this Day 2, the sight and smell of it were singularly depressing.

I took a steel tray, slightly greasy to the hand, and grabbed equally greasy silverware, then stepped up to the KPs behind the serving line. They stood, each one before his assigned steam table, and looked only from the stainless steel food receptacles to the next tray passed in front of them as they ladled their powdered eggs, limp bacon, gooey clumps that were sullenly identified as "hash browns" when someone timidly asked, orange marmalade, and lumps of margarine scraped off a knife. The last KP threw two pieces of cold toast onto the tray with huge tongs and filled a GI cup full of coffee that, as one moved toward a table, would instantly spill over the toast and ooze into the tray compartment to mingle with the eggs.

Carefully balancing my tray to minimize the flow of coffee onto my food, having already resigned myself to eating already soaked toast, I made my way to an empty table and put my tray and silverware down. The brown table was bare, its linoleum surface streaked from an early morning scrubdown but otherwise clean. I had forgotten a napkin and walked toward the front of the serving line. A KP held up his hand. "Other end of the line!"

"Just want to get a napkin," I said.

"Other end of the line, fella," he repeated; so I walked back to my table. It was a six-man table with benches, and I tried to pretend that it was a picnic table. But the linoleum smell and that sad tray in front of me permitted no such conjuring.

"When you're through," a loudspeaker croaked, "take your tray and silverware to the end of the serving line."

The food was as bad as it looked and as cold as the hearts of the KPs who had served it. Even the coffee was lukewarm. But I was hungry and I ate. I ate as fast as I could so that I would not have to stay any longer than absolutely necessary; I did not look up as I was joined by other men who, if anything, seemed even more eager to get through this factory breakfast than I. Again there was little talking. Only the clatter of trays and silverware, the rasp of benches being pushed or pulled, and the shuffle of feet were to be heard. Now and then a "Move it, buddy" from a cook or KP at the serving line was the only clearly audible human sound uttered without benefit of a PA set. I tried to look out of one of the windows in the far wall of the room, hoping at least to see a tree or a bird, but the curtainless glass simply stared blankly, the unshaded light inside the mess hall still dominating the gray dawn outside.

"When you're through, take your tray and silverware to the end of the serving line," repeated the voice through the loudspeaker. I picked up my tray and silverware, climbed over the bench, hitting a man with my elbow and mumbling, "Sorry," and walked toward the spot designated by the voice. A large barrel of corrugated steel marked "Edibles" was standing to one side and a cook in whites pointed toward it with a commanding gesture as I approached. "Scrape your tray. Then go through the wash line there." I scraped and proceeded to another barrel with hot water. A man in front of me dunked his tray in it and I did the same as he moved on. The next barrel held soapy water and the man in front of me handed me a small brush as he moved forward. I washed my tray off with the brush, sloshing brush and tray in the soapy water, then handed the brush to the man behind me. A substantial line had already formed to my rear.

There was one more barrel and one more cook standing by it. "Rinse your tray here, then place it over there, silverware in that rack." He pointed to a counter-type window behind which two sweaty KPs were stacking trays and rattling silver. I did as I was told. Another important Army lesson had been learned, and I hurriedly left the cold, smelly, inhospitable place.

Later after bedmaking, came the call, "Fall out for uniform issue!" The work for Day 2 was starting. As we tumbled out of the barracks, there was a distinct air of pleasant anticipation, even in those men who had quavered at the very thought of the loss of identity a uniform represented to them.

We entered a musty-smelling supply room that looked like a large barn. Supply sergeants and tailors were standing in stall-like enclosures, a four-foot-high counter running the length of the room in front of them.

I stepped up to the first stall. "Waist?" asked the horse in that stall; he then turned from a horse into a bartender. "Twenty-eight," I replied. "Twenty-nine," he said and placed a stack of five undershorts on the barcounter. Eyeing me clinically, he muttered, "Small," and stacked five undershirts on top of the shorts. Like a bartender in a Western movie sliding a beer mug to a customer, he slid the pile to his right and said, "Move on, soldier." At the next stall, a little man who really did look like a horse said, "Neck size?" "I don't know." Again the clinical eye. "Fifteen," he said and from the shadows behind him were handed two woolen and three khaki shirts that he piled next to the undershirts. "Move on."

By now I could discern the layout of the stall interior. It held immense shelves at which two men in T-shirts were in perpetual motion feeding things to the supply man at the counter who piled them up, made a check mark on a clothing form, and shoved the pile to his right at the precise moment when a new body appeared in front of him, the preceding body, me in this case, having followed the sliding pile of clothes up the line. The organization of the line, its speed, and its precision made an impression on me and I could not decide whether to admire it or be appalled by it. GI, Government Issue, moving through.

But then the line was halted. It was time for trousers and the rest of our outer gear. Here we were actually fitted. The result was a visual transformation of our civilian selves into soldiers. It was a bit Kafkaesque, but a feeling of pride prevailed over surrealism.

"The rest of your stuff," crowed our corporal as we tried on our uniforms, "fatigues and that kind of stuff, you'll get at your basic training station. OK, let me show you about the insignia and the helmet liner. Over here, you guys." The insignia went on the collar of the blouse. That was simple enough. And the mysterious little leather straps we had been issued were for the helmet liner. One was a sweatband that for me would never properly adjust throughout twenty-four years of Army service, and the other was a chin strap that we would be forbidden to wear.

By lunchtime we knew what a Class A uniform was, had turned in our civilian clothes for mailing, had learned something about the rank structure of the services (that one said "sir" to an officer but not to an NCO), and had had one hour of something called "school of the soldier," which seemed to be concerned mainly with the hand salute. After lunch our corporal had said we would go to "classification." There those of us who were crazy enough could volunteer for parachute duty and other weird assignments, and all would take the AGCT which was *very* important to our entire future in the Army. "AGCT," the corporal said importantly. "That's the Army General Classification Test. Kinda like an IQ test." The magic words "parachute volunteer" carried me through lunch, though it was a meal even more awful than breakfast had been.

A part of the classification section was in a long barracks with an entry hall and many individual cubicles that made it look like a maze. We were told to work very carefully at the test batteries because they would determine much of what we would do in the Army. For instance, an officer candidate would have to score at least 110, and so would a parachute volunteer. I could feel myself turn pale. Suppose . . . .

Herded into cubicles, we were given instruction sheets, test sheets, and special pencils along with verbal instructions about the work and the time we had to complete each battery. Then came the moment of truth, the command "Start."

To my surprise and great relief I found the first battery quite simple. It had to do with language, picking the right words for meaning, completing sentences without the bewilderment of grammatical terminology. I was finished and smugly relaxing in my chair long before the announcement "Time. Put down your pencils." Papers were collected and new ones placed on the desk. The new test measured general comprehension and seemed even easier than the preceding one. By the time I had finished, I felt like an intellectual giant. The feeling was not to last; next came the mathematical reasoning battery with its locomotives and trucks traveling at so many miles per hour to places so many miles away that would not be reached without delays or detours that would take so many minutes. . . . Problems like these had always deflated and defeated me. The frowning visage of my math tutoress in Hamburg rose before my mind's eye as I struggled and sweated. I was still at it when time was called. The AGCT seemed to go on for hours; and when we finally finished, I was sure that I had flunked miserably and would end up as permanent KP. Goodbye, paratroops.

The break passed in general gloom. Only older college men seemed happy. Then we went back to a different office for interviews and preparation of our personnel and other service records. Here I learned that my cumulative AGCT score was 114! Four whole points above the minimum I needed! Elated at having made it but still shaky, I volunteered for parachute duty. My records were duly marked and I was told that further airborne processing would be done at my next duty station.

Before supper we had time for an hour of close-order drill. Now officially a parachute volunteer, I executed still unfamiliar orders with exuberant precision, whether the response was correct or not. Even supper did not bother me. I went through the chow line and the multiphase wash line like a veteran, cursing Army food and greasy trays as though I had been at it for years.

On the morning of Day 3, I stood in formation, a soldier in uniform, and I knew what to do when our corporal commanded, "Dress right—*Dress*!" I knew what was meant by "cover down," correctly came to "at ease" and "attention," and generally felt that things were coming along as they should. In my euphoria at having passed the magic score of 110, the first barrier to the exclusive club of the paratroops, I was in a little world of my own and lost what slight identification I had had with my fellow draftees. Still I noticed, in our first formation in uniform, a subtle change in the men. They seemed to be conscious of the implication of their uniforms; they were trying to execute the commands correctly and without the contrived cynicism they had initially felt constrained to exhibit. We had all entered World War II, some willingly, most a bit apprehensively. But here we were, a part of it, embryonic, unseen by History, still quiescent in her womb but a part of her and destined to become her children.

Our corporal told us that from now on we were to check the bulletin board for assigned duties, announcements, and shipping orders. Then we were dismissed for breakfast.

The bulletin board became the center of our universe. Already there was a KP duty roster and there were shipping orders. I looked it over, not really expecting my name to appear yet because I imagined that I was destined for Fort Benning where I knew the parachute school was located and that we parachute volunteers were so special that it would take longer to get us on orders than the ordinary draftee.

Day 4 was almost a real training day. There was close-order drill. There was something called "interior guard" where we learned (but could not remember) general orders, how to challenge, how to call for

"Corporal of the guard—post number one!" and how to walk our post in a military manner. There was field sanitation and finally military justice. On the bulletin board that evening a guard roster for the next two days was posted, and my name was on it. That evening I wrote a soldierly letter to the folks on the home front, which was mercifully lost in the mail.

Guard duty started at six o'clock before sundown on Saturday. I approached that hour with a mixture of elated anticipation of my first real military task and anxiety about doing it properly. I was not at all sure that the two hours of instruction we had had and the additional two hours we were given to study the manual would be sufficient to sustain me and the others in what had been described to us as "the very serious responsibility of guarding a military facility."

Sitting on bunks in the guard room and receiving our instructions from the sergeant of the guard was, it seemed to me, introduction to the defense system of the United States. Even the most reluctant draftee listened as though his life depended on understanding the mission to its last detail. We were issued an armband with the word "Guard" on it and a billy club worn in a webb retainer fastened to a pistol belt. We fell in for inspection.

There we were! A regular formation in Class A uniform with helmet liner, and a billy club suspended from a pistol belt. We all passed inspection. Guard mount, in deference to our status, was kept simple. Yet there was the exercise of relieving the old guard and grouping the remainder of the formation into reliefs and reserve.

I was on post from ten to midnight, a walking post of about a hundred yards inside the perimeter fence. As I walked it, looking through the wire mesh toward the highway, I felt like a soldier (of the Foreign Legion?) doing his duty at a lonely but important outpost, dreaming of the loved ones he had left behind but ever watchful lest a saboteur or spy should attempt to breach that portion of the fence entrusted to his care and his billy club. It seemed incomprehensible that thirty-five miles west along that empty road out there was downtown Los Angeles.

By the time I mounted my post for the second and last time at four in the morning, I was convinced that I could get along without basic training because I felt thoroughly like an accomplished soldier. With a week more training, perhaps on the rifle range, I would certainly be ready for parachute school. I swaggered through the two early morning hours, swaggered with spartan indifference to the cold of a California morning—keen-eyed, a weary but watchful defender of a hundred years of a United States Army Reception Center.

On the tenth day the bulletin board informed me that I was on shipping orders. To my utter dismay, I was on orders to Fort Warren, Wyoming, a quartermaster center. I made my vehement protest to the highest ranking person I was allowed to contact, a staff sergeant in personnel, who assured me that my records were indeed marked "parachute volunteer" and that I would be duly processed for Fort Benning once I arrived in Wyoming.

I remember little about Fort Warren except that I was there for four weeks of their eight-week basic training cycle and that I met my first Army officer there, a young second lieutenant who was commander of my training company and who listened patiently to my twice-weekly inquiries about going to Fort Benning. I remember going to classification and assignment (C&A) where I was asked whether I was sure that I wanted to go to parachute school, and was reminded of the gravity of the choice, and was finally told that I would be scheduled for an "airborne physical" at the hospital.

I remember that when I was weighed and measured during the initial physical examination, I was two pounds under the minimum weight, that I pleaded to be rescheduled, and that a kindly old doctor who smiled at my plight rescheduled me for the following week and told me to eat bananas and potatoes. On my second try I made it by a half a pound and continued through a very long and exhaustive physical that included agility exercises, questioning by a psychiatrist who took longer than the one who had questioned me at the induction station, X-rays of every part of my body, and more and more lab work. I remember that, after I was informed that I had passed the physical, I was also informed that a "records check" with the Los Angeles Police Department had come back "clean" and that I was now ready for and acceptable to the Airborne Command. When I evinced surprise at the records check, the C&A clerk said, not without a touch of respect, "Three things you gotta have before you're assigned to the Airborne Command: AGCT score of 110 or over, parachute physical passed, and no police record of any kind except they don't say nothing about parking tickets." Apparently they had said nothing about two speeding tickets either.

And I remember that train ride from Wyoming to Georgia in late June, my rumpled khaki uniform, and the quartermaster braid on my cap that I could not hide and could not take off, though I considered trying. But I was sure that if I succeeded, the MPs patroling the train would arrest me for being out of uniform; then I would have "a record" and be disqualified from the parachute school before I had gotten there. So I suffered through that long train ride, one of quite a few lepers among the many soldiers of the combat arms. Only the handful of civilians on that train could have felt more uncomfortable than I did.

Transfer in Denver . . . transfer in Chicago . . . transfer in Atlanta. Atlanta—hot, humid, and a little frightening, for this was the gateway to Fort Benning. Here was the rail transportation officer (RTO) loudspeaker blaring, "Attention, personnel reporting to Fort Benning! Report to the RTO desk at track three." Travel vouchers and orders were checked, and we climbed onto a grimy, old, local train. After the pullman from Denver to Chicago, these dirty coaches that would carry us to our final destination at Columbus seemed to portend a severing from the simple luxuries of the past, a sooty shadow of things to come.

Most of the soldiers on this dreary, miserable train were as new to the Army as I was. Not many spoke. The tumbling, screechy train with its hard, uncomfortable seats was not exactly conducive to conversation as we lurched over the baked red clay of the Georgia countryside, dejectedly looking out of the windows that had to be left open because of the heat. Soot from the locomotive got into our eyes and settled on our khakis. With each mile the lure of Fort Benning lessened a little. At last the train screeched into Columbus, slowed, and halted. Even before it had come to a complete stop, loudspeakers on the station platform boomed their instructions.

"Casual personnel report to the RTO at the center of the platform. Airborne personnel report to the transportation NCO to the far right as you leave the train. . . ." Men in rumpled, begrimed khaki trudged in all directions to the places designated, were collected by guides along the way, and were finally assembled near trucks and buses in front of the station.

Sweating under the weight of my duffel and barracks bags, I stumbled in the direction indicated to me. A paratrooper with a red and yellow armband marked "RTO" directed us to some buses. Another trooper with a clipboard checked our names and loaded us aboard. We were expected. Enviously I looked the two troopers over. Both wore clean, starched khaki uniforms and highly polished paratrooper boots. Their silver wings over the left breast pockets were on a large oval red-white-and-blue background patch that, I was told, was worn by the cadre of the Airborne Command's TPS. The parachute school! One of the trooper-guides climbed into our bus and told the driver, "OK, let's go." To us he said nothing. We were clearly beneath his notice.

Although it was a relief to be out of that train, Columbus did not improve my morale very much. I was, after all, a city boy; small towns depressed me. We went down a characterless main street, turned past a surprisingly large hotel with an equally surprising green park across from it, drove down a residential street, and were out of town. The ten miles or so seemed to take hours before we reached the main gate of Fort Benning. The bus halted at last, and an MP checked the manifest before he waved us on.

3
Fort Benning: The Frying Pan

The parachute training towers that dominate the Fort Benning skyline came closer and closer as our bus rolled slowly through that immense Army post. Although the two-hundred-fifty-foot steel monsters claimed most of our nervous attention, we were curious enough about the legendary "home of the infantry" for an occasional look at its main street, a boulevard fringed with lawns and landscaping behind which stood the massive buildings of the Old Army.

On our left was the elegant officers' club with its cabanas flanking two large swimming pools and outdoor dining terraces. Directly opposite the club was the stately academic building that also housed the headquarters of the infantry school, its grounds richly landscaped with an expanse of carefully manicured green lawn extending from a semicircular forecourt to the street and along the considerable frontage of this handsome, two-story structure. Farther back stood the white infantry chapel with its red tile roof and Old World bell tower, surrounded by trees and rose bushes. I wondered what it would look like inside and resolved to visit it.

Farther down the broad, straight boulevard were the massive red-brick barracks known as the Quadrangle. Their fronts shaded by the thick, dark-green summer foliage of protective trees, these barracks were so much like their German *Kaserne* counterparts that I was startled to find them here in Georgia, reminders that America, too, had its military tradition with roots going back to Prussia's Frederick the Great, who had sent his General von Steuben to conduct our first infantry school.

The bus turned sharply to the left and I was suddenly looking straight at a menacing skeleton of steel that had taken on the proportions of the Eiffel Tower, its top with the four parachute release arms barely within our field of vision. The other towers, now huge, evil, and portentous, were farther to our left, a grotesque welcoming committee to the Army's version of the Inferno.

After a few more turns, the bus halted before a row of ugly, greenish wooden barracks, buildings as temporary as the brick Quadrangle was permanent, nondescript jerry-built hutments miserably hugging a dusty, treeless company street that seemed to run into an infinity of brownish fields totally devoid of vegetation and lying eerily silent, its edges swimming indistinct in the Georgia heat.

Here, in the midst of one of the largest and busiest posts of the United States Army, the traditional home of the Queen of Battles, was an area set aside for the New Soldier, the paratrooper. In the unbearably hot and humid summer of 1943, this area of calculated desolation was the newly plowed field the Army was seeding to grow a species never before encountered.

The significance of the contrast between the old, established Quadrangle sitting in smug permanence behind its old, established trees and this bare field hastily scraped to accommodate four ugly steel towers and rows of temporary wooden hutments did not escape us. One of us articulated it. "Hell," he said, pointing to the towers, "they were gonna tear down the Eiffel Tower right after the Exposition of 1889, too."

And many years after our "Exposition," two of those towers were still there: our monuments, functional reminders of what we were and what we can be.

"Here we are," said the driver cheerily and pulled open the door. "Out!" said the paratrooper-guide in our bus. "Your barracks for the next three days—if you last that long. Grab a bunk and stand by for further orders."

In the barracks were only bunks, nothing else. The unmitigated heat and humidity inside this wooden sweatbox were palpable, almost visible. This barren, ugly, oppressive structure was like no building I had experienced before. I dropped my barracks bag and sat down on a bunk. We waited in silence for what seemed like hours, our rumpled khakis, grimy from the soot of that awful train ride from Atlanta to Columbus, sweat-soaked and sticking uncomfortably to our bodies. The place sapped our energies. Even breathing was a chore.

There was a banging of doors and the command "Attention!"

Startled, we jumped to our feet as a sergeant crashed into the barracks, holding the door open for a young lieutenant, who followed him into the room. Both of these paratroopers were tall and slim. The sergeant looked cool in well-fitting khaki and gleaming paratrooper boots, and the lieutenant wore a perfectly tailored suntan uniform; both had their silver parachute wings fastened to black and red background patches over their left breast pockets. "At ease—rest," said the officer. "Gather round. Sit down."

We sat—grimy, sweating, and now even more conscious of our rumpled, sooty khakis—grouped around the officer in a semicircle on the wooden floor, looking up into his tanned, handsome face, awaiting judgment.

"You," he said, looking at us as though we were vermin, "are in the Frying Pan, the reception station of the parachute school. No one asked you to come here. You will not be welcome until we decide that you are fit to become one of us. You will have three days in which to make up your mind whether that is what you want. At any time during these three days you may quit and there will be no dishonor attached to your quitting. It would, in fact, be a sign of good sense because you have to be crazy to want to belong to us. Paratroops are the shock troops of the army. They are employed only on the most dangerous missions. They are dropped behind enemy lines, are expected to fight against overwhelming odds, and are not expected to get back. No one in his right mind would want to join an outfit like that." The young officer paused. He did not smile. He believed what he was saying.

Hands behind his back, booted legs spread apart, he stood before us like an omen. "Those we accept," he continued, "will be assigned to one of two experimental regiments, parachute infantry regiments. The experiment is to take parachute volunteer recruits, give them basic training, airborne training, and advance training all in one regiment, and then leave them right there in that regiment. Basic training will be known as parachute basic and will last for thirteen weeks. You will never again experience anything like it. Compared to it, combat will seem like recreation. You will then have three weeks of jump training instead of the usual four—B Stage, C Stage, and D Stage."

I had not expected this. I had been told that airborne training would last four weeks and that it would come after basic training. This was something new and quite ominous. Experimental regiments? No one had mentioned those.

The lieutenant did not bother to explain what B, C, and D stages were. He did, however, explain A Stage. That, he said, was the physical conditioning phase; he described the grueling training in blood-chilling detail. One would have to be in excellent condition to take just one week of it. (That was why we had been given a special airborne physical examination.) We, however, who were to be assigned to an experimental regiment would be given thirteen weeks of A Stage. We would be up daily at four o'clock in the morning and be physically conditioned until noon. From one o'clock in the afternoon until six, we would have regular infantry training. All this was to take place in what he called "the Alabama area," across the Chattahoochee River, in complete isolation from the rest of the post. "Look around you," he said. "Compared to the Alabama area, this place here is luxurious." We would come back to "this place" after thirteen weeks to complete our jump training. By that time, he guaranteed us, when the time came for jumping out of an airplane, no one would care whether he had a parachute on or not. But if we survived, which was very doubtful, we would be the best soldiers anywhere in the world. And then we could be employed on missions from which probably no one would return.

"Now," he concluded, "you see why we don't seriously expect you to want to join us. You may leave now or any time within the next three days. You will simply be assigned to a regular straight-leg infantry unit without the least blemish on your record or your honor. In fact, as I said, you'll be doing the smart thing. I will be in my office in the last barracks, next row. See me about leaving and we'll arrange your regular assignment. Any time between now and three days from now."

Silence and unbearable heat. I could hear my heart pounding. "But," said the paratroop lieutenant, and his cold, blue eyes rested briefly on each one of us. I could feel my heart pounding in my veins. "After those three days—*after* those three days—" he paused. I remember when as a small boy I had listened to a very talented aunt of mine telling a Grimm fairy tale and waited in utter terror, as she paused, for the beast to spring out of the pages. Now I held my breath and waited to be devoured by that very talented young lieutenant. "*After* those three days, you will be required to sign a quit slip. When you have signed that quit slip you will no longer be considered a man. You will have become a dog and you will be assigned to the Dog Company of your regiment. You will be dressed in blue denim fatigues and you will do KP and clean-up work for troopers of the regiment for the duration of the remaining training. You will clean barracks and latrines and work in the kitchen all day and you will live in separate barracks because you will not be fit to live with troopers. You will have become a dog. And when we no longer need you after training, we will kick you out into other parts of the army, with that quit slip forever on your record."

It was worse than any Grimm fairy tale I had ever heard. It fastened itself, almost word for word, onto my mind; ever after, the words "quit slip" and the sight of blue denim fatigues made me shudder.

"That's all," said the lieutenant. The command "Attention!" cracked through the dismal room again and we jumped up. At the door, the lieutenant turned his head and smiled a frosty smile. "Come see me, you men. Any time. . . ." Then he was gone.

I walked back to my miserable bunk. Out the window I could see the towers, those towers that represented C Stage, the next-to-the-last week of jump training, an impossible sixteen weeks away. Well, what did I expect? Just because I had had four weeks of the normal eight weeks of basic at Fort Warren—quartermaster basic—did I really think I would sweep through another four weeks and—presto—go through jump training? I had been told—hadn't I?—that parachute volunteers without infantry basic training would have to go through the whole cycle before being admitted to jump school. But no one and nothing had prepared me for this reception in the Frying Pan. I sat on my bunk, dejected, wondering how I would get through the first day, much less thirteen weeks—sixteen weeks—or whatever was to come after that.

The oppressive silence was shattered by a voice with a New York accent. "I don't mind dying for my country," it said from somewhere within the barracks, "but I sure as hell ain't gonna be no goddamn animal for it!" There was genuine fury in that voice, and its owner shouldered his barracks bag and walked out of the room.

Another man stood up and made ready to leave. This time I looked up. He was about my size, a little older, with a sad, intelligent face. "Look," he said apologetically to no one in particular, "this is a heathen ritual which has no place in the twentieth century among civilized people. Not even the Nazis would do this to a man who wants to serve his country." He, too, shouldered his bag. "I'm sorry, fellows," he said sadly, "I really am." Then he walked out.

I felt stupid sitting there. That man was not a coward. In his own, sensitive way, he was as deeply outraged as the man who had preceded him. Any intelligent, feeling human being should, it seemed to me, be offended to his very soul by this unspeakable reception. Why, then, I agonized, did I want to stay? Why did the others sit there, dumb like sheep? We were all presumed to be of above average intelligence, having been required to score at least 110 on the AGCT, the same score required of officer candidates. Why did we not all get up and leave? What were we? What was I?

Suddenly I shut it all off. What was I? Well, first things first! First I was going to go through the training. First I was going to get all the way up to where that goddamn superman of a lieutenant was snarling down. Once up there, I would indisputably have earned the right to follow whatever course I desired. And so, first things first. I was scared, but I was at peace. I would come home carrying my shield or I would be brought home on it.

The barracks were emptying and a chow line was forming in front of the mess hall. Eight ugly barracks, twenty men to each. How many would be there for supper tomorrow? Tomorrow, we had been told by a sergeant, we would fall out in khaki trousers and T-shirts. No one had dared ask, "What then?"

Bedtime was at eight, lights out at eight-thirty. By then I was asleep.

A whistle shrilled and I was instantly awake. It was exactly 4:00 A.M. "Outside! Hit it! Fall in in two ranks in front of your barracks. Go! Go! Go!"

No chance to wash, brush teeth, go to the toilet. Khaki trousers and T-shirt, low-cut boots hastily laced, and then outside. Floodlights in front of the barracks made the early morning darkness beyond seem even deeper and gloomier.

In front of each barracks, two rows of high school–age boys were forming in the dusty company street, two rows of boys who would, within days, be boys no longer.

"Fall in!" I had not had a chance to see what we were facing, who gave the commands, what went on left and right. I was in the front rank and surreptitiously glanced left and right to see a remarkably straight line of recruits in T-shirts at stiff attention. Facing us in front of each barracks complement stood a tanned, athletic-looking young man, also in khaki trousers and T-shirt. But his T-shirt had large black parachute wings stenciled on the chest, and his khaki trousers were bloused over paratrooper boots gleaming in the electric light, a creature from another world. Five steps in back of the paratroopers, in the center of the formation, stood another of these creatures. He had given the command to fall in. What rank they were we could not tell. Nor did it matter.

"When you get the command 'fall in,'" the creature boomed over our heads, "you will stand like statues. Like statues. You will not glance around or even blink your eyes. And when you do, you will execute twenty-five push-ups. When an instructor tells an individual to do push-ups, he will simply say, 'Give me twenty-five.' When addressing a formation, he will command, 'Leaning rest position—*Move*!' All right." He paused, then raised his booming voice an octave: "Dress right—*Dress*!" We did the best we could, most of us having at least been exposed to this command at the reception centers. Like sheepdogs, the assistant instructors prodded us into the proper stance, growling, "Cover down, goddamn it. Eyes right. Turn your head to the right. Not *you*, goddamn it! The first man on the right keeps his eyes front. Heads up, for Christ's sake!"

"Ready—*Front*!" Again the sheepdogs prodded and bit. "Snap your left arm down and eyes front at the same time. If you don't understand

English, get the hell out of this formation. Front rank—two steps forward—*Move!*" Then a short, oppressive silence.

"Leaning rest position—*Move!*" We scrambled to the ground only to hear the roar, "Recover! As you were! Goddamn it, when you hear that command, you *drop!* You don't *crawl!*" He demonstrated: body perfectly straight, muscles rippling, he had dropped to the floor of the slightly raised platform on which he was standing, looking like an Olympic gymnast. He sprang to his feet. "Leaning rest position—*Move!*" We dropped to the dust. "Ready—*Exercise!*" I had heard about the push-ups and had practiced. I thought that I did quite well as I executed the cadence. ". . . One—two—three—*Eleven*, one—two—three—*Twelve* . . . ." My body started to resist a little. One of the sheepdogs above me said, "Keep your ass level with your back. Keep it straight, goddamn it. All the way down—all the way up!"

". . . One—two—three—*Twenty-four*, one—two—three—*Halt!* Position of attention—*Move!*" My shoulders ached, but I had done twenty-five pretty good push-ups. It was a nice feeling. "At ease, not *Rest!* Detail: Atten-*hut*! Leaning rest position—*Move!* Ready—*Exercise!*"

No one completed the next twenty-five push-ups by the book, but somehow, arms and shoulders aching, constantly prodded by the assistant instructors, we clawed and wheezed and struggled our way to that "*one—two—three—Halt.*" My elbows shook violently and my head pounded. The sheepdogs were snarling, "Keep your back straight. Elbows straight. Head up." Then "Position of attention—*Move!*" We struggled to our feet, hot, dizzy, aching, sick to our stomachs. Three people remained lying in the dust. "At ease—*Rest.*" A medic we had not seen before walked over to each of the three men on the ground. Our first formation wasn't even over and we had casualties! My mind swam.

"All right," boomed the creature from another world, the creature in that spotless white T-shirt with the black parachute wings stenciled on the chest, the gleaming boots, looking down at us who were now dripping with sweat and covered with Georgia dust, filthy to the very bones, and still in our first formation of the day. "All right. It's OK if you faint. We won't dock you for that. But don't ever drop out of a formation or just lie there. Two ways to go: You walk out of here and get reassigned; no sweat during the next three days. *Or* we disqualify you. As you were told in your orientation, you can see the lieutenant any time. Nobody asked you to come here. All right. Detail: Atten-*hut*! Right—*Face!* Forward—*March!* Double time—*March!*"

Filthy, weak, aching, we ran around the perimeter of the Frying Pan, the sheepdog instructors, cool in their white T-shirts and gleaming boots, easily loping beside us, counting cadence without so much as breathing hard: "Hut—four, hut—four, hut, two, three, four, hut—four, hut—four . . . ." In front of me a man pitched forward, bounced on his right shoulder, rolled onto his back, and lay still. "Look to the front!" commanded a sheepdog. "Heads up! Elbows horizontal at your sides! Hut—four, hut—four, hut, two, three, four. . . ."

I could see very little of the area as we were running, and what I perceived was only dead grass and dust. I was on the verge of collapse. My legs did not want to function. Each step seemed to be my last. But somehow when a foot hit the ground, the leg did not buckle. My breath came in painful, short wheezes. The landscape, such as it was, gradually grew dim and indistinct.

"Quick-time—*March*! Detail—*Halt*! Left—*Face*! At ease—*Rest*!" We were back in front of our barracks.

We stood at "rest," swaying, heaving with labored breath, sweat soaked, filthy. The sergeant-instructor who had led us around this Godforsaken dust bin looked as though he had just come out of an air-conditioned NCO club. Without any apparent effect from the run, he said, "After you fall out, you will shave and shower, eat breakfast, and return to your bunks. You fall in here again at six. Detail: Atten-*hut*! Fall out! *As you were*—! At the command 'fall out' you execute an about-face in a sharp, military manner! What the hell do you think this is, a girl's finishing school? Leaning rest position—*Move*!" His gymnast's body went down like a board, his crew-cut head lifted above the rippling shoulder muscles, disdainful blue eyes sweeping the sorry mess of us in the dust. "Ready—*Exercise*! One—two—three—*One*! One—two—three—*Two* . . . ." The sheepdogs moved along the formation, growled, bit, snarled. Next to me I could hear sobbing. Down farther I could hear a choking cough. ". . . three—*Eleven* . . . ." Everything turned a dark red.

A buzz blended into indistinguishable human sounds. I was on my back in the dust, looking up at a medic. The medic disappeared from my view and one of the sheepdogs swam in. "You're all right." I could now understand. "Give me five more good ones." There was nothing left in me, not even the energy to quit. But I must have done something because I heard, very close to my ear, " . . . one—two—three—*Halt*! Position of attention—*Move*! At ease—*Rest*."

The formation seemed different. The men were standing, or trying to, but they were spread apart. Only minutes had passed, but I could feel a change. "Detail: Atten-*Hu*t! Fall out!" I executed an about-face, fell down, scrambled up, and staggered into the barracks, managed to find my bunk, and collapsed on it. I couldn't think. The red color had come back behind my eyelids. Then I heard people moving; water was running in the shower room. I remembered the words "shower, shave, mess hall" and knew that if I did not shower, shave, and eat, I would be disqualified. I got up from my bunk.

I managed the routine of cleaning up and eating, but I had no clear recollection of talking to anyone or hearing any voices until, at six o'clock, we were back in formation—to begin the day.

The formation had shrunk to about half of what it had been two hours earlier. This seemed to please the sergeant-instructor on his platform, who looked at us, nodded, and smiled that frosty smile I had seen on the lieutenant's face.

Our detail, now consisting of about seventy men, was double-timed to a field of the ubiquitous dead grass. We heard new commands. The sheepdogs growled and nipped us into the positions. "Extend to the right—*Move*! Arms downward—*Move*! Right—*Face*! Extend to the right—*Move*! Arms downward—*Move*! All right—cover down! Left to right—*Count off*! Even numbers to the right—*Uncover*! At ease—*Rest*. We are now going to acquaint you with the exercises you will be doing in the morning when you—if you—are assigned to one of the regiments in the Alabama area. The first exercise will be the squat thrust. I will demonstrate . . . ."

And then the now familiar "Detail: Atten-*Hut*! Starting position—*Move*! Ready—*Exercise*!" The cadence droned through the squat thrusts, the sit-ups, the bend-and-reach, the turn-and-bounce, the ubiquitous push-ups—the "Army dozen" as it has not been done before or since.

A favorite, second only to the push-ups, were the arm circles. "Arms extended horizontally, palms up, fingers extended and joined . . . arms rotated from the shoulders in small circles . . . ready—*Exercise*!" But no cadence. Just circles and the sheepdogs moving among the open ranks, doing the exercise while walking, snarling, "Keep 'em up, goddamn it. Keep those arms straight. *Circles*, soldier, not flapping 'em up and down. You ain't no seagull! Keep those arms straight!" After about a hundred twenty circles on top of just completed turn-and-bounce exercises of repetitions everyone had lost count of or was trying not to think about, arms and shoulders started to ache and because only the instructors knew how long they were going to keep us at it, the endless exercises without cadence became physically and mentally unbearable.

Finally, when the instructor picked up the count of "one, two, three—*Halt*!" and when we thought that it was over at last, there was no command of "Arms downward—*Move*!" They kept us there, our arms leaden weights, assistant instructors hissing, "Keep those arms straight, soldier. No one told you to bring 'em down. Up at shoulder level!" Again there was no telling how long they would keep us like that. "Arms downward—*Move*! At ease. Rest. Shake 'em out! All right. That was one goddamn sorry exhibition of lack of discipline. You don't move your arms down—not even a little—until the command is given to do so. Detail: Atten-*Hut*! Leaning rest position—*Mhove*! Ready—*Exercise*!"

Push-ups and double time: airborne staples. Push-ups were for regular exercise and for infractions real, imagined, or manufactured. Double time because that's the way the airborne units move.

Then there was the command "*Jab!*" encountered only at the parachute school. It was, we were told, a device to trigger instant, unthinking responses. It was given indiscriminately and when least expected. At the command "*Jab!*" we would strike our left breast with our right fist, insuring that the force of the strike would be audible to the instructor. The fist would remain where it was until the command "Recover!" If the command "*Jab! Jab!*" were given, the left-fist-to-right-breast was added. A slow response or one that was not sufficiently audible meant, of course, twenty-five push-ups. "All right. I'm going to ask one of you for the reason we use the command '*Jab*' at the . . . goddamn it! When you hear that word, what do you do? Detail: Atten-*Hut*! Leaning rest position—*Mhove*! Ready—*Exercise*!"

We exercised. "All right. Any questions about the command '*Jab*'?" Right fists were striking left breasts with loud, dull thumps. "Recover! Any questions?"

"Yes, sergeant. What if the command is given three times?"

"What's your name, soldier?"

"Hager, sergeant."

"Give me twenty-five, Hager."

That night, our first night at the Frying Pan, there were twelve men in our barracks.

By noon of the second day, two men had been medically evacuated and one more simply vanished. The smaller our formations became, the more pleased our instructors seemed to be.

By supper time of the second day, we had found out that the instructors were not from the Parachute Training Regiment (PTR) but belonged to the 507th and 513th Parachute Infantry regiments, those "experimental regiments" across the Chattahoochee River. The three-day "physical and mental screening" process at the Frying Pan was not a regular part of parachute school training. It was designed exclusively for those regiments and would be discontinued when the regiments were filled up. We were, in effect, guinea pigs. By then it was too late for those of us who remained to take any action. We were already committed.

After we were dismissed from our final formation on the third day and had stumbled back into our barracks to collapse on our bunks, there were nine exhausted, bewildered, and scared men left out of the original twenty volunteers in our barracks. At the formation we had been told that we had until 6:00 A.M. the next day to request a transfer without punitive consequences.

The deadline passed. We had breakfast in silence. What now? We would live in a different world, a world as yet unknown, the terror of a quit slip and the fear of disqualification always hovering in our awareness. It was now all or nothing.

For one brief moment that morning, the gloom of anticipating the unknown was dispelled. When we were in formation to board the trucks for the Alabama area, the young lieutenant with the silver parachute badge on a black and red background patch appeared in front of us and said, "Welcome to the Five-thirteenth Parachute Infantry Regiment."

4
Parachute Basic Training I

We sat on the hard benches of the two-and-a-half-ton trucks, bone weary, muscles aching from the three-day torture the sadists of the Frying Pan had called physical and mental screening, disheveled, nondescript bundles of bewildered misery in dirty khakis. We passed the Main Theater, the Red Cross building, the snack bar—manifestations of civilization that now seemed abstract and from which we felt irrevocably removed. We rolled through the Lawson Field area and wondered how it felt to be in the Air Corps. We watched the troop carrier crewmen stroll from cool, modern barracks to cool, inviting mess halls where, no doubt, they would take an hour for a delicious breakfast. Quickly we put such contemplations out of our minds as something downright unhealthy. Our trucks skirted the airfield, and we looked with momentary interest at the many C-47 aircraft sitting silently—waiting. We looked at the hangars, the rigger sheds, the B-Stage apparatus area, without knowing exactly what we were seeing. The road narrowed, went through some woods, seemed to dip downhill, and the trucks stopped. We had reached the Chattahoochee, our River Styx.

While we waited for the ferry to make its way over from the Alabama bank of the river, we were allowed to get out of the trucks. Silently we looked at the cheerless scene. Everything seemed to be olive drab or dirty-khaki colored: the trees of the sad little forest on either side of the road, the muddy banks of the Chattahoochee, the river itself, sluggishly laboring its way south to Florida.

Across the river, the civilian ferryman was casting off his little craft, pulling the ferry, which was nothing but a wooden platform with makeshift railings, along a sagging rope anchored to either bank. Slowly, crawfishing against the stream, the ferry made its way toward us. On it were two jeeps and a handful of paratroopers in jumpsuits. It was our first sight of these sharp-looking uniforms with the big, baggy pockets, and, as these smartly uniformed troopers came ashore, we gazed at them reverently. They climbed into the two jeeps without taking any notice of us and roared off.

The Chattahoochee ferry

Then it was our turn. Slowly, silently we crossed the muddy Chattahoochee. Back on our trucks, we went up the embankment, our engines whining in low gear, turned left onto the road running parallel to the river, and rode for four miles through the dismal countryside of peanut patches and anemic pine woods. Finally we reached the drab one-story hutments that were to be our home for the next thirteen weeks—an eternity.

We seemed to be one of the first groups of volunteers to be assigned; we were told that, while we waited for the regiment to be at full strength and ready to begin basic training, we would receive temporary assignments. To my dismay, I was assigned to Service Company and secretly suspected that it was because I had come from Fort Warren with quartermaster colors on my cap.

With the exception of one hour of the kind of physical training we had experienced at the Frying Pan eight hours a day, there was almost no formal training. Instead, we cleaned barracks, carried bunks and wall lockers, lugged mattresses, stacked sheets and pillow cases, and uncrated and stored webb equipment, steel helmets, mess kits, and fatigue uniforms. We ranged all over the regimental area and perceived, without ever being told, that we were helping the 513th cadre with the task of preparing our camp for the troops to follow. We were finally issued fatigue uniforms and turned our khakis in to the laundry, an act of transition that helped to acclimatize us somewhat. Then the crates with weapons arrived. Carbines, M-1s, Thompson submachine guns, Browning automatic rifles, .30-caliber light machine guns, all in cosmoline, brand new. We carried the crates and opened them but were not allowed to touch the weapons. We admired them from a respectful distance as the cadre armorers took them from their cradles and carried them deep into the recesses of the arms room. Then more crates arrived— .45-caliber pistols, bazookas, 60- and 81-mm mortars . . . . Again we lugged and shoved them in their crates to battalion arms rooms and stood aside as cadre lifted them out. Holy items may be touched only by the initiated.

For two weeks we swept, cleaned, washed, carried, stacked, and painted. Slowly the considerable labor pool of Service Company dwindled as assignments to permanent organizations were made; those of us who remained were beginning to worry that perhaps Service Company was to be our permanent assignment. When my orders finally came, I was relieved to find that I had been assigned to Company A, First Battalion—an infantry line company at last!

Two of us were taken to Company A by jeep and dropped off at the orderly room. It was just another drab hutment, but in front of it, planted firmly in the Alabama dust, was the infantry-blue guidon with the white crossed rifles, the white letter A, and the number 513 in it.

We walked into the orderly room and waited behind a barrier, still clutching our heavy bags. A clerk looked up and told us to put our bags down and step over to the barrier. He had our records on his desk and asked which of us was which. We gave our names and he picked up my records, saying, "One at a time. You—come in here and report to the first sergeant."

I opened the barrier gate and followed the clerk to the first sergeant's desk just beside a door marked "Company Commander." The clerk placed my records on the desk and the first sergeant picked them up, rising from his chair. "Welcome to Company A, Gabel," he said and shook my hand. He was what I expected a first sergeant of a rifle company to be, and more. He was a type: professional, serious without being unfriendly, ever conscious of his responsibility. He would be fair and he would try to be just. He would be respected first and then liked. We were in good hands.

No interview. Welcome to Company A was enough for now. The rest would come later. "Let's meet the company commander," he said. "Do you know how to report?" I got nervous. I had reported to the Service Company commander, but this was different. "Yes, sergeant," I said dubiously. The first sergeant knocked on the door marked "Company Commander" and a hard voice said, "Come in." It was a command rather than an invitation.

The first sergeant opened the door and almost gently motioned me forward. For a moment he blocked my view as he stepped up to the company commander's desk, placed my records on it, and said, "Private Gabel, sir." Then he stood aside and I faced my new commander, Captain John H. Spears.

I was immediately unnerved. There sat the first "real" parachute infantry officer I had so far encountered except for that young lieutenant at the Frying Pan. He was a grim-looking man, his clear, deep-set eyes mustering me under perpetually contracted brows. He was a lean, strong, old-looking young man and scared me by just sitting there, saying nothing. I felt that I would never be able to report properly to this stern, old young man, that he would find me unfit to be one of his riflemen, and that he would send me back to the limbo of the Service Company.

I came to attention, saluted, and croaked, "Private Gabel reporting to the commanding officer, sir!" A couple of long seconds elapsed before he returned my salute, seconds during which I felt I was being inspected, evaluated, and rejected. Then he rose from his chair, walked around his desk toward me, and put out his hand. He looked at me grimly with those clear, inspecting eyes and said, "Glad to have you, Gabel." He did not smile as he shook my hand, but I thought I detected a slight change around his eyes. "Thank you, sir," I managed. I did not dare add, "I'm glad to be here," although I was. At last I had officially arrived.

The training cycle began—thirteen weeks of parachute basic.

I had had a brief look at basic training when I was exposed to four weeks of it at Fort Warren. Many years later, during the Korean War, when I was an officer, I watched troops going through their twelve-week cycle of infantry basic and I saw them again during the Viet Nam era. But never have I seen or experienced the likes of parachute basic, as never again have I seen the product of such training, given within a line regiment and administered by the officers and NCOs who would lead the same men in advanced training, in maneuvers, and in combat.

I was awake when that strange, musical, Prussian-sounding bugle call rang lustily through the darkness, and out of bed by the time its last, long note was interrupted by the roar, "Hit it! Out of the sack! Go! Go! Go!"

Company A sprinted outside, practically from bed to company street, and formed quickly into its platoons and squads. "Fall in!" That was the first sergeant. We could barely make him out, there in the dark in front of the company, but we snapped to attention as though we were being individually inspected by him.

50   Training

Capt. John Spears, commanding officer, A Company, 513th PIR, in 1946. He was Gabel's first commanding officer.

Platoon sergeants took the report from their squad leaders and wheeled about to face the first sergeant. "Report!"

"First platoon present or accounted for!"

"Second platoon present or accounted for!"

"Third platoon present or accounted for!"

It seemed unremarkable and accepted as normal that even in the early morning darkness commands were executed with precision, salutes were sharp and exact.

Only dimly seen, the first sergeant made an about-face and reported to our company commander. "Sir, Company A is formed!" The salute was returned. Platoon leaders were posted. Then the hard voice of the company commander cracked through the early morning: "Right—*Face*! Forward—*Mharch*! Column right—*Mharch*! Double time—*Mharch*!" They wasted no time. One hundred and eighty seconds ago, I thought, we had been in bed.

We had not been told how far we would run. Only the cadre knew. The run was therefore made more excruciating by its apparent endlessness. Platoon sergeants counted cadence. By the time we left the regimental area and reached the dusty road leading to the river crossing, we were sweating and breathing hard.

Three men abreast, the platoons of Company A in meticulous formation beat a rhythmic tattoo on the dusty Alabama road. After only three days of basic training, the men looked infinitely better than the recruits at Fort Warren had looked after three weeks. By the crunching rhythm of boots striking gravel, it was clear that not one man of the company was out of step.

Behind us we could hear the commands of Company B as it moved out onto the road. Behind it would be Company C.

The sound of the battalion, its muffled rhythm already indicating the latent power in its ranks, did much to help my legs move in the way they were expected to move, though thighs and calves ached. The cadence, shouted effortlessly by the young platoon sergeant, who occasionally ran backward to survey his platoon, also helped—for a while.

Dawn was breaking. Sweat was running into my eyes and my aching legs grew weak and rubbery. Worst of all, I had lost control of my breath. It was now coming fast and wheezing through my wide-open mouth, and my insides seemed to flutter. How far had we come? How much farther? How long? We were not allowed to wear watches, but a look at one wouldn't have helped me run.

There was some commotion in the third platoon. It broke stride momentarily, then quickly regained it as the platoon sergeant commanded, "All right, pick it up! Hut—four, hut—four . . . ." A man or two must have fallen. They did not fall out or simply quit because the platoon would not have lost its stride in that case. They must have fainted in ranks where they ran and the platoon had to run over the fallen forms, thus breaking its stride. "Look to the front, goddamn it! Heads up! Hut—four, hut—four, hut—two—three—four. . . ."

An ambulance, following the battalion like a vulture, would pick up the ones who had fainted. Lucky guys.

I was afraid that my legs would buckle and that I would cave in without fainting. What then? What would the medics do? They said you'd have to faint or die or . . . . "Column left—*Mharch*! Column left—*Mharch*!" The company was making a U turn. The sweat-soaked first platoon passed us before we, too, made our turn. Their heads were up, eyes to the front, elbows at their sides in the prescribed manner. The "rsh—rsh—rsh" of their boots in double time on the dirt road was as precise as it had been at the start of the run. I marveled at them and could not understand how they managed to do it.

"Quick time—*Mharch*!" There was a sliding and tripping motion as we slowed to a walk and my knees actually did buckle, but I stiffened them fearfully at the shout of the platoon sergeant, "You're at attention! Pick up the cadence! Hut—four, hut—four . . . ."

Once again we double timed; by then I had gotten my second wind. Quick time again and the battalion marched back into the regimental area.

In the shower that morning, I heard Hager's booming voice over the rush of the water, "What the goddamn hell did we get ourselves into here, anyway?" But he was grinning, the idiot! I just knew it.

The line for breakfast started forming in front of the battalion mess hall at 5:54 A.M. By then it was light, hot, and humid.

As we inched into the mess hall, a jukebox not far from the door started to play. Someone had dropped a nickel into it. For the first time in three days and ten meals, I noticed that it was playing the same song it had played before, the only song on it. It was "Boogie Woogie." I knew the song, of course, in Tommy Dorsey's arrangement. Soon it would be the most hated song in the first battalion, and there would be a concerted effort to catch the phantom lover of "Boogie Woogie" who managed to activate that God-awful jukebox at each and every meal without being detected. After a while we were sure that the phantom was cadre—that "Boogie Woogie" was just one more device to drive us out of our minds and into the orderly room for a quit slip. Only our great hunger, fresh eggs, sausages, lots of toast, and good coffee managed to neutralize that song.

It had been one of those special moments when the rifles were issued. Our platoon sergeant had made a ceremony out of it. "When you step up to receive your rifle, receive it as you would a wife. Treat it gently. It will be yours to have and to hold until death do you part. Only for inspection or on orders or when you yourselves secure it, must it part your company. In the field, you will sleep with it. You will come to know it intimately and will always keep it clean and in superior functioning order. Learn its serial number as you have learned your own. All right . . . ." Then each man was called and handed his rifle. It would be a long time before we would fire it. There would be a long courtship first.

Although the first hour of the afternoon was in a classroom, it relaxed no one. The classroom was simply another barracks with field tables and chairs instead of beds. By the time we took our seats, the Alabama summer sun had made a baking oven out of the wood-and-tarpaper hutment. We had brought our M-1 rifles and had placed them on the field tables before us. We sat down.

And there I was, an embryo rifleman in an embryo rifle company, my M-1 on the field table. Much as I wanted to be a good man to my rifle, I was afraid I would never be able to remember all its parts or master its disassembly and assembly in the time required. I watched one of our squad leaders as he pulled down a chart showing the three main groupings and a multitude of parts.

"Yesterday I went through this thing by the numbers and you people learned how to break it down into the three groupings which are . . . Gabel?"

Thank God, I was the first one and for the easiest question, too. I stood up and came to attention. "The trigger housing group, the barrel and receiver group, and the stock group, sergeant!"

"Very good." I sat down. I would not be called again for some time and I felt better. "So that's where we'll start. Break down your rifles into the three main groups." I picked up my rifle, pulled back on the trigger guard and separated the trigger housing, pulled up on the barrel and receiver, and laid the three groups side by side on the table. I was quite pleased with myself for having done it smoothly and fast.

"Now for a quick review before we go any further," the sergeant said and turned to the chart. His pointer tapped the parts as he named them. I became dejected again.

"That's all there is to it," he concluded. "Now, you will disassemble your rifle as I tell you. What will be the first thing you do? I just told you that, remember? All right, Leverson."

"Remove the bullet guide, sergeant?"

"Don't ask me, I'm asking you."

"Remove the bullet guide, sergeant."

"Give me twenty-five, Leverson. Benny?"

"Disengage the follower rod, sergeant."

"Very good. Sit down, Leverson. All right, people, do what the man said. Disengage the follower rod."

We went through it from follower rod to gas cylinder lock screw and I worried all the way. The sergeant went through the disassembly on his own rifle, holding each part and asking what it was. He held up the trigger and separated a part from it, holding it in his left hand. It was my turn again. "Hammer spring housing, sergeant."

"All right." That one had been easy because I could associate it with the spring behind the trigger.

And *that* was an easy question, too. "Hammer spring," said Otto.

"Brilliant, Hager," said the sergeant without smiling. Otto grinned broadly. "Give me twenty-five, Hager," said the sergeant in the same tone of voice. "Twenty-three, twenty-four, twenty-five. Sit down, Hager. There is absolutely nothing funny about the M-One rifle."

After a ten-minute break in the meager shade of the hutment, we assembled the rifle. Again we named each part and I felt increasingly inadequate. I knew fairly well where the parts belonged, but many of them I simply could not remember by name. Even later, when I became proficient at field stripping the weapon, its parts remained a stumbling block to me, and people who could glibly name them at random gave me an inferiority complex. I respected the M-1, took good care of it, and qualified as a sharpshooter on the range with it. But I never loved it—ours was a marriage of convenience.

In England, we parted. I became a battalion scout and was issued a Thompson submachine gun that was considerably less complicated. There was, I confess, some sadness as I handed my M-1 to the armorer, for we had served each other well and I had been proud to be a rifleman. But it was better for both of us that we parted. We remained friends and I remained respectful, but I never quite lost my inferiority complex, noticeable each time I watched a rifleman at care and cleaning, even after I had become a rifle platoon leader.

Those afternoon hours until 6:00 P.M. consisted of intensive, highly concentrated infantry training. Many subjects on which regular infantry basic spent much precious training time had been woven into the morning hours and into each spare minute. Close-order drill, for instance, was almost taken for granted. Wrong moves during formations would cost twenty-five push-ups; split-second execution of commands became a way of life within days. Fast paced, filling every minute, the weaponry tools of trade were presented to us by the experts who were to lead us. Examinations after each hour insured that we fully understood what had been taught. Classroom instruction was followed by field application. Everything was done with extreme care and on the double at the same time. First aid, map reading with its signs and symbols, scale and coordinates, squad tactics, field fortifications, cover and concealment, chemical warfare, mines and demolitions, combat in towns and cities, hand-to-hand combat, scouting and patroling, communications, night problems, combat intelligence, firing ranges . . . on the double! Learn. Remember. Do it *right*, or we'll disqualify you. Can't do it? Sign a quit slip!

We had squad formations, each of which was executed at a dead run. From a squad column we galloped into a squad diamond and from there into skirmishers and back into a column. For a short while we would march in a column, grateful for the respite, only to see the squad leader's arms signal for a diamond again. There were no breaks in the sense that we could sit out our ten minutes on our own time. The ten minutes were spent in reviewing hand and arm signals and in practicing the signals ourselves. Then we sprinted out into the heat and dust again.

Showers were as mandatory before supper as before breakfast; so, as we stood in the evening chow line, we were clean, though tired. And we were tentatively happy. We had made it through another day, and a dim outline of parachute basic was becoming faintly discernible. There was reason to believe that we might make it. But it would be quite a job each day. Then we braced ourselves as we entered the mess hall. Any moment that damn song would begin.

The jukebox was located in the line of traffic of the people leaving the mess hall and of cadre coming in by way of the exit and in the traffic lane of cooks and KPs. The corner was always crowded and from our position at the entrance we could never see exactly what was going on near the machine. Even as I looked toward that corner, "Boogie Woogie" spilled into the room and no amount of cursing would turn it off. But again the food was good and plenty and, though it seemed longer than it had ever been, the song finally came to its end and we could enjoy our dessert in relative peace. Most of us were in bed by 7:30 P.M. and fell asleep immediately.

It was during our first week that most quit slips were signed. Those who signed them simply could not believe that what had been threatened at the Frying Pan would actually be carried out. Or if carried out, that it could possibly be worse punishment than the prospect of going through three months of the agony unmercifully imposed by the physical and mental demands of parachute basic.

As they fell out of formations to trudge dejectedly, sometimes defiantly, to their orderly rooms to sign a quit slip, the rest of us waited apprehensively for their fate. It struck instantaneously. They had been moved from our barracks even before we stood our formation. Uniforms were taken away from them and they were issued blue denim fatigues. On the same day they reported to the kitchen and relieved most of the KPs on duty there. During our last formation of the day of the first exodus, we were told that several "persons" had signed quit slips and had been reassigned to the regimental Dog Company, not to be confused with the line company of the same designation. They were, we were told, no longer members of the regiment and would remain on the rolls only for the purpose of performing menial tasks for the regiment. They were no longer considered men and we, who were training to become paratroopers, would have no further contact with them and would not talk to them except when giving them directives for service in the mess hall or for cleaning latrines and common areas of our barracks.

At supper time we had our first look at these poor creatures in their blue denims. They seemed to be in a state of shock as they circulated among the tables and served coffee, picked up dirty trays, and wiped up food spills. Only this morning, I thought, they had been a part of us, running on that hot, dusty road toward the Chattahoochee ferry crossing. I shuddered.

This diabolical innovation, implemented only once, even in wartime and under experimental conditions, had a double-edged effect: It illustrated to us most horribly that there was, indeed, a fate worse than parachute basic and galvanized us to efforts beyond what we had imagined we could be capable of. And it subtly bred a sense of respect, of superiority, of belonging, of pride, of brotherhood with those who remained—it bred a spirit that would evolve and grow, as other, more somber events enveloped us throughout the life and much of the physical death of our regiment, into an esprit de corps of enduring magnitude.

The noon meals, after almost a normal, full working day of strenuous physical training, were a welcome break that we anticipated with pleasure despite the competition of that blaring jukebox. "It's one of those goddamn dog KPs," Benny speculated as the song started. "I just bet it is. Revenge is what they want, those goddamn quitters!"

"Hell, those poor bastards wouldn't have the guts," someone said. "It's just part of the shit they try to rattle your cage with. Probably activated from battalion headquarters."

"Oh, for Christ's sake—it's just one of our stupid, goddamn people right here who get his rocks off over that song, that's all. I'll catch the bastard soon enough and stuff his ass right into that machine!"

"Let's just disconnect the goddamn thing or smash it up."

"Yeah, and get disqualified." Silence. Again the jungle strains of "Boogie Woogie" with its hopping rhythm (ever after sending visions of Zulu warriors with spears in a long chow line rocking up and down whenever I heard that song) dominated the first half of the meal. When it was finished, many eyes remained riveted on the jukebox, watching for the phantom to drop a second nickel. He never did.

Each day was different. Each day brought at least one little surprise, at least one more step in the graduating pressures of this strange smithy where a new weapon was being forged.

As we fell out for our morning run on Monday of the fifth week, our company guidon came with us for the first time.

Platoon leaders had been posted and the company commander was facing his company. One step to his right front stood our first guidon bearer. He had been selected from our ranks because he had excelled in training subjects and military appearance, the latter truly a difficult achievement given the uniformly excellent appearance of the company.

Each week a new guidon bearer would be selected on the same basis, and each week no one was either surprised or resentful when the selection was announced. He was our representative. But our first guidon bearer seemed to feel awkward. His shy smile and slightly cocked head conveyed that he did not really want to be different, that he would rather be in his platoon, and that he himself had nothing to do with his being there, rigidly holding the guidon staff to his right side, the blue pennant lazily curling outward in the early morning breeze.

"Right—*Face!*" In the blink of an eye, the awkwardness had disappeared. At the preparatory command of "Right," the guidon had shot straight up, propelled by the right arm and steadied by the left hand with such precision that we thought it had been secretly practiced all night. The smile had disappeared, replaced by concentration and a touch of pride, pride with which I, too, was touched. That blue pennant, with its white crossed rifles, the letter A, and the numerals 513, was *my* guidon. As we executed the movement at the command "Face," the pennant shot back into its carrying position.

The company commander strode to the head of the column, the guidon bearer one step behind and to his left. "Forward . . ."—up went the guidon again—" . . . *Mharch!*" Down it went once more, rhythmically moving with the marching column. When we went into double time, it fluttered before us at the "port arms" position, placing an extra load onto its bearer, who would now have to run eight miles with it. For this day was the day we would run to the ferry and back without a marching break. This was the day we took our first tangible step toward becoming a rifle company. On this day, not one man fell out of the column, though two were medically evacuated after the company was dismissed from its morning run.

PT was not easier than it had been before. What no one seemed to notice was that repetitions had been steadily increased until the fifth week. From here on, the incredible pace would simply be maintained. An apogee had been reached and the regiment would now catch its second breath.

Again, in the afternoon our spartan classroom provided no real respite from the physical exertions of the morning. We were reviewing map reading and had reached the subject of the grid-magnetic (G-M) angle. I had to struggle with it almost as much as I had to struggle with the parts of the M-1. According to the instructor, naturally, there was nothing complicated about the G-M angle. Simple: It is the angle between grid north and magnetic north. It is always measured *from* grid *to* magnetic north and is written as a magnitude and a direction, as in five degrees east. See this map? Now, in the marginal information you always find this declination diagram, OK? See it? Good. Now let's determine the G-M angle for this map. As you can see, this diagram is for 1940, mean declination 1940. Annual magnetic change two feet westerly. In this case, magnetic north is east of grid north, so the G-M angle is east. Now this one is for 1940. What would it be for 1943? All right. Annual magnetic change is two feet westerly so each year the size of the G-M angle decreases by two feet. *Decreases.* East is least and west is best. Remember that. All right. So this one decreases two feet each year. So now, in 1943, it's what? Right. You subtract. East is least. Suppose it were a westerly declination? West is best. You add. All right, east is least and west is best. Remember. So now we have the G-M angle for this map. Let's see how we use it. Suppose you're a patrol leader out there in the boondocks and you see an enemy machine gun position. You take your compass and read the azimuth from your position to the enemy position and it's one hundred twenty degrees. Now, that's a *magnetic* azimuth so if you want to locate that machine gun on your map you've got to find the *grid* azimuth, the one on your map.

I was soaked with sweat, only half of it caused by the nearly intolerable afternoon heat. I kept my finger on the declination diagram and stared at the map on my field table in front of me. I grieved. Not only couldn't I run without gasping for breath, or do PT properly without hurting all over my body afterward; I wasn't any good with my brain either, no matter how hard I tried. Just look, I sighed, how all the others are sitting there with their protractors, cool and confident and competent and intelligent, the G-M angle clearly fixed, not having the least trouble with plotting that machine gun.

Our young instructor liked map reading and his voice was full of enthusiasm. "We're going to put that machine gun on the map and then eliminate it," he said. "All right. Our G-M angle, now, rounded off, is nine and a half degrees east. Let's draw that on our paper. OK. Azimuth to the gun is one hundred twenty degrees. That's the magnetic azimuth, right? Now, the *grid* azimuth is going to be larger by how many degrees? Right; nine and a half. So now you've got a grid azimuth of one hundred twenty-nine and a half. Draw that on your map. Now you estimate the distance to that enemy gun from your position and you've got him fixed. Now let's take another one. . . ."

Damn it! My sweaty hands fiddled with the protractor. Sweat was dripping onto my map. Stupid! The G-M angle is simply the angle between grid north and magnetic north. Just figure the declination and that's what you work with. East is least and west is best. Line up the protractor to the vertical grid line, curved portion in the direction of measurement. . . . There has *got* to be an easier way to eliminate an enemy machine gun. I'd rather walk up to it and send smoke signals back to DivArty than go through this. And now that Einstein of an instructor asked me a question. I stuttered out an answer that appeared to persuade him I might possibly be on the way to understanding at least the principle involved. I didn't even have to do push-ups. But I was still unhappy.

And the aerial photographs weren't much better. I could simply not remember whether you hold the photomap or photograph with the shadows toward you or away from you. And if it's not read correctly, streams become ridges and ridges become streams. So it was pure luck when I identified a ridge as a ridge.

Then we double timed out into the dismal, hot, shimmering terrain for some range estimation, compass practice, and map orientation by terrain features. Maps were of the standard large-scale type of one over twenty-five thousand. Those were the maps we would usually be working with in the future. My gloom persisted right up to supper time. In the chow line, bracing myself for "Boogie Woogie," I gave vent to my frustration by attacking Otto with the snarl, "Anything I hate is a smug bastard who can sit there and look at a declination diagram and just put down the G-M angle." Otto tried to look very blank and asked, "What's a G-M angle?" I nearly hugged him and hardly noticed that the jukebox had begun to play.

Before I drifted off to sleep that night, protractors swam around in my tired mind. And map scales. And G-M angles. Large-scale map. One over twenty-five thousand. Or is it one over fifty thousand? That must be a bigger scale because it's a bigger number. No, it's a fraction, remember? One twenty-five-thousandths of something is bigger than one fifty-thousandths of something. And east is least and west is best and the curved end always points toward the machine gun and shadows point toward you. . . . Shadows point. . . .

Even while fast asleep, I heard the first notes of that long, strange, special bugle call at 4:00 A.M. I knew perfectly well that I should hate that bugle call and I tried to hate it properly but never really managed. I knew it was a recording, but I always imagined a bugler standing on a hill out there in the dark of the early morning, his bugle as shiny as his boots, perhaps a corporal of the cadre or maybe even one of us but special as our regimental bugler. Though I knew almost nothing about the Army outside my regiment and therefore had no basis for comparison, I felt that this particular bugle call was nowhere else in the Army repertoire and was meant only for us. As it turned out, I haven't heard it again since leaving the 513th Parachute Infantry Regiment, not in twenty-two years of subsequent service; nor have I ever found anyone outside the regiment who has ever heard it.

If it was a recording—I was never one hundred percent sure of that or perhaps never wanted to be—it was an excellent one. If it was amplified, it was amplified to perfection. Sharp and clear and lustily martial, it must have been composed for light infantry or chasseurs or uhlans or hussars; time had merely placed it on a record to be played through an amplifier for parachute infantry without altering its spirit.

Someone said, "God *damn* that guy!" and noisily jumped out of bed. He probably meant the charge of quarters (CQ) who had put the record on; but I preferred to think that he, too, meant the bugler with the shiny boots.

It was to be our first day on the rifle range. On this day there would be no classroom work.

The morning differed from others only in that there was a general surprise, more felt than expressed, at repeating the eight-mile run. We had done it once, and apparently success was not to be a record-breaking one-shot affair. That run was to be accepted as the routine way to limber up for the morning's PT. Every morning, for the rest of basic, and probably after that, too. Perfectly normal for Company A of the 513th Parachute Infantry Regiment. No one fell out and no one was evacuated.

The afternoon formation was in Class D uniform, steel helmets on heads, rifles slung over left shoulders, the uncomfortable webb equipment drawing sweat the instant it was put on. There was a short orientation by the first sergeant. Then he said, "You guys know the song 'I Got Sixpence'?" For a moment there was just a "Huh?" hovering about the company before some of us nodded. "How about 'I've Been Working on the Railroad'?" Again some of us nodded and now I started to get the idea. "OK," said the first sergeant, "after we move out I'll give you a signal and we'll sing 'I Got Sixpence' and we're going to sing it loud."

For me, this was a pleasant surprise. I had never heard American soldiers sing on the march; only German soldiers. I could hardly wait. But I noticed that no one seemed to share my enthusiasm. They grumbled—not very audibly—that maybe Girl Scouts sang and that they themselves may have learned little songs in kindergarten, but, Jesus Christ, who ever heard of grown men singing like that except in a barbershop quartet? It was all right maybe to count cadence, but to sing?

"Fall in!" The soft grumble stopped and Company A came to attention. After the reports and posting the platoon leaders, Captain Spears moved his company out, the blue and white guidon fluttering ahead. "Column left—*Mharch*!" and the first sergeant counted cadence. "Hut-four, hut—four, hut—two, three, four; all right. 'I Got Sixpence.' Go!" He sounded almost like a German first sergeant.

As my left foot hit the ground I started to sing and I didn't care whether anyone else sang or not. To my surprise, all officers and NCOs started to bellow out the song and quite a few others in our ranks seemed to feel the way I did. The result was electrifying. The sound of perhaps thirty men singing on the march with the unit in step, arms swinging, heads high—that sound was almost irresistible and the entire company was caught up in it. From one hundred sixty throats, that marching song went aloft, preceded the company and left its infectious trail behind it, beckoning the units that followed:

>"I got sixpence, jolly, jolly sixpence,
>I got sixpence, to last me all my life.
>I got twopence to spend and twopence to lend and
>Twopence to send home to my wife—poor wife!
>No cares have I to grieve me,
>No pretty little girls to deceive me!
>I'm happy as a king, believe me,
>As we go rolling, rolling home!"

Behind us, Company B had taken it up. Then the whole battalion was singing. From then on, those who only moments before had felt awkward about singing would hear the battalion in later years whenever someone whistled that marching song.

The rhythmic crunch of boots on gravel seemed a little more pronounced than before; right arms seemed to swing just a little wider, left hands seemed to tighten their grips on rifle slings, and those rifles didn't seem to weigh anything like nine and a half pounds. The miserable discomfort of webb equipment and steel helmets in the summertime South was forgotten as the young voices carried the battalion to the rifle range. I was sure that we could be heard on the main post across the Chattahoochee River:

>"Rolling home, rolling home! Rolling home, rolling home!
>By the light of the silvery moo—oo—oo—ooon!
>Happy is the day when the trooper gets his pay,
>And we go rolling, rolling home!"

We bellowed through all the stanzas until the trooper of the song had no pence left but remained happy as a king anyway. And then we sang, "I've Been Working on the Railroad," which nearly exhausted our repertoire. By then it was clear that we would have to learn all the marching songs we could find because singing, like so many other unheard-of innovations, had become a part of the tradition of our regiment. And learn them we did—first our own and later, in England, the ribald songs of the British and Australians and New Zealanders.

But that's another story.

5
Parachute Basic Training II

We swung into the range area, where an advance detail had already begun work on setting up targets, and halted behind some equipment sheds. Again there was no formal break. "Break time" was used to organize the battalion into pit details, firing units, dry-fire or preparatory marksmanship groups, and miscellaneous work details. Throughout the day and in the days to follow, these groups would be rotated until the battalion had completed its rifle qualification.

We had already spent many hours on preparatory exercises that seemed to be a continuing—and somewhat less than engrossing—part of our overall instruction usually woven into the intricate pattern of the schedule as "concurrent training." This training included sighting and aiming with a sighting bar, position exercises, trigger squeeze exercises, windage adjustments—in short, all the dry-fire preliminaries in our courtship of the M-1 rifle. On this day, then, we were to consummate our marriage to our rifles; even those of us who had fired rifles as civilians experienced a touch of nervousness. It was mandatory for each man to qualify as a marksman, expected of each man to make sharpshooter, unmistakably stressed as desirable for each man to make expert. Dr. Freud would have shaken his head; a teenager was not only expected to be a good lover, he was enjoined to be expert.

Company A was first on the firing line of the "known distance" range at the three-hundred-yard line, using the standard battle range on our sights. We were to fire nine rounds for zero in groups of three. After zeroing our rifles, we would fire the standard courses. On subsequent days, all courses would be fired "for record" and scores would be entered on our service records. To qualify as a marksman, we needed one hundred sixty points, for sharpshooter one hundred eighty-seven points, and for expert rifleman two hundred twelve points. At each target position, one man would fire and one would coach. As usual, Otto behind me in line was my team member and he was first to coach. He had blackened the sights of my rifle, had gotten the ammunition and checked it, and would now watch me to detect a flinch, check my position, and insure for trigger squeeze; he would adjust my sling and help me figure windage. He would also handle the score book.

Targets were up because there would be no timed firing for zero. Platoon leaders walked up and down the line, checking. Then the range officer's voice came over the PA set: "For zero! Prone position. Three rounds ball ammunition. Lock and load!" Safeties clicked, clips were inserted, and bolts slammed shut. "Three rounds for zero group one," boomed the PA set. "Ready on the left . . . ." A safety NCO on the left of the line signaled an all clear. "Ready on the right . . . ." The signal was repeated from the right. "Ready on the firing line!"

I looked through my sights and brought the front sight into the position below the bull's-eye the way I had been taught. A perfect sight-picture. "Commence firing," said the PA voice. Down the line, two shots cracked out. I squeezed the trigger, heard the loud, sharp report, and felt the force of the recoil slam into my right shoulder. I grinned to myself. She was a virgin no longer. Other shots crackled along the line.

Otto went over to one of several field tables on which EE8 telephones were already in steady use as coaches asked for target pit information. "Mark four," Otto yelled to the operator. We watched our target. It disappeared into the pit and came back up, followed by a white disc with a black cross. The disc was attached to a long handle, and the trooper on the pit detail moved it to the "three" ring, down and left of the bull's-eye. Damn! I sighted again, again setting a proper sight-picture. Come on, baby. Don't make a fuss, and don't kick so hard. I squeezed but flinched as the shot cracked out. However, this time I had held her closely to my right shoulder and she didn't kick quite as hard as before. "Mark four," Otto requested, and again it was that black and white disc, again in the same position. "One more in that position," Otto said, "and you've got a good zero." And so it was. The rifle was firing left and low. I went through the adjustment and waited.

Firing slowed to an occasional shot and then the PA voice commanded, "Cease firing!" Then it asked whether anyone had not completed the first group.

My second grouping got the red disc, fairly well in the "four" ring but still slightly to the left. On my third and final try, one was in the bull's-eye. The white disc hovered precariously toward the lower left edge of the black, but I was happy. My marriage to my M-1 was successfully consummated and I lovingly patted her stock. Then I changed places with Otto.

Otto fired his first three rounds in rapid succession. "You dumb son of a bitch," I shouted at him, "this John Wayne shit is going to get the lieutenant down on us," and then to the telephone operator, "Mark four." Down went the target and up again, followed by the red disc, which pointed three times to a tight grouping at just eleven o'clock. The next two groups were either in or at the edge of the bull's-eye. They, too, had been fired in rapid succession. "Why don't you get off my back," I said to Otto. "Go someplace else," Otto laughed.

For the rest of the day we went through the firing tables and kept informal score. "From standing to prone! Nine rounds ball ammunition. Lock and load!" But this time, after the firing line was cleared, the command was "Targets—*up*." And we would have fifty seconds to take the prone position and get our nine shots on target. Then the targets would be pulled down and the command "Cease firing" would boom along the line.

When the day was over I had accumulated enough points for sharpshooter and I felt confident of making expert for record. Otto, of course, had fired expert with points to spare. Damn it. He was good at map reading, too.

We went to the cleaning tables and swabbed down the barrels of our rifles, first with solvent, then with lightly oiled patches, and finally with dry patches until the barrels were gleaming. Back at the barracks there would follow an hour of care and cleaning that would not be merely the military equivalent of our high school study hall; it would be a closely supervised field stripping and by-the-book cleaning of rifles in preparation for a minute inspection.

On the return march I carried my rifle with a different air. She was really mine now and we would take good care of one another. I was certain that she would no longer make me flinch or kick me in an unexpected way and that she would try not to jam or misfire. And I would clean her without griping quite as much as before. Needless to say, on that return march I felt like a rifleman.

The next day we were in the pits pulling targets, marking the strikes, and pasting up the bullet holes. The eight-foot-deep trench with two troopers at each target position, interspersed with the field telephones, made me think of World War I trenches. And we were told to listen to the firing directly over our heads and to either side. This is what aimed rifle fire sounds like when it's coming at *you*. Good old cadre. Even here they tried to squeeze additional training in!

Otherwise things were boring at our end of the range. The telephone operator nearest us would say, "Mark five," and I would haul down the target, look for the newest hole, put some glue on it, stick pasting paper over the hole, haul the target back up, get the pole with the appropriate color of disc, and point it over the strike. There would be the inevitable military hoodlum (very few among us if only because of the constant fear of disqualification) who would fire at the marker while it was pointing to the strike. We all took such undisciplined behavior as personal affronts and would send messages threatening to report the clown back to the firing line. There were equally few misses, and for those we would wave a red flag back and forth across the target—Maggie's drawers. And, invariably, the soldier who missed would not believe that he did so and would request a recheck.

After a while we became quite efficient and sensitized to the marksman firing on our target and would haul it down for marking without having to be told. But life was still very boring in the pits.

Generally, lunch in the field was almost as pleasant an interlude as it was in the mess hall, even when this little break, too, was used to make training points. There were those exercises, for instance, when we were told that feeding would be "tactical."

I always had trouble with the word "feeding," probably because I was brought up speaking German. In German, people eat (*essen*); only animals feed (*fressen*). Cows in a barn or pigs at their troughs or horses in their stables feed. "Tactical feeding" would send my imagination rampant. I imagined myself as a horse, a well-trained cavalry horse.

Marmite cans with hot food were lined up at five-yard intervals and one man at a time would be allowed to approach each one so that there would be no bunching up, no lucrative target for the enemy artillery forward observer (FO). After getting our food, we would disperse and sit in groups of not over three, using the cover and concealment principles we had been taught. Once, when I stood before a marmite can full of steaming, delicious-smelling steak, I snorted and whinnied. I didn't even have the excuse of doing it for the benefit of the man behind me because there was no man behind me. Luckily, a Dog KP had temporarily relieved a cook on line. Cooks were cadre, and cadre would certainly have reported me as a potential Section 8. I was very careful after that, particularly when feeding tactically.

But on the rifle range there was no tactical feeding. We didn't even have to bring our mess kits but were served on trays. Marmite cans, the relatively new invention that Napoleon would have ranked very high in the arsenal of infantry, were close together, steaming, beckoning from the chow line. As usual, the food was the best available, expertly prepared, solicitously served.

It is difficult to overemphasize the importance of food as a morale factor in any institution, be it in marriage or in the Army. But to an infantry unit it has a significance quite beyond its high priority status in military logistics (not by coincidence are rations designated Class I). The mere anticipation of "chow time" often lightens the many considerable burdens of the infantry, and a consistently good chow line is an indispensable element of morale and, by extension, of esprit de corps. And it had been carefully calculated in the equation that produced the 513th.

We ate, griped about the pit detail between bites, washed our mess trays in the wash line, and stacked them for the KPs to wash again. And we still had a few minutes of leisure to smoke and talk and finish our coffee and revel in the ritual that was, is, and ever shall be "chow time."

At last the day came for us to fire for record. It was serious business and was universally treated as such. Although coaches no longer had to worry about such things as sling adjustment, trigger squeeze, or flinching, they looked carefully at the blackening of sights, the condition of the ammunition, the calling of shots, and, most important, the score book. Those who fired did so with the utmost concentration. Gone were the jokes, the complaints, and certainly the isolated hoodlums who would take a chance at firing on a marker. Each firing position was almost constantly monitored by a cadre member. Every position was spot checked by an officer throughout qualification firing. Even in the pits, the detail was commanded by an officer but, even without the lieutenant, they would have worked silently and without that almost obligatory griping. They worked with the efficiency they expected from those on the firing line who would take their places as soon as qualification was completed.

We fired at the two-hundred-, three-hundred-, and four-hundred-yard lines, standing, kneeling, sitting, and prone, anxiously peering at the marker discs, occasionally asking timidly for a recheck and watching the figures in our score books with trepidation.

When we were done, I had almost enough points for expert, but not quite. So I only made sharpshooter, but I was happy.

And when the battalion was through there was a high percentage of expert riflemen, a majority who had made sharpshooter, a low percentage of marksmen, and not one who had disqualified.

On Saturday there was a formal presentation of our qualification badges, our first awards ceremony. And Saturday night we had several celebrations within the meager resources offered by our spartan environs in the Alabama area. We drank beer in shifts in the wooden hut, which must have been the smallest service club ever thrown together, and we crowded into the tiny movie theater, which was hot and stuffy and showed awful movies.

There were many more hours on the range. We had to qualify with the carbine and fire familiarization courses with all automatic weapons, grenade launchers, recoilless weapons, and mortars. And then there was the hand grenade range.

The hand grenade worried me. We had had the requisite classroom instruction on grenades (including smoke, concussion, and fragmentation grenades) and had practiced throwing the training grenades in the field. But it was remembering the lecture on the fragmentation grenade that made me sweat when it was my turn to stand in a hole with a three-foot parapet, holding a live grenade in my hand, waiting for the command "Pull pin." The lecture on the fragmentation grenade was particularly chilling because it was delivered in a cold, matter-of-fact way without a trace of the dramatic. It was almost as though the instructor was trying to be dull, trying for an antidote against this spine-tingling subject.

The grenade, hand, fragmentation MK 2, he explained, contains an explosive charge in a serrated metal body that is designed to break into fragments on action of the explosive charge. It is a curved trajectory weapon used by the individual soldier at short range against sheltered enemy personnel, particularly weapons crews, who are protected from rifle and other flat trajectory fire. It has a bursting radius of ten yards, and stray fragments are effective up to fifty yards. He explained safety pin and lever, fuse assembly, primer, igniter, explosive charge, cast-iron serrated body, and other parts as he pointed to his chart, and we followed on our training grenades on the little field tables in front of us. He explained that the deadly device weighs approximately twenty-one ounces, has a fuse delay of three to six seconds, is easily thrown, and is an excellent casualty-producing piece of equipment that may be viewed as the infantryman's personal artillery. We would, he continued in the imperative, become thoroughly familiar with it because it would become almost as much a part of us as our individual weapon.

At a sawdust pit we were shown how to grasp it, safety lever under the thumb, fingers spread evenly between the horizontal serrations, forefinger of the free hand in the ring ready to pull the safety pin. And we were shown how to throw it. "All of you people have played ball, right? Football, baseball, what-have-you. There's no one way to throw a grenade and so you football players throw it like a football and baseball players like a baseball and you other guys however you throw a ball. What counts is distance and accuracy." In throwing it for distance we could see how close we would have to be to the enemy, and how far we would have to throw it in view of the "effective stray fragments." And in cases in which a soldier drops a grenade after the safety pin has been removed, or drops the grenade and freezes, or freezes and allows the safety lever to separate—well, these were not applicable to the 513th Parachute Infantry and should be completely disregarded.

So there I stood, neither a football player, a baseball player, nor even a handball player. And I was sweating.

"Pull pin," said the range NCO next to me. With the prescribed twisting motion of my left forefinger I wrenched the pin from its hole through the lever. "Prepare to throw." I drew back my right arm, the NCO watching me through half-closed eyes as though he were bored to tears. "Throw," he said in the same tone of voice he used when telling someone to pick up a cigarette butt. I threw as hard as I could, barely hearing the ping of the safety handle as it flipped off the grenade, or the hiss of the primer that activated the timing—but hear both I did! We ducked below the parapet and I counted. Then came the explosion down range.

There was a slap of fragments, but none seemed to have reached the parapet. "Fair," said the sergeant. "Now try for accuracy. Pull pin." I had barely enough time to reach for my second grenade on the wood-covered shelf dug out of the dirt wall and pull the pin, this time without being conscious of using the correct form so I could wrench my arm back as he commanded, "Prepare to throw," followed instantly by "Throw." The sequence was executed almost as though there had been no commands. After the explosion we checked for accuracy and the sergeant nodded and marked his clipboard. "Fair," he said again. "Next one just pick up and throw without commands. Distance and accuracy." I was no longer worried and went through the sequence. Not bad, I thought. Really nothing to it.

The sergeant looked at me with the utterly bored look and said, "This time let the safety lever go and count two seconds before you throw it. One thousand, two thousand. Go ahead." I felt myself go pale. Why can't they *ever* leave well enough alone? Just when you thought you had the problem solved, bang—they have to throw shit into the game. I sighed involuntarily and hoped that the sergeant hadn't heard me. They put all kinds of remarks on those damn clipboards. The sigh seemed to settle the butterflies a little and I reached for the grenade. Might as well get the damn thing over with and blow the two of us sky high.

I pulled the pin and let go of the safety lever. The striker, bent back under the handle by a spring, came up and over, flipping the lever off the fuse T-lug with that characteristic ping noise and simultaneously setting off the fuse action with a soft primer explosion that sounded "phtssss." I counted my one thousand, two thousand, and threw, then ducked. The sergeant was still standing and after an eternity he, too, ducked—though it looked more like a slow bending motion. At that point the grenade exploded.

As we straightened up he said in that bored voice, "Notice how many seconds you had left on that fuse? Count was too fast. Last grenade coming up, so do it right and don't forget accuracy. That's what it's all about, you know. OK, go."

Something came over me. That bored, blasé bastard of a sergeant had finally gotten to me. I picked up the last grenade, pulled the pin, and let the handle go with its "ping, phtssss." Then I looked at the sergeant and said slowly, "One thousand, two thousand." Then I looked down range and threw the grenade. Silently I continued to count to four thou . . . at which point the grenade exploded. The sergeant had ducked at the same time I did, I noted with some pleasure, as we both came up again to check for accuracy.

Without any noticeable change in his bored look and voice he said, "OK," and marked his clipboard. Then he called the next man over as I double timed back to the concurrent training area where we threw training grenades until I thought my right arm would come off.

At chow time that evening there were many hair-raising stories, none of which included any reference to the possibility of "freezing." One would almost believe that everybody *liked* hand grenades. "What a weird bunch," I thought, again feeling that touch of warmth at the thought of belonging here.

The weeks suddenly started to rush by. We were becoming proficient in the skills of the individual infantryman and slowly shifting to team and squad activities without really being aware that we did so.

Morning PT after the daily eight-mile run had taken on a different character. The "Army dozen" were still there, but they had been condensed to allow for the addition of team rope climbing, tug of war, hand-to-hand combat by squads, and, finally, running the obstacle course, first individually and then in teams.

The obstacle course made maximum use of some very difficult terrain where steep banks had to be climbed, gullies had to be traversed by means of a single-strand rope bridge, water barriers had to be crossed "Tarzan" fashion by swinging over on suspended ropes and—during team runs—high walls had to be scaled. There were, of course, the usual devices where one had to twist and crawl and slither and balance, but those presented no problems for us and seemed to have been included simply in deference to some training expert, probably a civilian, who had to put his two cents' worth in somewhere. It went without saying that the course was traversed at a dead run and that we were timed. And, finally, we had to run the course wearing gas masks.

We seemed to race time in everything we did. When we reached the live-fire machine gun course, familiar to every infantryman who ever clawed his way under barbed wire while machine gunners fired live ammunition in long bursts three feet above his head, our standard joke was that we would cross down range above the wire and move on the double toward the machine gunners and blow them up with hand grenades. Live-fire exercise 513th style. Anyone left alive was disqualified. As it turned out, the joke wasn't too far off. Two men actually were hurt when they tried to improve their time, but my recollection is that they were hurt by barbed wire rather than by gunfire.

Later, when we had "combat in cities" training in England where certain bombed-out sections of Southhampton had been set aside for the purpose, we were to experience the ultimate in realistic live-fire training. But even in Alabama, our early introduction to conditions approximating those we would eventually encounter in combat was handled with a degree of realism that effectively prepared us for each succeeding step toward that first enemy contact. By then our training had made us predictable. We were already veterans.

During small unit training, the lessons we had learned were subtly put to use. New subjects such as scouting and patroling incorporated old subjects such as map reading, range estimation, camouflage, and enemy identification. Squad tactics required all the skills and physical endurance we had developed during the previous weeks. In forced marches with a forty-pound pack, steel helmet, rifle, bayonet, gas mask, canteen, entrenching tool, and webbing, we would march along dusty, hot Alabama roads and trails to our training area, always singing.

Here and there we would pass the hovels of tenant farmers. Small, flimsy wooden huts with tarpaper-covered roofs, they were as dismal and poor as the meager land they stood on. Occasionally a door would be open and we could see inside what must have been a living room. More often than not, the floor was packed dirt and the furniture painted crates. Rarely would we see the farmers or their families; when we did, they were listlessly, disinterestedly leaning against their rotting wooden fences waiting, it seemed, for us and for the war to go away so that they could get on with their poverty without the constant reminder that there were other things in the world.

It was a shock each time I saw them and their ramshackle houses and outhouses, their bleak, dusty yards and their randomly plowed, eternally thirsty fields. And I wondered why it was that the American Army, or at least the likes of us, would see only the poor, unfriendly shacks of tenant farmers in the poor, unfriendly South of the military reservations as we marched to and from our training areas. The Army always seemed to be hidden away from the civilian communities except during Fourth of July parades down Main Street. Unlike the German regiments I had seen—or their English and French and Belgian counterparts that we came across later—which would march from their town garrisons through the streets and the clean little villages along the highway to their training areas, admired by friends and relatives lining the sidewalks and roads, we were kept hidden away in the depths of Fort Benning and Fort Bragg and Fort Campbell. No wonder most of the American Army doesn't sing on the march and makes a martial appearance in public only on the Fourth of July.

Most of the American Army. But not us. We were new and young and proud and on the way to becoming parachute infantry! We would march in step for *us*, sing for *us*, excel for *us*, endure for *us*, and—when the time came—suffer and die for *us*. For each other. We would be impelled by the awesome meaning of the first two words of West Point's motto: Duty and Honor. Somewhere down the line there would be a confluence of the long columns of infantry and armor and artillery and engineers—perhaps on the Fourth of July behind the American flag—where the word "Country" is added, where the trilogy etched on our shield might convey the source of our collective strength to friend and foe. But it starts with us; and without us the shield would buckle under the first hostile blow, regardless of the glorious motto upon it.

But such ruminations would not come for another twenty-five or thirty years. In the summer of 1943 we knew only that we were different from all other soldiers and that we liked it. I would have liked it more had we marched through clean little villages and towns where the children would stare at us in wonder, where the pretty girls would look at us in admiration, and where the old folks would look at us with pride. They, the people; we, their Army. But in America that experience was reserved for the Fourth of July. Perhaps it was because the rest of the year we would hold up traffic or take too much training time or would otherwise squander time, resources, and money—there certainly were valid enough reasons for not marching through a town—but it would have been nice. It would have been nice to share *something* with the people, even though most of what we had could not be shared.

And so the things we could have shared, the marching, the singing, the proud, military bearing of the unit, we kept for *us* on the dusty Alabama road on our way to squad tactics to learn how to keep the American people safe.

One of the many things we could not share started immediately after we arrived in the training area—"the rifle squad in the attack." It began with a review of what we had learned during the block of subjects called squad tactics and included movement to contact, passing through long-range fires, getting to the attack position, fire and movement, execution of the assault, and reorganization on the objective.

We sat in a semicircle while our platoon leader gave his brief review and introductory lecture on the rifle squad in the attack. As usual, that was all the "ten-minute break" we would have. Well, we *were* sitting down, weren't we?

Some things I didn't seem to get straight, and not until I became an officer much later did the terms become a routine part of my vocabulary. What the lieutenant said seemed more applicable to the man who would have to lead the assault; and it was only when he said, "I'm spending time on this because after the medics pick up the squad leader *you* may have to lead the assault and reorganize . . . ," did I try to clear my mind of whatever had crept into it at the beginning of our pretend break.

The lieutenant explained what a line of departure (LD) was—what purpose it served. He said that between the LD and the assault position there would probably be well-registered enemy artillery fire, a barrage, that would be intended to break up our attack—remember the rifle squad in defense?—and that this bit of terrain had to be traversed as fast as possible. "Yes, as fast as *possible*, people, because you will literally be running for your *life*! Once you're through the concentration, the enemy forward observer (FO) will stop the fire because ain't nobody on that bit of real estate now. He will have to shift fire, probably to an area that has not been as well registered. That takes time. All right: by then you're in the assault position, that last covered bit of terrain within a short distance of the enemy from where you assault. And once the order for the assault is given, you *move* and you don't stop until you reach the objective. All right: tempting though it will be, the leader must *not* allow his men to lie down in a barrage to seek cover from the artillery because there *is* no cover. *Move through fast* and that's the way to salvation. All right. You get to the assault position, catch your breath, and wait for your artillery fire to lift from the objective; and when you get the order to move, you *move* and don't stop. Usually you move in a line of skirmishers and fire your weapons to kill the enemy or, failing that, to keep his head down and prevent him from firing an aimed shot at *you*. All right; that's what we're going to do now. On the objective you're going to do what you learned in your classes on intelligence. You're going to take prisoners, segregate them by rank, search them for documents, and secure them. You'll get as much front-line information as you can from them while you reorganize on the objective. Any questions? OK, squad leaders; take'em out!"

We moved through the pine wood in a tactical formation until we came to a small clearing. Our squad leader halted us and spread out a one-over-twenty-five-scale map—large scale, I thought smugly. No longer conscious of the teaching points, we concentrated on orienting the map to the terrain features and listening to the attack order of our squad leader. He told us where the enemy was, where our own people were and what our other squads were going to do, what kind of support we were going to get, that we were going to use the line of skirmishers as a formation for the assault, and how we were going to reorganize on the objective—"that bare-assed hill here, see it on the map? And there it is over there. Now, here's the LD and over there—see it on the map and over there by that line of trees?—that's the assault position. Any questions?"

"How do we know when we get to that barrage?"

"I'll tell you. Right now we dry run the whole thing almost by the numbers. I'll tell you everything that's goin' on and you guys take action. We're gonna go through this many times and later there's gonna be demolition charges and all that. Any more questions?"

"Anybody up there?" the questioner pointed to the objective.

"Negative. This time we simulate POWs and all that. I'll tell you how. More questions? All right. Let's move out!"

And there we were, the lowest organized tactical unit in the infantry, as we had often been told—the unit that would close with and destroy the enemy, the point of the lance. We were the final point behind which stood the companies, battalions, and regiments of infantry, the armor and artillery, the divisions, corps, armies and army groups, the Air Corps and the Navy, the generals and the admirals, theaters of operations, communication zones with the supply complexes and harbors, the factories and war plants, the immense, complex war machinery that had been assembled for one purpose alone: to enable us to close with and destroy the enemy. Whatever earth-shaking convulsion would be set in motion by an order from Franklin Delano Roosevelt, its force emanating from that unbelievably broad base described as the Arsenal of Democracy would narrow down (fixed by operational and logistic parameters) to the triangle pointing in the direction of the enemy. And at its point would be the rifle squad in the attack!

All this we had been told by one of our young West Pointers, one of the select few who had been entrusted with the platoons and companies of this extraordinary regiment. There was fire and pride in his words and deep, abiding respect for the rifleman. Though we may not have understood all of what he said, the main message was abundantly clear. And now, after many weeks of grueling training, we had become riflemen and were ready to use what we had learned. We were almost ready to take our position at the point of the triangle.

We crossed the LD in a squad diamond formation and the squad leader yelled, "Artillery fire!" He thrust his right fist up and down in the signal for double time, and we broke into a dead run across the clearing to the line of trees. Then the command came, "Fix bayonets!" and we carried out the final assault, just as we had been told to. We simulated prisoner processing and organized the objective for defense against counterattack. And as soon as we were in position, we began a new problem. This time, after crossing the LD, we would have to eliminate enemy machine gunners in a woods before we could get to the assault position. That meant fire and maneuver. And, finally, it was chow time. Tactical feeding, of course. Here, too, was a change; for we had gone on the march to the training area without first eating.

In the days that followed, each of us had to command the squad in attack and defense, maneuver it, pick the approach routes and types of formations, and manage all the minute details we would have to manage in combat should the squad leader be out of action and the responsibility become ours. The entire squad treated this exercise as the serious business it was, and we suddenly had a new appreciation of our squad leader and of the crucial point made by the entire block of instruction. We could see the shadowy outline of the irrevocability of a decision reached at this point of the triangle, and the awesome consequences of a wrong decision loomed on the horizon of our new understanding. A corps commander may make a wrong decision and lose divisions and regiments, and perhaps he could still go to bed that night and sleep. But a squad leader who makes a wrong decision would lose men, men who trusted him implicitly and obeyed without question. There would be no sleep for the squad leader.

When it came my turn to lead the squad, the shadow of those as yet inarticulated perceptions enveloped me and made me insecure, sapping my confidence.

There was, I was told, an enemy position of three men with one or more automatic weapons over there, behind that little embankment next to the woods. It had to be taken out before the platoon could continue its movement to the assault position. And it had to be done fast!

The word "fast" dominated my decision. I had yet to learn how fast "fast" was in a case like this. Uneasily I pointed out a spot in the tree line to the left of the enemy position and designated four men who were to go with me. We would move to that spot at a dead run. While we were running, the remaining three men would give us covering fire. Once we were in position, we would give *them* covering fire and they would join us. We would then assault the enemy from the flank. Questions? The men had been intent on understanding their orders and were not prepared to ask critical questions. They understood the order and were ready. We ran to the spot I had indicated, three hundred yards more or less in an angle dominated by the position we were supposed to take out.

At this stage in our training we were using "enemy details." Initially, these details were made up of cadre; but as we completed certain phases of tactical training, we ourselves started to assume the role of enemy. On occasion, we would be given quite a bit of latitude in that role and we found it interesting, almost fun. But most of the time there would be tight control so that the teaching points would not get lost. And always—even in our role as "enemy"—those teaching points would be hammered home. The corporal directing the three men of the enemy position facing us made the best of this splendid opportunity to make his points.

A whole belt of blank ammunition was run through the enemy machine gun, and the rifleman with them fired his blanks as fast as his M-1 would let him. In contrast, the fire of the three men I had left behind sounded puny and halting. The BAR that could have answered the enemy with some authority was at a dead run with me.

We got into position and fired while the rest of my men ran toward us. As we started to assault the enemy position, our sergeant waved us off.

He told us to sit down. "That was fast all right, Gabel," he said. "Only trouble is you now don't have a squad. So now the platoon has to do the whole thing over again but with one squad the less." I felt sick, and gloom settled over all of us. The sergeant explained that we had a perfectly good, covered approach route if we had taken our time instead of using the stupid shortcut across an open field. And several short moves would have been better. And the BAR should have given us initial cover—and the squad leader should be in a position where he can direct his men, not charging off across an open field . . . .

There was more. We listened in dejected silence. Ours was a collective gloom and not for one moment did the others feel like neutral observers simply because the decision had not been theirs. A rifle squad is something special. Each member is a part of its body. Before it is decision-making time, when questions and comments are asked for, each member will consider what is ahead. "Question, sergeant! Any reason why we can't move up that way over there? Seems shorter. . . ." "Goddamn— you're right. Change one." The process is the same all the way up the chain of command to the president of the United States. There is no such thing as a collective decision. Only the leader can decide, and he is responsible—be he squad leader or president. But the process of making that decision takes in all the experts and their expertise.

What makes the squad special is that the experts test their expertise in immediate action; at the point of the triangle, the chances are that the leader will make no more than one mistake. After acting on the decision, the BAR man cannot say, "Damn! I should have told him when he asked," because the BAR man may not be among the living by that time. At the command "Go!" all considerations and alternatives have been exhausted and only one thing remains—the one, all-important act without which the point of the triangle would be blunted and useless: immediate execution of the order regardless of consequences. And only the man who gave the order—if he lives—must live with the consequences. Though the squad shares equally in his grief and may reach out to him to comfort him when he has erred, the leader remains weighted with the responsibility. Doubt remains to deepen the grief. Had he done all that should have been done, asked all the questions that should have been asked? Had he looked at the terrain carefully— here was his last chance before giving the fateful command. It would be executed in unquestioning, reflexive, desperate response and there would be no going back. It had to be *right*! When all is said and done, there remains one awesome, final objective in the training of an infantryman: instantaneous, precise execution of orders regardless of consequences. In the confusion of battle, this may mean blind trust in the person giving the order, literally trusting the leader with life itself. The infantry leader must therefore be a master at his trade. And since the men under him may have to assume his responsibility under combat conditions, they, too, must be experts at their trade.

All this was brought home with peculiar clarity: the sudden realization at the end of basic training that I, the individual rifleman, must be prepared to assume the responsibility for the lives of others. Later, as an officer, I would be taught that my major concern as a leader is accomplishment of the *mission*. That doctrine, of course, expresses the raison d'être of the Army. But even a rifle platoon leader or company commander executing an independent mission dreamed up at a remote headquarters may have the agonizing conviction that the mission is not worth the life of a single one of his men, that it will serve no purpose other than to provide spectacular material for a war correspondent and hasten the advancement of the commander who dreamed it up. Yet the mission must be accomplished. The doctrine is valid and must not be changed. Only the position of those who exploit it for their own ends must be changed.

Down at the squad, however, no such murky considerations weigh the soul. The order is executed with trust in leadership. It is in the process of execution that the squad leader's prime concern will be to bring his men safely to the point ordered. The infantry squad leader worth his name will grieve for a dead man more than he will rejoice in accomplishing the mission that cost the man his life. And the entire squad will mourn the loss of their own more than they will rejoice in victory. The infantryman is the last to smile when victory has come. So at the end of basic training, which marked our beginning as infantrymen, we became conscious of what the squad would mean to us and of our responsibility to it. I know of no one who took it lightly.

Basic training ended with a regimental review, the regiment on parade with its colors flying next to the American flag. On the reviewing stand stood at rigid attention our regimental commander, his executive officer, and a brigadier general whom we did not know. At the command "Eyes—*Right!*" I looked into their faces. We were marching eight abreast and I was deep within the formation, unknown and unseen. Nor could I see the regiment except for steel helmets and for bayonets fixed on rifles in front of me and to my right. I could only feel it. But I saw its reflection on the faces of the officers in the reviewing stand as their right hands snapped to the brims of their helmets in salute. That salute was no mere courtesy. They were saluting me and my squad and my platoon and my company, and each had the look of a parent whose child had been singled out for some great honor.

6
Jump Training: B Stage

The truck ride from the Alabama area back to the Frying Pan was nothing less than a motorized graduation procession. Like a graduating class, we felt joy and a great relief, mixed with a touch of nostalgia and a dash of anxiety. Goodbye, you God-forsaken Alabama area, you miserable tarpaper and plywood hutments, you scrawny pine trees, you dusty peanut patches—if we *never* see you again, it'll be too soon! And yet—strange how one gets used to something. Anyway, it's behind us. The worst is over. Jump training would be a mere formality after that.

It was amazing how different the Frying Pan looked after thirteen weeks in the Alabama area! The place we had feared so thirteen weeks before, the place where we had lost nearly 50 percent of our original volunteers in just three days, now looked positively inviting! Why, it was practically in the middle of the main post. We could walk to the theater and the PX! But best of all, now it belonged to *us*. We were no longer unwanted transients. Now we *owned* the place!

The 513th had taken over the entire area in the time it took three battalions to go through jump training, one battalion at a time. The dusty company streets were *our* streets now; the orderly rooms, where people like that inhospitable, arrogant young lieutenant had made their headquarters, now had our guidons at their entrances. Even the forbidding towers seemed to belong to us—just elaborate pieces of equipment now. Well, almost . . . .

We settled in for our final three weeks, confident and happy. After jump school we were to go home on furlough. Imagine: home on furlough as paratroopers! I looked around the barracks and wondered how I could ever have found them ugly.

Dawn had already come when I awoke on the first day of B Stage. Startled, I looked at my watch. It was five o'clock. I looked around. Sure enough, we were all still in our beds. Most of the troopers were awake. One waved at me languidly and I waved back. Then I settled down again. So now we were going to keep banker's hours. There would be no more four o'clock bugle ever again. Good riddance, you Prussian bugle call! But I shall always remember you.

After ten more minutes of this unaccustomed luxury, I got up to shave and shower. Most of the others did, too. By the time the charge of quarters (CQ) came in, we were dressed.

Reveille was at six-fifteen. With characteristic speed and precision the company formed and squad leaders reported their squads to the platoon sergeants. Then we stood at ease, waiting for our first sergeant.

Wade Allen, first sergeant of Company A, strode out of the orderly room and to the center-front of his company. I wondered whether any of the cartoon writers or movie directors who depicted first sergeants had ever seen a real one like Wade Allen. "Company A—*Fall In*!" And Company A snapped to attention before its ranking noncommissioned officer. How different from that first formation on this street! "Report!" Platoon sergeants reported, holding their salutes until returned by the first sergeant. I liked these formations before the officers took over. I liked it when sergeants saluted sergeants. I didn't know exactly why, but I liked it when there seemed to be no difference in the attitude and appearance of the company whether the first sergeant stood in front of it, or the company commander, or the colonel—or the president of the United States, should he ever visit us.

The battalion was formed and stood at parade rest, waiting for the duty officer. The battalion duty officer, a young lieutenant picked by roster, rapidly walked from our temporary battalion headquarters and took his place. He called the battalion to attention and commanded, "Report!" The young officer stood at attention, it seemed to me at respectful attention, trim and immaculate in his jumpsuit and boots, and took the reports. He was one of the *crème de la crème* selected as cadre for the 513th and had watched us young volunteers rapidly turning into soldiers. Pride was manifest in the way he returned the salutes of the reporting first sergeants. The battalion report was complete. "First sergeants, take charge of your companies!" After a final exchange of salutes, the officer made an about-face and walked back toward battalion headquarters as the first sergeants faced their companies. "At ease. After breakfast there'll be a formation in front of the supply room. You'll draw your two jumpsuits, new helmets, and jumpliners . . . ." Draw jumpsuits! Finally! Happy murmurs of "Wow!" and "Hot *dog*!" and "*Son*-of-a-bitch!" rippled through the formation. "At ease, *God-damn* it!" bellowed the first sergeant and tried to scowl. The murmur stopped but a Cheshire-cat grin hovered above Company A. "We fall in back here at zero nine hundred hours for transportation to Lawson Field. You're then turned over to the First Parachute Training Regiment for their orientation and then you men start jump training with them. We pick you up each night when they get through with you. All right. Company—Atten-*hut*! *Dis*missed!" With deafening whoops the units swarmed to the battalion mess hall where two long lines at its two entrances formed immediately.

I was happy, waiting in this long line. It was just like "downtown." There was a jukebox in this mess hall but no need to anticipate that awful "Boogie Woogie" of the Alabama area. Instead, soft, sophisticated rhythms wafted over the chow lines.

The man in front of me, a man from another company, turned around and said, "Well, we're getting there," and I knew he wasn't thinking about the line moving toward the steaming breakfast inside.

Drawing our jump uniform was an event surpassed only by the little ceremony of putting it on for the first time. Now we not only felt special; we looked it. Even our helmets and helmet liners were different. The steel helmet, although of the exact same shape as all others, was modified by a snap-fastening device to which the liner was anchored. It was the liner that departed sharply from the helmet liners of other troops. A parachute helmet liner had reinforced chin straps and a leather cradle that fitted over the chin. Fastened or unfastened, this rigging added to the wearer's "airborne" appearance. Alas, regulations called for chin straps to be tucked away under the liner when the wearer was not on an airborne exercise. It was just one of a number of annoying petty regulations promulgated by unsympathetic higher headquarters in an attempt to reduce our airborne forces to the level of "straight-leg" GIs. Back in our barracks we changed from fatigues to our new jumpsuits, bloused our trousers over our boots, dug out our caps on which we had had the parachute patch sewn by the PX tailor shop during the past weekend, and mightily admired one another.

The nine o'clock formation was a sight to behold. Parachute basic was over. Jump training was about to begin.

The second our truck convoy came to a halt in front of the Lawson Field packing sheds, tailgates were dropped by the two men sitting closest to them and the troops spilled out of the vehicles. "Company A, over here!" "Company B, move, move!" "Ho, Company C!" The battalion formed, it seemed, even faster than usual. "Close interval, dress right—*Dress*! Ready—*Front*! Pa-rade—*Rest*!" This time the battalion officers were present to turn their units over to the Parachute Training Regiment. The PTR cadre, standing in front of the packing sheds opposite their new charges, watched in silent admiration. It was the first time in their experience that a full battalion had been assigned to take jump training as a unit.

"Battalion—:" "Company—:" "*Atten-Hut!*" The sound of the battalion obeying, that one loud "thud," never failed to send a shiver of pride down my back. The battalion commander faced the officer commanding the PTR, saluted, and reported, "Sir, First Battalion Five-thirteenth Parachute Infantry present for training!" Again I felt that little ripple, as though the officer had said, "For a while I leave my family in your hands. You had better take good care of them!" The answer, "Thank you, sir!" seemed to acknowledge that trust. And now we belonged to "them." "At ease!" commanded the PTR colonel. "Rest." We loosened up and waited. There was the man responsible for all parachute training in the Army. He was only the second colonel I had ever seen in front of our formation.

"Welcome to the First Parachute Training Regiment," he said. "Although you are new to the airborne family, we have heard about you. This is something new for us, too. You are not a class; you are a battalion of a parachute infantry regiment, and you look every inch the part. All of you, without exception, look like paratroopers. And there is not the slightest doubt in my mind that, in three weeks, you *will* be paratroopers. Now, I've never said that before when addressing a class. But this time I'm not addressing a *class*; I'm addressing the First Battalion of the Five-thirteenth Parachute Infantry." There it was again, the sound of my unit. In thirteen long weeks the regimental idea, its name, the number 513, and the magic sound of "parachute infantry" had germinated, taken root, and sprouted in our consciousness. Even at this early way station it had entrenched itself as something like a home. The sound of it, like the sound of "California" or "Sunset Boulevard" heard in far-off places, gave me a pleasant start. Much later, the sound of it would touch other corners of my heart. "I won't bother to wish you good luck," the colonel continued, "because what you are about to learn here has nothing to do with luck. But I wish you Godspeed and I hope that your stay with us will remain with you as one of your more interesting memories." At that, the colonel smiled wryly, came to attention, and commanded, "Battalion—*Atten-Hut!*" And to his cadre, "Take charge."

Headquarters and Company A were assigned to Shed 1, Companies B and C to Shed 2; we filed in for our orientation.

The cavernous rigger sheds looked like the airplane hangars they had once been. Rows of long parachute-packing tables dominated the center of the shed. Along one of the walls, riggers were working at heavy duty sewing machines repairing harnesses and backpacks. Opposite the entrance—it seemed a mile away—a row of fairly spacious offices and supply rooms huddled like dwarfs at the foot of the giant hall. The only nondwarf at that end of the shed was the parachute shake-out and drying room. Actually it was more of a tower than a room; for here parachutes were hoisted to their full length after they had been used in a jump, to be shaken free of branches, dust, and dirt or to be left to dry overnight prior to repacking.

Just in front of this loft, at an open area clear of the packing tables, we were assembled and told to sit on the cold concrete floor. A PTR captain began the general orientation.

"The First Parachute training Regiment of the parachute school here at Fort Benning is responsible for all individual jump training of the United States Army. It is a department of the school. Other departments include riggers, jumpmasters, demolitions, pathfinders, and air transport. Some of you will be taking one or more of these courses at a later stage in your career as a paratrooper. A good number of you can count on taking the demolitions course after you get back to your regular training." The captain had our undivided attention. Up to this point, most of us had heard only about the First PTR. That it was akin to a department of a larger school had not occurred to us. What else was in store?

"As you must have heard a hundred times," the captain continued, "we normally have four stages of training at the PTR—A, B, C, and D. A Stage is the physical conditioning stage. Here the student gets into shape for the jump training to follow. Since you as members of a parachute infantry regiment have already had this physical training during your basic training, you will not take A Stage.

"B Stage is the ground training phase of jump training. Here you will learn the anatomy of a parachute and how to pack it. Remember, your training includes packing each of the five parachutes you will jump, so I'm sure you will pay close attention to your rigger instructors." At this revelation some troopers shifted in their places and murmured.

"You will learn the jump commands and how to exit from a mock-up of a C-47 aircraft. You will learn parachute manipulation on a suspended harness device that has the reputation of being somewhat less than comfortable." The captain smiled. We had seen that device. The harness was lovingly known as the ball breaker.

"You will also become acquainted with the parachute landing training which, after the manipulation harness, will be kind of fun. Further, we have the wind machine which will inflate a parachute and drag you across the ground a bit so you will learn how to collapse a parachute in a ground wind. Finally, we have the forty-foot jump tower that com-

A forty-foot mock-up tower

bines exit training with parachute manipulation and the good old parachute landing fall—the PLF." More troopers shifted and murmured. From the ground, the forty-foot tower didn't look too terribly high; but it, too, had a bad reputation.

"That about covers the week of B Stage. A pretty busy week.

"C Stage involves the real towers. You've seen our two-hundred-fifty-foot towers." He grinned. "You will get a ride on the 'buddy-seat' first. That's the device you had to pay a lot of money to get a ride on at the World's Fair, and here you get it for free. We haul you up just to give you an idea of height. We haul you up a second time in harness, and again you experience a controlled descent. The third tower is a 'free' tower. This one counts. You are attached to a thirty-eight-foot canopy and the only thing controlling your descent is *you*. Then you'd better do what you've learned during your manipulation training because you're on your own." This time the general murmur seemed approving. C Stage sounded interesting.

"Since the actual tower descents and the necessary rigging at the free tower will take relatively little time, you will have quite a bit of concurrent training. That will include the art of unarmed defense, knife attack training, and bayonet training." There just had to be a catch, the murmur conveyed; too good to be true!

"Finally we get to D Stage, the third week. Here you will exit an aircraft in flight. And just to get it out of the way, everyone will be saying that you will exit an aircraft in fright." General laughter with an edge of nervous anticipation.

"You will make five qualifying jumps, the first four in the morning. In the afternoon you repack the chute you have jumped for the next day. The fifth jump is a night jump and you don't have to repack that one. After that jump you're a trooper and the riggers will pack your chutes. Questions?" There were none. "End of orientation." The captain stepped aside and made room for an elderly warrant officer from the rigger section. They certainly wasted no time getting us started.

"Platoon sergeants, take your platoons to the rigger tables marked with your number. We're going to tell you a bit about the parachute and then make table assignments. Move out." We moved. There was not even a ten-minute break.

Our entire platoon fitted easily around the long packing table without anyone having to stand behind someone else. Curiously we stared at the smooth, shiny surface on which a parachute with its harness and pack was stretched out. At the center of the table stood a rigger sergeant, the instructor for our group. He was slightly older than we were, perhaps twenty-two or twenty-three, well organized, and intelligent.

"This is a T-7 parachute," he smiled and waved his right hand as though presenting us to a princess, bowing slightly. He walked toward the canopy and lifted its very top by a small loop. "The apex," he said, putting it gently back on the table. "The canopy," he continued, running his fingertips along its length as he walked back along the table. "The skirt," he explained as he held what we would have called the hem. He lifted a section of the skirt and said, "A panel. There are twenty-eight panels in a T-7, troop-type parachute, each twelve inches at the skirt. That gives you a twenty-eight-foot canopy." He continued his walk. "Suspension lines," he said and again followed the long, silken bands toward the harness. "Civilians call these 'shroud lines.' If you ever call them that, you will do twenty-five push-ups. They are suspension lines." I have never once heard a paratrooper call them anything else.

The sergeant and the suspension lines had reached the harness. "Connector line," the sergeant said and picked up a steel connector to which some of the suspension lines were fastened. "Riser," and he picked up what we would have called one of those straps you guide the parachute with. He continued, "Four connector links, four risers. Pull on one, and the suspension lines attached to it pull down that part of the skirt to which *they* are attached. And that's the direction you go in." He showed us chest and leg straps. Clearly, indelibly, the anatomy of the parachute fixed itself in our brains.

The way the contraption worked was simplicity itself. The canopy was to be folded and placed into its cover with the apex on top. I had my doubts about this operation. Those yards and yards of nylon would never fit into a cover the size of the one we were looking at. On the outside of the cover a packet contained a fifty-foot length of webbed rope called the static line. One end was attached to the cover; the free end terminated in a hook called the snap fastener. Aboard the aircraft, the free end of the static line was hooked to a cable running the length of the plane. When a person jumped, the static line as it ran out pulled the cover free from the parachute, and the propeller wash inflated the canopy. There she goes, safe and sound; happy landing! I could *see* it.

Suddenly the sergeant said, "Take ten outside. There's a coffee machine in front. See you back in ten minutes." For one of the few times in our military lives, the ten-minute break seemed too long. A short blast of a whistle, and we filed back into the shed to our positions around the table.

"What do I hold in my hand, Gabel?" the sergeant asked.

"A rubber band, sergeant," I replied innocently.

"Give me twenty-five!" said the sergeant, not unkindly. I assumed the leaning-rest position and started my twenty-five push-ups. "This is *not* a rubber band. This is a retaining band. What does it retain, Johnson?"

"The—uh—static line?"

"Right. What else does it retain, Hager?"

"The suspension lines," Otto said proudly.

"Very good. Suspension lines. Twenty-three, twenty-four, twenty-five. OK, Gabel." I got off the floor and rejoined the group. The review continued. "And what is *this* called?" There was a small "thinking" pause. The sergeant glanced at his clipboard. "Cullen?"

"The apex, sergeant."

"Well, yes. But what I really wanted is *this* thing here. OK, Benny."

"That little string, sergeant?"

"Right. What's it called?"

"I don't know, sergeant."

"Give me twenty-five. Class?"

"Breakcord," roared the platoon while Benny executed twenty-five perfect push-ups.

The review lasted twenty minutes. It was surprising how much we had learned in this very short time. The remaining period was allocated to table and locker assignments. Then the actual rigging instruction began.

Step by step we were taken through the intricacies of packing the T-7 parachute for a jump. Each instructor at each packing table stayed abreast of the others as we received our first taste of the well-orchestrated and highly professional way in which the Parachute School went about its business. And by some miracle, everybody's canopy actually did fit into the parachute cover. I couldn't believe my eyes or my hands.

We double timed from apparatus to apparatus at speeds that seemed to blur what we saw on arrival and yet imprinted knowledge permanently on the subconscious, ready for instant recall when needed.

There was the mock-up of a C-47 interior. With dummy backpacks and reserve parachutes strapped to our bodies, with hot and uncomfortable steel helmets on our heads, we climbed the ramp of the mock-up and took our seats in stick formation, a row of us along either side facing each other.

"All right, no grab-ass here! We're gonna have jump commands, and you men exit and execute as though we're in the air because this stuff *is* gonna keep you alive!" The instructor was a technical sergeant who, we were told, had made quite a record for himself in Africa. He was tall, lean, and blond, and he did not hide the fact that he did not at all care for any of us. I for one was afraid of the man and resolved to stay as inconspicuous as possible.

"When you hear the command 'Get ready!'" he bawled as he unceremoniously began the instructions, "you take and grab the static line snap fastener in your right hand, making sure it is open for instant hook-up to the cable, that one there running the length of the aircraft. Number two command is 'Stand up!' You do that like this." He demonstrated by getting out of his bucket seat, turning toward the exit door of the mock-up, and grasping the static line above him with his left hand. "So you're all standing there facing aft, everybody holding the cable with the left hand. Then comes command number three: 'Hook up!' You now snap the fastener to the cable like *this*. You *yank* it down and make sure the safety button sticks out from the hook because that means it won't unhook again. Then you secure the hook. You take this little cotter pin tacked to the end of the static line and insert it into the little hole just below the safety button, see? Now there is absolutely no way that that hook is gonna come off the cable."

He took a breath and glared at us. "Now comes command number four: 'Check equipment!'" He glared some more. "Now you know and I know that the riggers will check your equipment two million times before your scrawny asses ever get on the aircraft. But things happen up there when you're flying around all cramped and hot. Static lines uncoil, silk gets worked outa the pack, rip cords on reserves get pulled, leg straps even get very mysteriously unbuckled. So when you get the command 'Check equipment!' goddamn, *check* equipment."

"You," the tech sergeant pointed to the first man near the door. "Stand up." The man got to his feet. "First you check the backpack and harness." As he explained, the instructor smoothed straps and pointed to the areas he was discussing. "Look at the packcover. Static line secured? Lacing OK? Any silk sticking out? Risers smooth and tucked in? Turn around, you," he growled at his mannequin, and the man quickly turned. "Bellyband tight? Rip cord OK? Silk sticking outa the reserve? Sit down!" The man sat. "You check your buddy in front of you just as close as you want your buddy in back of you to check *you*! The last man in the stick is checked by the next-to-the-last man. All right."

"Fifth command: 'Sound off for equipment check!' If all is well, the last man in the stick yells, 'Twelve OK!' and taps the man in front of him on the leg. That man will yell, 'Eleven OK!' and so on. When the check is completed, the jumpmaster will usually ask, 'Is everybody OK?' or maybe, 'Is everybody happy?' You guys will then yell at the top of your lungs, 'Yes!' The reason for that is, it relieves the tension." The sergeant paused as though he expected some disagreement.

"Now a quick look at the jump lights," he continued and turned to a panel at the right edge of the exit door that displayed a red and a green bulb. The red bulb was on. "Usually this red light goes on three minutes from the drop zone, the DZ. Usually. It's on while we go through the jump commands.

"OK, next command is 'Stand in the door!' Now remember, you guys are all standing facing aft, left foot in front of the right. First man in the stick now simply pivots on the ball of his right foot, left foot halfway out the door, hands out and straight, head up. Foot of the next man in line is flush up against the first man's right foot, forming a T. Everybody else closes up and shuffles, always left foot first.

"OK; now the red light goes off." The sergeant manipulated a hidden switch and continued, "The green light goes on." I was at the edge of my seat with anticipation. I had to tell myself that this was just a mock-up; the rapid-talking sergeant had me living a jump. "Final command is 'Go!'" He shouted the word and whirled around facing us. "All right, let's run through it!" And without further ado he commanded, "First stick—get ready!"

Then there was the manipulation harness.

Steel hoops suspended from wooden beams over an oblong sawdust pit had parachute harnesses attached by their four risers. The hoops were lowered by pulleys; the hapless trooper strapped himself into the harness, trying hard to place the leg straps flush against the insides of his thighs. Alas, when he was pulled off the ground and suspended over the sawdust pit, the leg straps closed on his scrotum like a vise. "Slip to the front," came the first command, and thirty troopers suspended in agony grasped the front risers and pulled, dipping the steel hoops above them forward. "Recover! Slip to the right!" The pain between my legs and the Georgia heat of late summer had me drenched in sweat. I pulled the right set of risers and strained to hold that position until the command came, "Recover!" Assistant instructors, reminders of the Frying Pan in brilliant white T-shirts with the black parachute wings stenciled on their fronts and creased jump trousers tucked into polished boots, stalked among us and mustered each move. They all looked alike. Cool, slender, cleancut, they walked among the bundles of suspended misery with unconcealed contempt. One of them was standing next to me, legs apart, fists stemmed against hips. "Don't just hang there, trooper! Get those risers down!" I thought there was no reserve strength left in me and was surprised when, with the thought of "You sadistic son of a bitch!" the steel hoop quivered on the right side. "Recover!" came the command from the senior instructor on the platform; but there was no rest yet. "Slip to the left!" I executed the maneuver, suddenly getting very angry. The assistant instructor next to me said, "Better," and walked over to the next man. "Bastard," I thought as I clawed the risers at chest level. "Recover!"

Time crawled by as we executed all the guidance maneuvers two or three times. Then the pulleys creaked us back onto the sawdust. As we shed the harnesses and waited for the command to fall out, we secretly glanced at one another to confirm that all was well and that these PTR bastards would have to wait for a cold day in hell before any of us would show a sign of what we felt.

"Fall in on me!" a white-shirted assistant instructor shouted, holding up his right arm. I was still in pain as I ran toward him and took my place in the formation. We stood, fatigues soaked with sweat, faces flushed. "Right—*Face*! Double time—*Ho*!" The white-shirted superman took us over to the landing trainer. Here the inevitable dummy harness would be attached to a trip-release device on a rail that started from a raised platform and descended slanting over and beyond one of the ubiquitous sawdust pits. Over the pit, the trip release would be activated just as we would sail at what seemed to be fifty miles an hour, and we would slam into sawdust that seemed as soft as concrete. "Unsatisfactory PLF," an instructor at the pit would say and direct us back to the platform. How anyone could make a school-approved PLF from that contraption was beyond me.

Lunch in the battalion mess hall did for us what a fine restaurant does for the harassed businessman who manages to get away from the pressures of his office at midday. Somehow our own cooks and other mess people, who had taken over the big, ugly mess hall from the PTR for the duration of our stay here, had made it as attractive as an Army mess hall could be made. They had placed curtains on the windows and each of the four- and six-man tables had a real tablecloth. Napkins with silverware, salt and pepper shakers, and a sugar bowl were on each table. Meals were consistently well prepared and our trays were filled in a manner close to tender loving care as we took them through the cafeteria-style chow line. The Dog KPs circulated among the tables serving steaming coffee.

Conversation centered on the events of the morning. The suspended harness generated the most four-letter expletives, followed closely by the wind machine that we had experienced just before lunch and that had dragged each of us over thirty yards of Georgia clay-dirt while we struggled to collapse the fully inflated parachute canopy. Still, there was an undercurrent of pride in each expletive. Each of us quite naturally assumed that we would all make it through this phase of our training; this unspoken confidence, which would grow as we grew within our regiment, imposed the obligation of maximum effort on the part of each man. More and more, we became a family; more and more, individual excellence accrued to the unit and was reflected back to each of us.

It was passed around the tables at lunch that the afternoon would be exclusively devoted to the forty-foot towers.

The tower looked innocent enough from a distance. Even when we were lined up beneath it and gazed straight up at its jump platform with looks we hoped showed nothing but professional interest, it seemed only moderately high. But as we climbed the wooden stairs inside its frame, glancing down occasionally, it grew to the height of the Empire State Building.

As each man stepped onto the deck of the jump platform, two assistant instructors snapped riser webbing onto the D-rings on the shoulders of our harnesses. The webbing arched out the jump door to a cable, but my eyes did not linger on the pulley in space out there. It is safe, I said to myself. The Army simply could not afford to have it otherwise. But the thought did little to mitigate that elevatorlike feeling in my stomach.

I looked at the sergeant instructor with the spaniel-type look he probably encountered each time a trooper first stepped onto that platform. I thought that the sergeant would probably make a first-class hangman.

"All right," he said, and I wondered (as usual) why they always started their more unpleasant instructions with an "all right." "Left foot in the door, ball of the foot on the line. Toes are outside. Right foot behind, knees flexed. Both hands outside against the sides of the door and straight. Head up. *Don't look down.* At the command 'Go!' bring your right leg forward, push off with your left, make a quarter-turn left, bring your hands in front of your reserve, put your head down and count. I want to be able to hear 'One thousand, two thousand, three thousand' loud and clear. Questions?" I shook my bloodless head, resigned to my fate. "Stand in the door!" I stood as I had been told but could not help looking down. Way down there below me—that can't be only thirty-five feet—stood the men of my platoon looking up. "State your name," said the hangman sergeant, bored as ever.

"Private Gabel, sergeant!" I yelled toward the ground and noted that the instructor in front of my platoon down there was marking his clipboard.

"Go!" said the hangman sergeant in a dry, flat voice, utterly without compassion, not caring that the cable was going to snap and that I was going to hurtle to the ground to die in a pool of blood in front of my platoon. At the same time he slapped my thigh. "Goodbye," those things in my intestines gurgled, and I did what I had been instructed to do. I even kept my eyes open, though with great effort, because the platoon was watching. There was a sensation of falling. "One thousand," I screamed, head down and staring at my dummy reserve. The cable took hold, the D-rings slapped against the sides of my helmet, and I was spinning in at least two directions at once. "Two thousand," I croaked as I sailed downward toward the sawdust pit where the release point was. Two more bounces of the long cable carrying me down, and I managed to get out "three thousand" before my feet hit the sawdust. Two assistant instructors unhooked the riser webbing, which was instantly pulled back up the cable for the next man. I double timed over to the tower and stood at attention in front of the principal instructor. Without looking at me, he read from his clipboard, "Feet not together, hands improperly on the reserve, poor PLF. Fall back in." In positive terms, that meant that my exit had been proper, my body position was generally acceptable, my count was all right, and on the whole I had done rather well.

"How was it?" whispered two men who had not had their turn.

"Nothing to it," I managed to grin and tried to suppress the sigh of relief about to surface from deep within my bowels.

"Stop the chatter!" shouted the instructor. "Now look at that man. Damn it, watch. That's how you're supposed to learn. OK, that trooper up there is looking down. Looking down gives you a tendency to fall forward when exiting an aircraft even though here you don't have enough space to do that. Now watch that man!" With a mixture of pride at just having beaten the tower and a feeling of anxiety for my buddy in that same door, I watched as he went through his paces.

Once again the groups made a tower exit, and then it was time for supper. We sat in the open trucks on our way back to the Frying Pan and sang ribald songs. Dust and grime stuck to our sweat-soaked fatigues and our faces were streaked as though we were Indians in warpaint. But our eyes shone; we were getting closer and closer to wings with each piece of equipment we conquered.

The end of the day at the parachute school was a vacation in miniature. Just standing under the shower and feeling the grime run down under the awful-smelling GI soap while anticipating dinner in clean khakis was a cure for the soul. The naked, trim, muscular young bodies under the eight showers in that steaming room stretched and turned to get all the hot water while those waiting for their turn yelled, "OK, you guys! Quit playing drop-the-soap and make room!" "You been in there two hours now, so get the hell out!" "Hey, leave some hot water, you guys!" "OK, Hager. Gettin' clean don't do you no good anyhow, you ugly son of a bitch!" The shouted replies from inside the shower room were uniformly obscene, but each one of the bathers took only the minimum time to wash so as to make room quickly for his buddies.

In the large mess hall, groups from within the squads and platoons, the same people who had shouted at each other in the shower, put their dinner trays on the four- and six-man tables, careful not to spill sauce or soup onto the clean tablecloths. We were sparkling clean in our uniforms, happily anticipating the unhurried evening meal and perhaps a movie at the main post theater after that, as though we were at a resort, ready for an evening of entertainment after a full day of golf, tennis, and swimming.

Alone within the Army, we paratroopers were authorized battalion, not company, messes. The jukebox was playing, just audible over conversations at tables and in the serving line. Unlike our Alabama area jukebox, this one had a wide selection of popular numbers, weighted in favor of romantic rather than boogie-woogie and country music. Over the clatter of silverware came Dorothy Lamour's sultry voice, "They can take the moon away, hide the stars from sight; Time can take a holiday for one romantic night . . . ."

I walked aimlessly from the serving line through the mess hall, threading my way around tables and troopers, savoring the contrast of this clean, easygoing world with the sweat and grime of just an hour ago. My eyes swept the tables for no one in particular. I still had no close buddies, had not become attached to any group, and was simply looking for an empty chair.

It was not that I found no one I liked. On the contrary, I felt a close kinship with the men of my regiment, and I liked most of the troopers of my squad, platoon, and company. My sympathies were simply diffused and until there came a clearer focus I preferred to remain by myself insofar as that was practicable. In a battalion mess hall, it was decidedly not practicable; so I was glad to spot an empty chair at a table occupied by Otto Hager, Mark Leverson, and a soldier from Headquarters Company whom I did not know. "OK to join you?" I asked.

"No," replied Leverson. "Only airborne types allowed."

Otto looked up from his overloaded tray and added, "And sure as hell no Krauts are gonna sit here."

I kicked Otto's chair leg and said, "OK, Otto. Get your Kraut ass off this chair and make room for an American trooper." I put my tray down at the empty table setting.

Between slurps of soup, Otto mumbled, "These Krauts ain't got no manners," and I suggested what he could do in the classic two words without one of which the soldier's vocabulary would barely qualify as functional.

"Here, here," said Leverson, raising his blond eyebrows in mock horror. "I shall call the head waiter. We insist on civilized language." I was introduced to the other man at the table, Leo Beaulieu, who, of course, was called Frenchie.

Frenchie, born in Canada and retaining a heavy French accent, was a short eighteen-year-old, slightly built, with large, yellow teeth, dark, scraggly hair, and a generally unkempt appearance, though he obviously tried to look neat and clean. He had small, greenish eyes that seemed to look rather stupidly out of his gray face. But when he talked, his eyes became kindly and gentle, and one forgot his unlovely appearance.

And Frenchie talked a lot—mostly about food and girls, not necessarily in that order. I had interrupted his description of a girl he had met at the Alabama area service club, but he soon regained his stride. Although we could understand only half of what he was saying in that rapid, accented speech laced with French words, the description was vivid enough and kept us highly entertained. Without so much as a pause, Frenchie switched from the girl to our soup. "Do you know zat what you are eating iz ze real French onion soup?" he asked as though he had just made a profound discovery. "Zey really deed well, ze cooks. Must be a French chef zey 'ave."

The soup was, indeed, excellent, hot and well prepared, as was the rest of the meal. There were generous helpings of crisp, plump chicken, fresh peas and carrots, and new potatoes. For dessert we had strawberry shortcake topped with real whipped cream. When the food was served in our line, it was carefully placed onto the tray so that the entrée, as one of our cooks called it, would not have dessert on top of it as seemed the rule rather than the exception in the usual Army mess. Dessert was invariably served in a separate dish; after we finished our meal, a Dog KP took our trays, placed the dessert in front of us, and scurried back to the kitchen to bring us hot coffee.

Mess supervision was meticulous. On the serving line, the first cook walked back and forth watching his underlings like a hawk, seeing to it that the food was attractively and carefully served. The mess sergeant, tall and trim and atypical—not at all what the movies usually portrayed—walked the perimeter of his domain, missing no detail. And crisscrossing the mess hall, stopping here and there at a table, was the battalion duty officer. Although all officers seemed to me to have descended for a time from Olympus, here in the mess hall that young second lieutenant seemed like the owner of a fashionable restaurant. He'd stop at your table to ask, "How's the chow? Everyone got dessert? Is the coffee hot?" It was, though slightly intimidating, viewed as a flattering solicitation after our well-being.

Otto lit a stogie, tasted his coffee, and leaned back in his chair with a grunt. Leverson wanted to know who was going to the movies. From the jukebox Frank Sinatra was crooning, "I couldn't sleep a wink last night, because we had that silly fight; I had to call you up this morning, to see if everything was still all right." A falsetto voice at the next table squealed, "Oh, Frank-eeeee!" to the delight of everyone within hearing. The only thing missing in our Army life, I thought, was girls.

We discussed the musical spectacular playing at the main post theater and, except for Otto, who was going for a few beers and talked big about picking up a Red Cross girl, decided that we would go to see it.

A trooper from the great open spaces had finally managed to drop a nickel into the jukebox to get some relief from the big city music, and Farrin Young replaced Frank Sinatra with "Way down . . . in Columbus, Georgia . . . take me back to Tennessee." From practically every table, including ours, came the inevitable, high-pitched "Ahh Haaaaaaaa" and "Sing it, Farrin," and "That's *mah* kahnd of music." It was clearly time for us city boys to go to the movies.

Mark, Frenchie, and I crossed the Frying Pan area to Lumpkin Road and ambled toward the theater. We walked slowly, enjoying the luxury of leisure even though we knew the early show would be starting in minutes. But if it came to a choice of double timing or missing the cartoons, Bugs Bunny would simply have to carry on without us. Although it was still hot and muggy, the sun was going down and, compared to midday, it seemed almost cool.

As we approached the theater, I said, "You guys wait. I'll get the tickets," and collected the money from them. There were some ten people ahead of me in the box office line, and I watched the reaction of the pretty red-headed ticket seller to each man's approach. No soldier seemed to be able to buy his ticket without saying something to the redhead. She would punch the button of the automatic ticket dispenser, look up, and either smile or look stonily at the man in line. Once she threw back her head and laughed, showing even white teeth in startling contrast to her deep tan. I thought of Ruth Walton at Grauman's Egyptian Theater and how on our upcoming furlough I would nonchalantly step up to her window in full paratrooper regalia and say, "Two, if you can spare the time." It was my turn and only partly to practice I said, "Two, if you can spare the time."

The girl looked up and chuckled. "Oh, brother! *That's* a new one!"

"OK," I said sadly, "if that's the way you feel about it, give me three, please. I'll just take my buddies instead." She laughed, shook her head, and gave me the tickets.

The line waiting for seats was exclusively made up of men in khaki. Most of them were from regular infantry and armored units. Their uniforms had wilted during their walks or rides from barracks and service clubs to the theater, the heat and humidity having taken its usual toll. Here and there were groups of paratroopers or PTR students, who, with trousers bloused over shiny paratrooper boots and their field caps (universally known by the obscene name for a critical part of the female anatomy) sporting the blue and white parachute patch jauntily tilted over the right eyebrow, somehow made the work-clothes-like khaki outfits look like military uniforms. One or two troopers, contrary to regulations, were wearing their jump jackets. That was considered "mixed uniform" and was not allowed for off-duty wear. Although the nonairborne MPs would usually not attempt to stop airborne soldiers, the CPs (courtesy patrols, or chute patrols, as we called them), who belonged to our own units, would make the troopers take those jackets off and carry them or sometimes even issue a delinquency report (DR), which spelled trouble from the company commander.

Slowly the line moved forward. As the trooper in front of us—wearing a jump jacket—entered the lobby, two CPs standing slightly to the side of the candy counter shifted their position. They didn't really move, but their attitude clearly conveyed that they were about to take action.

The CPs were older noncommissioned officers, one a sergeant, the other a technical sergeant. They were paratroopers from the 507th Parachute Infantry Regiment, dressed in the regular khaki uniform but with a blue arm band on their left sleeves showing the white letters "CP." On their pistol belts were a billy club to the left and a .45 automatic pistol in a highly polished holster to the right.

The tech sergeant gestured toward the trooper in the jump jacket. That hapless soldier, who instantly realized that playing dumb was out of the question, left the line and walked to the patrol. A few words were exchanged, softly spoken so that we could not hear. The trooper took off his jacket and, carrying it over his arm, left the theater. He was lucky. No DR had been written.

We walked past the two NCOs and they nodded to us in a big-brother manner that we rather appreciated. Then we stood in another, shorter line for popcorn. Once more the simple pleasures of "civilization" registered. I felt the carpet under my feet, saw two or three ladies in light dresses walking through the lobby on the arms of their officer husbands, and smelled the popcorn and candy mixed with the heavy perfume of the young woman dispensing those items at the counter.

Popcorn bags carefully balanced, we made our way down the dark aisle. Bugs Bunny had indeed started without us. Except for a section of seats midway down the aisle marked "Officers Only," the large theater looked no different from theaters in Los Angeles, Denver, or Atlanta. And the ritual of finding a seat with its accompanying "Excuse me" and "Oh, sorry" on one side and the tolerant, good-humored responses on the other was wholly civilian. There was something about a theater at the beginning of a film that seemed to relax any audience as it settled down to be entertained, willingly suspending its disbelief in Hollywood's glamorous fantasies.

Conversely, "The End" and the credit lines waving goodbye from the screen brought us back to the sweltering Georgia evening. Our "mini-vacation" was nearly over, and tomorrow would be another day of B Stage.

The rest of B-Stage week passed quickly, partly because of the multitude of new training devices that continually kaleidoscoped past and that, each time we worked on them became a little less uncomfortable, and partly because we thoroughly enjoyed our new freedom at the end of each day. When the battalion was dismissed at noon on Saturday with only two men hospitalized for injuries sustained at the wind machine, we had achieved our first victory as a unit.

Saturday afternoon the schedule called for care and cleaning, with the customary inspection in barracks closing the week out. Since no weapons had been used during B Stage, care and cleaning primarily meant shining our boots. The ritual turned into a social occasion, like a washday in an apartment-house basement where "the girls" could gossip at leisure. Unlike weapons cleaning, which demanded a certain concentration, shining boots and brass gave everyone leisure to dream or talk or both. Talk, of course, reviewed the week in rowdy commentary on the equipment, the instructors, and the training routine and in warm praise of the mess hall and its food. Inspection by the platoon leader and the platoon sergeant was almost a pleasure. In spite of its usual formality, the inspection of wall lockers, footlockers, barracks bags, and bedding progressed in an atmosphere indefinably different from that of previous inspections. The faces of our young lieutenant and our platoon sergeant seemed to glow and their voices were gentle. "They really *like* us," I thought with some amazement.

Saturday night I wanted to be alone with my happy thoughts. I felt that the worst part of jump training was over; the tower stage next week was considered a "fun" stage, and D Stage, the actual jumping phase, was still too far away to worry about. It seemed appropriate to do a quiet bit of celebrating which I always preferred to do by myself. And so I went to the snack bar instead of to the mess hall for dinner, took a long walk, and then went to the main service club. This, I thought, was really living. And indeed, compared with the Alabama area, the main post of Fort Benning was Broadway and Forty-second Street, Sunset and Vine, and the Etoile all rolled into one. I reveled in this military downtown until well past nine o'clock before heading back to the barracks.

7
Jump Training: C Stage

The march to the towers for our C-Stage orientation was a short one. We didn't even have enough time to sing, and most of us felt very much like singing. Here they were, those towers that had seemed so unreachable when first I looked at them from my barracks window. Now they loomed immediately over us, the final obstacle to be conquered before we would board an aircraft and, high above the post, actually and unimaginably jump out of it.

Our orientation began beneath one of the "free" towers where a first lieutenant, the senior instructor, took charge.

Most of the instructors who had become airborne characters by 1943 seemed to be assembled at C Stage. They were the legendary figures, the heroes, combat and otherwise, that we had heard about from our own cadre and through rumors. They came from the original parachute battalions, some even from the test platoon. The most famous was "Flash Gordon," a blond gorilla so personally formidable that he needed no combat record. No one seemed to know his real name, nor did I ever learn his rank, though I suspected that he was a noncommissioned officer. And next in line was the senior instructor, Lieutenant Stanley A. Galicki.

Galicki was relatively small for a paratrooper, about my height but much heavier. His weight was all in muscle and he looked musclebound until he moved. He was exceedingly lithe and fast on his feet, with a dangerous feline quality about him. We were seated in a circle around him and he was making a whole turn inside that circle, crouching slightly, looking at each trooper as though he were selecting his next meal before he spoke.

"You're here primarily to learn how to manipulate your parachute during actual descent," he finally began without any change in his loping, feline progress—a lethal mixture of Groucho Marx, Peter Lorre, and Tarzan. "Second, you will go into some of the refinements of your job after your parachute has deposited you in enemy territory. So those of you who are not either stepping off the free tower or rigging up for it will be engaged in hand-to-hand combat training." The intensity of the man momentarily made us forget that he was talking about concurrent training, which would take up the slack on the waiting line at the towers. Moreover, the subject had already been thoroughly covered during our first weeks in the Alabama area. But something about Galicki told us that there would be a new and interesting twist to his instructions.

Galicki paused, turned, and continued his crouched loping in the opposite direction. "Now, about the towers," he said in that staccato, attention-getting voice of his; "there are two types: controlled and free. The control tower has you on cables and is mainly to familiarize you with height and the harness. In fact, the first one you'll go on has the buddy seat. You just sit there, two of you, and we'll haul you up so you can see what it's like at two-hundred and fifty feet and won't worry about it. Then there is a controlled descent in harness. It's almost the same thing except that you will be in a harness and your attitude will be graded. Then comes the free tower. You're hauled up with a thirty-eight-foot canopy rigged to a lift hoop and released. The canopy, of course, will be partially inflated at the moment of release and then you take over. All right." He stopped, clapped his hands sharply, and said, "On your feet! Off to the buddy seat. That ought to be *fun* for you." And to an assistant instructor, "Move 'em out."

We double timed to one of the control towers and were grouped into buddy teams for the ride up. Otto Hager, who always seemed to be immediately behind me, shared my seat. Up we went and I decided that two-hundred and fifty feet was a goodly distance from the ground. But it *was* fun and we had a fine view of Fort Benning from the top. We peered at the platoon at the foot of the tower. "They sure do look small, though," Otto mused. Before I could comment, there was a slight rocking motion and down we plunged.

Our platoon rushed up at us. The seat bounced to a halt, and we returned to our squad. Within minutes the entire platoon completed its orientation and jogged to the controlled harness tower.

Another tanned giant with black parachute wings on his spotless white T-shirt started his lecture the second we were given the commands "At ease! Rest!" "You've just had an enjoyable ride to two-hundred and fifty feet," he said, looking at us with utter disdain. "And on the way down, after looking around at beautiful Fort Benning, you looked straight down at your buddies, didn't you?" We stood in silence, wondering what that had to do with anything. "Well, goddamn it, I asked you a question," the giant bellowed at us. "Didn't you?"

"Yes, sergeant," we shouted in unison.

"All right. Now, in a live situation you prepare to land between one hundred and fifty feet above the ground. You've been told time and time again to look at the horizon and not straight down. If you *do* look down, you will *not* make a good practice landing fall (PLF) and you are liable to break your asses. And then you will be absolutely no good to anyone and we will have wasted our time on you. So again: Look at the horizon when you prepare to land. You are *not* up there for the fun of it! All right; you get into the harness this time. And this time do what you're supposed to do! Clear?"

"Yes, sergeant!" the platoon roared.

The World's-Fair-carnival mood of the buddy seat now gave way to the decidedly uncivilian harness. "Grasp your risers," the giant hissed and looked at me as though I were a particularly vile cockroach as I stood waiting to be hauled up. My hands moved and flattened against the front set of risers. "Think," he rasped, his white teeth gleaming like those of a snarling wolf. Then he flipped his right thumb up, and the harness tugged at my shoulders as the cables lifted me off the ground. Swinging free between the whirring cables, all alone and without Otto's chatter, I decided to make "official use" of my time. I recited the points of descent while cautiously looking around. One: Check canopy. Of course there was only this old loosely rigged simulator flapping above me, but I strained dutifully to look at it. Two: Check your descent. Well, I was still going up; so I looked around once more. Three: Watch other men in the air. I tried to imagine a sky full of troopers. By now I had reached the top of the outstretched arm of this ugly tower that I was just beginning to respect. Four: Prepare to land. There was that slight upward rocking and the sensation of falling as I was released for the descent. I glanced down but then quickly riveted my eyes on the horizon and bent my knees in a "prepare to land" position. Five: Land. By God, that cable was actually rigged so that my feet hit the padded platform with some force and my legs strained to absorb the great shock I was sure would follow. But there was no shock—only the rocking motion of the cables catching me. I unbuckled and stood at attention. "OK," said the giant, fixing me with cold eyes, and it sounded like a compliment. I returned to my squad and said, "Whew!" Otto chuckled and said, "Yeah."

That afternoon, after two more tower descents interspersed with landing fall practice, we assembled at the free tower again. And there was the second most famous of the PTR characters once more: Galicki.

"Whatever you may think, two-hundred and fifty feet is plenty high," he began while moving within the semicircle in which we sat, a lion in an open area separated from the human onlookers not even by a ditch. "It's so high, in fact, that you can open your reserve at that height in case of a malfunction and still make it safely to the ground. Observe!" While he was talking, two assistant instructors had fastened a dummy to the lift cables of the free tower. On the dummy's chest was a reserve parachute with its rip cord rigged for opening on descent. The dummy was now lifted up; the higher it went, the more human it looked. "What we want to do here," Galicki continued in his harsh, staccato voice, "is to show you the relative safety of free descent from the tower *and* to demonstrate the capability of your reserve parachute to function properly at two-hundred and fifty feet." He looked over his shoulder and said, I thought superfluously, "Watch."

One-hundred sixty pairs of eyes were glued on the diminished human-looking dummy swinging from one of the four tower arms, hovering high above us. "Release number two," Galicki commanded. There was a small, metallic sound as the cables lifted the dummy a few more feet to its release mechanism; then it fell.

We saw the small pilot chute spill out of the reserve pack, and we saw it drag out the reserve canopy as the figure plummeted to earth. For a few seconds the unopened parachute flapped in the air like a huge white rag; then the dummy plowed into the ground at one-hundred fifty miles an hour. We watched, wide-eyed, as it bounced three times and came to rest just outside our spectator semicircle, the skirt of the limp canopy partially draped over its legs.

Into the stunned silence Galicki's voice crackled, "Well, it usually opens. We don't have enough time to try it again; but anyway, you noticed how well the chute deployed. With just a little wind it would have worked OK." We were never to know whether the dummy's reserve parachute was meant to open or whether its failure was a special demonstration for possibly overconfident rookies of the 513th.

Galicki's thoughts could not be read from his face, no matter how hard our anxious eyes searched, as he continued his lecture. "Depending on the direction of the wind, you will descend from two of the four tower arms. To check wind velocity and direction we shall give you a very sophisticated device which you will activate at the top of the tower prior to release."

He fumbled in his pocket and said, "Ah, here it is," as he pulled out a scrap of white paper that he tore into four pieces. He dropped three of the scraps and as they fluttered to the ground he held up the remaining one. "This is the meteorological device you will take along with you each time you go up. When you reach the top, we will ask you over the public address system to drop it. If this little piece of paper drifts into the tower, we will haul you back down because we do not, of course, want you to be smashed against those steel beams."

This device at least seemed foolproof.

"Still," Galicki went on, "even if the paper floats away from the tower, you must remember that the wind may shift after you've been released. *Therefore*: Climb your front risers hard immediately after your release to make sure you put some distance between you and that steel. We will then call out the maneuvers you are to execute. And one more thing. When I say climb your risers immediately after release, I mean, of course, after the canopy is fully inflated. You don't want to collapse your chute, do you? As you know, you won't have a reserve; and anyway, even under the best of circumstances . . . ," his voice trailed off dreamily, "much below two-hundred and fifty feet the reserve really does become excess baggage . . . ." Then in his normal lecture voice: "All right. We use the same buddy teams as on the seat. Tomorrow if the wind holds we use arms number two and three. Hand-to-hand combat is in this area. All right. On your feet!"

The next morning we were beneath arms number two and three and, after a brief explanation of rigging procedure, we gathered around the large hoop to fasten the skirt of our first free-descent parachute. On command of our instructor, we stepped back as the first two men were lifted. Up and up they went, to the hum of the cable. Finally the hum stopped and the troopers, tiny forms dangling high overhead from those outstretched tower arms, swayed gently in the breeze, as the dummy had swayed the previous day.

"Number two," the tower instructor's voice boomed over the public address system, "drop your paper!" Through his binoculars the safety NCO watched the drift of the paper and the "attitude" of the trooper, then without a word or gesture, took the binoculars from his eyes and picked up a clipboard from the field table next to him. "Are you ready, number two?" the loudspeaker voice asked.

A tiny voice from above replied, "Yohhh!"

"Release number two," the monotone loudspeaker voice said. The short cable sound, the barely perceptible "click" of the release mechanism, and our fellow airborne student half drifted and half fell away from the tower, his partially inflated canopy filling and becoming taut seconds after the release. Then he floated gently, almost majestically, toward the landing area.

"Number two," the PA voice came again, "slip to the left." Instantly the parachute changed direction and drifted left. "Recover! Slip to the right!" There was a tiny rocking motion as the left set of risers were released and the right set pulled down. The chute obeyed and drifted right.

"Recover! Prepare to land. Good work. Execute a good PLF!" Even before he hit the ground and the oversized canopy gently collapsed on top of him, the PA set turned its attention to the other trooper waiting for his descent. "Number three! Drop your paper, number three." The exercise took its course; in just over two minutes from the time both of the troopers had been hauled up to their positions on the tower arms, incredibly the free descent practice for the first two men was over. Then came the rigging of the two chutes for the next descents, with a squad of us working in a large circle around the lift hoop to which the canopy was to be attached.

Two more troopers went up; two more chutes were rigged to the hoops. Then it was my turn, and I trotted to my station at number three. The principal tower instructor, a tall, young second lieutenant, watched me in silence as I got into the harness. He too was bronzed from the sun, cast from the same mold as his fellow C-Stage cadre and distinguishable from his noncommissioned officers only by the rank insignia on his cap. After a moment the young officer turned and strode to station number two, leaving me in the care of his assistant.

After a brief harness adjustment by the NCO, I was told to place my hands on the risers; I stood there, hands over my head flat against the front set, waiting for the lift.

With a tug on my harness, the lift mechanism went into action. This time I was not surrounded by the confining cables of the control tower and a song from the movie "Pinocchio" echoed briefly in my mind— " . . . there are no strings on me." Up I went, looking straight ahead over the Fort Benning panorama, at the sandy hills in the distance and at the small white clouds sailing above my head and passing behind me. Behind me? Behind me was the tower! The freedom from the confining cables, the sand hills, the blue sky lost a good bit of their charm as I glanced over my shoulders and saw the ugly steel beams of the tower slowly, menacingly passing by. The hum of the lift cables stopped. For a moment all was silent except for the soft whisper of a breeze wafting through the deadly tower beams. The Fort Benning panorama rocked as I oscillated gently at two-hundred fifty feet.

"Number two," squawked the PA set from below. Although it no longer boomed at that distance, it remained the voice of authority, of the unseen, all-seeing PTR controller. "Drop your paper, number two!" On arm number two, outside my field of vision, Otto's scrap of paper would be fluttering to earth. I struggled to reach into my pocket for my scrap. "Are you ready, number two?"

"Yahhh!" Otto's characteristic yell could probably be heard at Lawson Field over the roar of the C-47s.

"Release number two!" I strained to see Otto but could not. "Good forward slip, number two. Recover. Slip to the left! Recover! Slip to the rear! Recover! Prepare to land . . . watch your PLF!" There was scarcely a break as the voice continued, "Number three!" I gave up trying to locate Otto.

"Drop your paper, number three!" I let go of my scrap and watched it flutter toward the tower like a wounded butterfly. "Are you ready, number three?"

"No!" I yelled with all my might, as the little piece of paper made its painful way through the steel beams.

"Release number three," commanded the unseen instructor in that same monotone squawk, as though I did not exist, as though I were yesterday's dummy-human. Luckily I was more furious than afraid and exploded silently in a string of obscenities as the release mechanism clicked above me. So they wanted me to get smashed up on that tower, those goddamn bastards! At once I pulled down on the front risers, reckless, not caring whether the canopy collapsed or inflated. The elevator feeling, the sensation of falling, calmed my fury and stayed my arms in their effort to pull the risers down to chest level. As the canopy fully inflated, the falling sensation ceased.

"Climb your risers, number three! Get away from that steel!"

"What do you care, you filthy bastard?" I thought as I struggled to get the risers down.

"Atta way! Recover! Slip to the left!" I let go of the risers and seemed to hang motionless in air. Then I pulled at the left set and for the first time noted the response of the parachute. Now, too, I noted the changing horizon, saw the red roofs of the Quadrangle, the low green barracks huddle around the Frying Pan. By God! I was really up there with a parachute! My anger melted like ice cream in the Georgia sun.

"Recover! Slip to the right!" I executed the command and delighted in the chute's obedience. "Recover! Good job. Prepare to land. Watch your PLF!" I let go of the risers and the canopy skirt snapped up, stabilizing the parachute into that momentary attitude of hovering. Had the instructor just said, "Good job?" Well, maybe those guys aren't so bad after all, I reflected as I prepared to land.

My hands flat against the front set of risers, arms stretched out above me, I flexed my knees and forced myself to stare at the horizon. It didn't seem to do much good; I saw the ground rushing up to claim me. Then the horizon was gone and the ground slapped against the soles of my feet. I tumbled forward onto the grass at the edge of the graveled area radiating from the base of the tower. The shock of landing was considerably less than I had anticipated, but I ascribed that to the oversized canopy used on the tower. An assistant instructor appeared from thin air even before I had scrambled to my feet, glared at me as he marked a sheet on his clipboard, and growled, "Poor PLF." But I felt good. Besides, I could not imagine that in the history of the parachute school any one of these types had ever used the word "good" to describe a parachute landing fall. Nor could I imagine anyone ever really making a "good," classical fall. Regardless of any instructor's evaluation, in the future if I could walk away from a landing uninjured, I would be satisfied with myself.

As I got out of the harness, four men of my platoon ran up to help carry the canopy back to the tower. Lest we expected such luxury at a "live" drop zone, we had been carefully told that only at the towers would we find a recovery team and then only because it saved time and rigging effort.

"Looked kind of funny," one of the men said while we were running back toward the empty hoop under arm number three.

"Felt kind of funny," I replied.

"Think they ever hauled anyone back down?" asked the soldier carrying the apex.

The man next to him said, "Hell, no! Those bastards don't give a shit!"

I felt good enough to play the devil's advocate and said, "Oh, for Christ's sake, it's just a big goddamn show. Think of the paperwork the bastards would have to go through if we really got smashed up. Nobody goes up there unless there's a weather clearance."

And I almost believed it.

In stylized confusion, elements of Company A shuttled in crisscross patterns between towers and landing areas as the unit shifted its training activities. Now the hand-to-hand combat element was at the towers and we were on the meadow, delivered into the hands and the power of First Lieutenant Galicki.

"At ease. Rest. Sit down in place," said Galicki with a sardonic smile. This was his forte and, though he was principal instructor at C Stage, his favorite training was right here on the ground.

"I'm told you gentlemen have already had some unarmed defense in the Alabama area," he began. "So our refined techniques here will not be entirely strange to you. The object of hand-to-hand combat, you remember, is to render an opponent *hors de combat*. What does that mean?" There was general silence. Galicki paced around our circle, looking at us contemptuously, and softly said, "It means . . . ," his eyes half closed, he continued looking at us as the lord of the manor appraises his lowliest charwoman and softly repeated, "It means . . . ." He stopped pacing, threw back his head, and bellowed, "Kill him!" We jumped—we couldn't help being galvanized—and we stared up at the Great Galicki like chickens at the fox. "In case you gentlemen have forgotten while engaged in the glamorous business of learning how to be a parachutist," Galicki's voice had sunk almost to a whisper, "You're being paid to be killers. That is your primary, your only function in life: to be *killers*!" As he shouted the word, Galicki looked lethal—a killer and an instructor of killers. He could no doubt take on a German platoon single-handedly.

Although we had quite gotten the point, Galicki continued: "The parachute is only a means of transportation by which you are delivered to the ground. And once you're there, you do what?"

"Kill!" we yelled.

"What?" Galicki hissed.

"*Kill*!" we roared. Galicki nodded and relaxed.

"All right. Here's how you do it unarmed," and he launched into the principles of jujitsu, pressure points, critical body areas, and attack techniques. His enthusiasm was infectious and made us forget that we had been taught almost the same thing a few short weeks before. Then came the demonstrations of defense against knife attack, bayonet attack, and pistol attack. After that it was "approach and dispatch" with the knife, the garrote, the rifle butt, and the hands as instruments to effect the silent, rapid, efficient rendering of the enemy permanently *hors de combat*—a ballet of death, superbly performed.

Before the training day was done, we had time for only two student teams to practice what the Great Galicki had preached. When the attack victim went down, Galicki would bellow: "What do you do when he's down?"

We would respond, "Kick him in the head!"

"And then?"

"Kick him again!"

"And *then*?"

"Wipe our boots!" We were getting into the spirit and found it exhilarating. The next day, Galicki assured us, we would all have our turn, and by the time C Stage was over, we would be as good at dispatching an opponent as Galicki himself. When we assembled to jog back to the tower, we had almost forgotten that the primary training at C Stage was concerned with the manipulation of a parachute during free descent.

At dinner time, the mess hall buzzed happily with our first "jump stories" and with blood-curdling tales of the Galicki victims. In our animated state, few noted the Dog Company KPs in their blue denim fatigues dejectedly making their rounds with hot coffee, enduring the humiliation of their assignment, which became increasingly painful the closer we others came to the end of airborne training. From deep within the safe haven of Company A, I watched their sad movements, their shy, furtive, fugitive glances, and shuddered at their thoughts of the what-might-have-been. How would they live through their Army service? What would they tell their children and grandchildren? And had we not been the same when we started; had they not been our buddies only weeks ago? There but for the grace of God . . . .

"Kraut," yelled Otto from across the table, yanking me out of my contemplation of the unimaginable.

"Yes, Heinie?" I replied gently.

"Pass the goddamn cream!"

"Yes, *sir*," I said, relieved to be diverted from the murky track my thoughts took almost every time I watched those KPs.

"You speak good English, Kraut," Otto commented and continued the hilarious story of the little piece of paper that floated into the tower.

Frenchie, Mark Leverson (the cool, blond, handsome Scandinavian with his impenetrable reserve), and I were on some mundane errand in the orderly room. While we waited to be taken care of, Frenchie eyed the framed motto of the 513th hanging on the wall—*Sequitis bastatii*, hand lettered with loving flourishes—and went into profound concentration.

"What do you think it means?" I asked him.

"Zat is seemple. *Sequitis* is like 'sequence.' It must mean 'after.' *Bastatii* must mean 'basting.' Ze French chef bastes a fowl while he cooks it. *Sequitis bastatii* means 'after basting.' After basting he can serve his roast duck." Frenchie's eyes rolled and he licked his lips.

Leverson groaned. "Not 'after'; it means you 'follow.' *Bastatii* is dog-Latin for 'bastard.' The motto means 'Follow the son of a bitch.'"

Frenchie and I exchanged glances. I said, "Sure I follow the goddamn sergeant. He still outruns me in the morning; of course I follow him—what else can I do?"

Leverson drew himself erect. "It doesn't mean to follow your leader. It means get after the bloody enemy. It means get the Krauts whether a sergeant is in front of you or not. It means—it means—'Flash Gordon' knows what it means. Even Galicki probably knows what it means. The

Dog KPs don't understand and never will. You guys—you guys better learn what our motto means. It gets important after a while."

An outburst from Leverson? Emotion from *him*? Frenchie and I shut up. We had some thinking to do. I was still thinking that night after lights out, and on and off for many days to come.

The remaining days of C Stage went by almost faster than those of the preceding week. We were now straining forward toward the goal. There were more tower descents and the subsequent rotation to rigging, recovery, landing fall practice, and hand-to-hand combat. The latter had become our favorite source of entertainment, and only as we approached the end of the week did we realize that we had perfected the attack and defense techniques learned in basic training. We accepted the fact without examining the training principles that brought about a perfect dovetailing of physical and mental skills taught us from the very beginning, from our first close-order drill to the final stages of airborne training. We knew nothing of the painstaking staff work that implemented master training schedules, that housed, clothed, and fed us, that figured, scheduled, coordinated, and supervised. Only in those secret grins on the faces of our officers would we occasionally perceive that things were going well. But according to plan? Within the framework of policy? That had not entered our minds, which were solely and totally engaged in the objective of becoming paratroopers.

As with the Alabama area, the Frying Pan had become home. It had become home as other dismal places would become home simply because our regiment was there to inhabit them—the barren camps, the wind-swept tent areas, the foxholes dug in frozen ground, the bombed-out buildings. And so the concluding days of C Stage saw us almost comfortably nestled in the same place where we had feared the unknown horrors of parachute basic and airborne training on our arrival at Fort Benning under a searing southern sun before we had become soldiers.

Then C Stage was over and we were ready for the finishing touches.

The weekend was particularly long. At mail call Friday night I received a bubbling letter from my mother, who had all sorts of things planned for my impending furlough, and that reminded me that I still had not bought a suitcase for the trip home. So I tried to use up all of Saturday for the acquisition of a suitcase and perhaps one suntan uniform. But even though the PX was crowded, my purchases were completed shortly after lunch. The long weekend dragged on.

Sunday I went to church. I went to the infantry chapel that I had admired from the bus window on my first day at Fort Benning, but I almost gave up trying to get a seat when I saw it filled to capacity. As I turned to walk back up the aisle, not without visible embarrassment, a lady waved to me and smiled, indicating a seat from which she had just taken a small boy onto her lap. Red-faced, I excused my way past several officers and their families, thanked the lady who had made room for me, made a Europeanlike bow toward her colonel husband, and sat down. After being reassured by my benefactress' smile that I need not feel awkward to be in the officers' section, I relaxed a little and started to follow the service. It was simple and dignified, like the chapel itself. When the chaplain said, "Let us pray," I took the opportunity to ask God to take care of the battalion during D Stage.

After the service I went back to the Frying Pan and waited for Monday.

8
Jump Training: D Stage

The first day of our last week with the Parachute Training Regiment was gray, hot, and humid. Company A marched silently as lead company of the battalion toward Lawson Field. Coming over a rise, we could see the gray hangars in the distance and, with a skip of the heartbeat, the long line of gray C-47s squatting silently—waiting—on the apron in front of the rigger sheds. Everything was grayed—the helmets in front of me, the faces to my left and right, and the rigger sheds looming now directly in front of us, blocking the view of the dreaded field and apron.

Now we marched parallel to the rigger shed, which had grown to look so friendly and familiar to us during the past weeks. This day it looked inimical, evil. All too soon we were halted. The merciless drill during the past weeks had made precise, flawless movements a matter of habit and there were only company sounds of company movements in unison. The sounds of Company A executing a "left face" with perfection must have warmed the hearts of the regimental commander and his executive officer, both of whom were watching. But I felt dull and weak and gray, and I could not understand how all the other men in the formation could calmly and precisely execute these mundane commands as though they were doing morning close-order drill in the nice, safe Alabama area.

Captain Spears turned us over to the captain of the First Parachute Training Regiment, who, with his instructors, would now take command for the rest of this long, long morning. "At ease!" the PTR captain commanded. "You will move in stick formation to your lockers, pick up your parachutes, and move to Shed Two. You will put your parachutes on in the fitting area of Shed Two, after which you will receive a rigger check. You will then move to your ready area and sit down until further orders." I was trembling and cold under the muggy, gray Georgia sky. "All right. Fall out, and fall in in stick formation." There was a slight readjustment as squads became sticks, the units in which we would make our jumps. "Company—Atten-*Hut*! By sticks, column left—*March*! Route step—*March*!"

We filed into the yawning bleakness of the rigger shed and past the packing tables, which now seemed like rows of morgue slabs, to our lockers. Even my locker no longer looked familiar. Its horizontal air vents leered at me as I mechanically turned my lock combination. I gingerly pulled my main parachute out of the kit bag and slipped my right shoulder into its harness, then picked up my reserve pack by its carrying loop and pushed the locker door shut with my left knee. It occurred to me that I was being very neat.

The sticks followed an unseen rigger to Shed 2. In the gloom of the fitting area we were halted and told to put our parachutes down. Ahead of us, farther into the gloom of the cavernous shed, were the four sticks of the First Platoon, the first two being fitted into their parachutes. We stood silently, waiting. Here and there a pale face under a gray helmet would turn in the direction of another pale face under a gray helmet and smile tentatively. Shyly, the other face would smile back. Somehow that was reassuring. It was really us standing there, and perhaps this whole thing would work out all right after all.

But the only people talking in the shed were the riggers and the instructors. "Pull those leg straps tighter. Well, get your balls out of the way or you're gonna castrate yourself. . . . It'll loosen up when you get your opening shock. . . . You can't breathe? Good! That means you're in there. . . . Pull a little more of that bellyband through. After you hit the ground you won't be able to get outa the goddamn harness unless you get the goddamn reserve chute off. . . . Pull a little more static line up—don't unravel the whole goddamn thing, for Christ's sake. . . ." The words floated over my head, just so many meaningless sounds.

"Sticks five and six, over here!" That was us. We picked up our parachutes, moved forward, and watched as the last of the preceding sticks moved through a door into the ready area. Three or four riggers and a sergeant were facing us. "All right, put 'em down," the sergeant said. "Get into your main chute and make everything tight. We'll check you and then you get your reserve on. You can take your helmets off now."

I climbed into the T-7 harness the way I had been taught, folded my kit bag and stowed it under the chest straps, clicked the snap fasteners in place, adjusted my leg straps, and made sure all the important parts of my anatomy were securely settled. A rigger came up to me and spun me around by my leg straps.

"Christ, man! You can drive a goddamn truck through here," he said and yanked at the leg straps to get the seat of the main lift webb further under me. "Well, get the reserve on!" I stood, unable to move and bent over. He picked up my reserve, threaded the bellyband through it, and snapped its left fastener to the harness D-ring, mumbling, "Hotshot goddamn troopers. You guys ain't no better than the PTR slobs comin' through here." He pushed the right side of the reserve parachute against my chest in an effort to connect the other snap fastener. I reeled back, barely able to stay on my feet. "Stand still, goddamn it!" growled the rigger and pulled me forward by the left harness strap. As the fastener finally clicked in the D-ring, nearly crushing my chest, it occurred to me that the 513th might be getting some special treatment from these PTR types. "Pick up your helmet," said the rigger. I stood hunched over, unable to bend down or straighten up, and looked at the rigger from below as a tired bull looks at a matador. "Jesus Christ," said the rigger, picking up my helmet and handing it to me. Then he turned his attention to my shadow, Otto Hager.

Just as I was sure that all circulation had stopped and that I would collapse on the concrete, the sergeant said, "All right, make a right face. Follow the corporal." Nobody executed the command with precision. . . . I waddled painfully after the man ahead of me and stepped through the door into the ready area, known at the parachute school as the "sweat shed." It had no windows; it was very sparsely lighted by two naked bulbs. Several rows of benches stood on the concrete floor, and on the first four benches sat the first four sticks. As we took our places, an instructor called, "Sticks one and two, put your helmets on!"

Whether it was the effort of getting into this nearly unbearable equipment and having to maneuver in it, whether it was the stifling, humid Georgia autumn, whether it was the enclosed shed with its wooden sidings and partitions, or whether it was a combination of all those factors as well as the anticipation of the jump ahead, the sweat shed was rapidly justifying its name.

"Kee-rist," said Otto, sitting next to me. It was the first time I had heard one of *us* say anything since entering the rigging area.

"Sticks one and two," called out the instructor, "stand up!" As the two sticks lurched to their feet, a large wooden hangar door at the front of the shed was rolled back just far enough to let through two squads of men side by side. We could see the apron and two or three of the C-47s still waiting for us.

The two sticks waddled through the open door toward the squatting aircraft, and the door was rolled shut again. It was as if something had just swallowed two entire sticks. I briefly thought that there must be a valid reason for keeping us here in the gray gloom, in the sticky air, with the door closed. Surely at this stage of the game they wouldn't practice any more psychological warfare on us. . . . There was a noise from outside, the whine of an engine being started, and finally the muffled roar of first one, then the other of a C-47's engines. The roar intensified, then grew fainter.

Behind us, we heard two more sticks shuffling in. Before us, the voice said, "Sticks five and six, put your helmets on!"

It was not an easy task. I had to twist my entire body just to get the helmet onto my head, and then there was the matter of hooking the chin strap and fastening the jump strap while my arms were restricted by the reserve pack.

"Stand up!" We struggled to our feet, turned, and followed another unseen rigger. The hangar door rolled back and we moved out toward the apron.

My body was twisted in a Quasimodo shape. We were halted at a right angle to the plane, each stick facing the other on either side of the jump door for one more rigger check. "Open your rip-cord cover for a seal check." Somehow I managed it. A corporal stopped in front of me and said, "OK, close it." Then he walked around me, tugged at my harness, checked the break cord and pack cover, smoothed the risers, said "OK," and moved to the next man. It was only slightly reassuring.

"Stick five, move aboard." Our stick labored up the steps to the aircraft, grasping the guide rails with both hands and pulling our bulk into the interior. On the last step we were helped by an Air Corps crew member and by the static jumpmaster, both of whom pulled the men in sharply, saying to each, "Starboard side, all the way back . . . starboard side, all the way back . . . ." The interior was not, after all, quite like the mock-up. The mock-up had been level, the training chutes were not "live," the flooring had not been of slippery steel. We waddled and slithered to our seats and sat down. We were told to fasten our seat belts. Stick six joined us.

The static jumpmaster, a PTR instructor, moved up and down the aisle, propelling himself hand over hand by the static line cable while he talked to us in a pronounced Brooklyn accent, always addressing the stick whose direction he was swinging in at the moment. "No smoking at all. When I get tru, we start engines, rev up, and go to twelve hunnerd feet. Youse already know de commands. Dis is an individual tap-out jump. I will give de command 'Go!' and tap youse on de rear. Right leg goes out foist, quarter toin left, feed togedder, head down, hands on de resoive, count tree tousand—you've hoid it a million times. Good luck!" By that time he had reached the jump door and was putting on a headset. He gave us a "thumbs up" and said something into a mike.

The jumpmaster, wearing a soft, comfortable-looking free-fall parachute backpack, stood in the door and looked back at us. His communications headset was plugged into a box by the door. On its right were

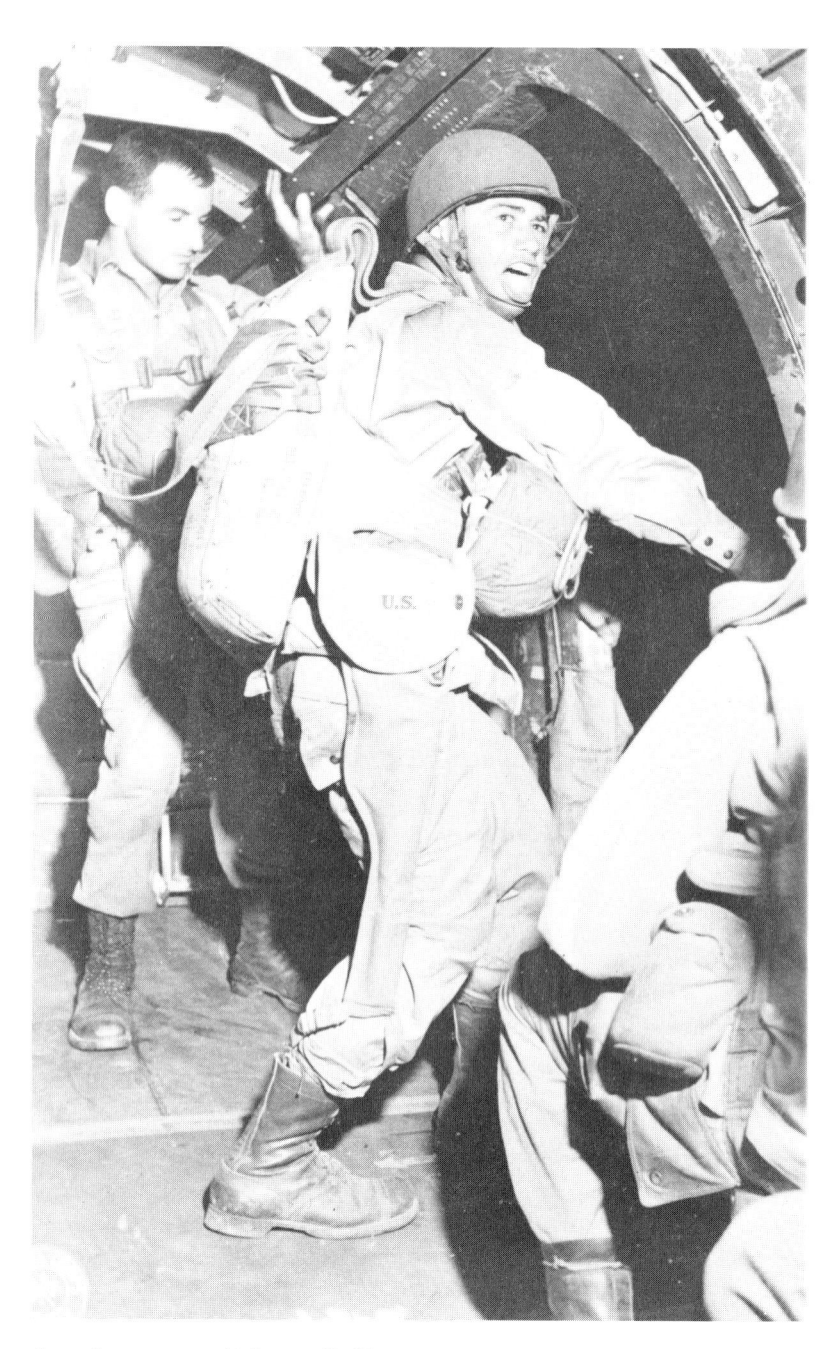

Learning proper exit from a C-47

two lights that now flashed on in a test—red and green—then went out again. It was silent in the aircraft. Again, each set of eyes searched out an opposite set of eyes; there were the shaky smiles, the tugging at chin straps. Then a high, penetrating sound whined from starboard. The plane rocked slightly as the starboard engine started, immediately followed by the port engine. Smiles faded. Each man retreated into his fear. The aircraft taxied toward the end of the runway. The express elevator feeling in my stomach subsided a little because I was thinking that this was the first time I had ever gotten on an airplane to fly, not just to see relatives take off. That amused me. The feeling was immediately spoiled when the C-47 turned sharply at the end of the runway and halted for the engines to rev up, one at a time. I tried to let my mind turn into an insensitive leaden ball, leaving only enough awareness exposed to recognize and follow commands.

There was the pull of extra gravity as the airplane raced over the runway to take off. "Airborne," someone said. I wanted to look but could not muster energy for the struggle of a glance out the plastic window behind me. "Unfasten safety belts!" the jumpmaster shouted over the roar of the engines. The Air Corps crewman walked up and down the aisle to supervise that task while the aircraft was still climbing. Someone across the aisle pointed toward the jump-light panel. Though I couldn't see it, I realized that the red light must have gone on.

"Stick five—get ready!" So soon. God almighty, so soon! We had just taken off! But then we all knew that we were to jump on a drop zone near Lawson Field. I unsnapped my anchor-line snap fasteners from the reserve-carrying loop and held it in my right hand. "Stand up!" We all got to our feet at once. I grasped the cable overhead with my left hand and faced aft. "Hook up!" My right hand went up to the cable and the snap fastener caught. The safety button was protruding; I yanked on the line a few times, inserted the cotter pin, and held on just below the hook.

"Check equipment!" It was a perfunctory exercise. The man in front of me, like everyone else on the aircraft, had a flawless pack. I checked him anyway, and the man behind me dutifully tugged near my own shoulders. "Sound off equipment check!" From behind me came the nervous, high-pitched young voices yelling, "Twelve OK . . . eleven OK . . . ten OK . . ." over the roar of the propellers. "Five OK!" shouted Otto, and I felt his slap on my right leg. In turn I slapped the leg of the man in front of me and shouted, "Four OK!"

A dull, all-over tingling made me feel as though I was trembling deep inside. I held my left hand out with fingers spread and examined it; it was steady as a rock. I looked down at the men of stick six sitting and waiting, wide-eyed and pale. "That must be tough," I thought without any particular feeling, "having to sit there and watch before going out."

"Stand in the door!" There was a movement forward. I shuffled two steps, left leg forward, right leg driving behind. Fear was attacking my throat, making it feel tight.

"Is everybody happy?" roared the jumpmaster.

"Yeahhh . . . !" we yelled. This was supposed to relieve the tension, I remembered. It didn't even faze mine. Fear balled itself into my throat and chest.

"Go!" The man in front of me was in the door; so my left foot was now supposed to form a T with his right foot, and my right hand was supposed to let go of the static line and grasp the right edge of the door. Suddenly joy replaced fear for a moment as I noticed I was doing all that, exactly as I had been trained. I felt the prop blast on my right hand and noted the detail of the masking tape at the door's edge. Near the door at eye level I saw the green light.

"Go!" The jumpmaster slapped the man in front of me and he disappeared. I pivoted into the empty space, left foot forward and toes over the edge of the door, right foot behind, hands straight and outside the door, head up, looking straight out. Propeller blast and wind combined into a force that pulled the skin of my face into ripples like a flag. There was a numbness now. I thought perhaps fear had dropped into my legs, but I could not detect it anywhere because of the numbness. I was supposed to see only sky, and I forced myself to concentrate on its color. But in my peripheral vision the trees and fields a thousand feet below flowed by like a great, textured brown mat. Otto Hager's boot slammed into mine as he formed his T and it annoyed me.

"Go!" Well, what do you know! I actually felt the tap out. My hands pushed away from the bulkheads and my left leg propelled my body out. The right leg followed and I was thinking "quarter turn left" when the prop blast caught me. I could see my hands on the reserve; so my eyes were open, just as I had been taught, and my head was down, out of the way of the risers. There was no sensation of falling. It was rather as if a huge wave had caught me and was pushing me down.

"One thousand . . . two thousand . . . ," I counted. I was being conservative and counted slowly. There was a tugging on my shoulders, not unlike the tug I had felt on the thirty-five-foot tower but considerably harder. I recalled the instructor's admonition: "If you've got a good body position when you exit the aircraft, your opening shock is going to be pretty easy . . . ."

I was jarred to what felt like a dead stop. My arms went up and I

A trooper glides down during a practice jump at Camp Mackall, 1943.

could feel the taut risers confining my helmet between them. I managed to squeeze my head back to look at the canopy above. There it was—white, beautiful, and *open*. The idea was to check for blown panels, suspension lines forming a "Mae West" over the canopy, and other aberrations; but all I could see was that beautiful expanse of nylon.

My hands, palms out, were now resting on the front risers. I decided to manipulate the chute. So . . . left hand on right front riser, right hand on left rear riser, and pull; that's a left turn. Ah! Now I could see three other parachutes nearly level with me and slightly above. I let go of the risers and made a right turn. More parachutes. This was what I was supposed to be doing. "Upon receiving the opening shock, check your canopy. Then check your descent." You do that by watching the other parachutists. If they're way up there and you're way down there, you're falling too fast. I tried slipping backward. It worked.

The ground was coming up, so I grabbed the front risers. "Prepare to land." You do that by grasping the front risers, looking out at the horizon, putting your feet together, and bending your knees slightly to absorb the shock, I instructed myself mockingly. All right; just one more pull on the front risers so that I have gone through the forward drift maneuver . . . and now time had run out. The horizon was gone; the ground rushed up. Fear came back and tensed my body almost to the point of cramps in the "prepare to land" position. I was oscillating gently and remembered the final point of descent: "Land." This was where the PLF came in. Depending on the motion of your parachute, you either tumbled forward right or left or to the rear . . . .

The ground hit me hard. My knees buckled and I slammed into the dust somewhere on my right rear, a sack of potatoes. The rim of my helmet dug into my right shoulder. "PLF, bullshit!" went through my mind. Even in C Stage I had never been able to make a school-approved PLF. "Collapse your canopy. Get out of your harness. Roll up your parachute." The canopy is collapsed either by running around it to its apex or by hauling in the near portion of its skirt, pulling the front risers, and gathering up the suspension lines. Otherwise the full canopy will drag the parachutist . . . but either action had been necessary only during B Stage at the wind machine. This time my canopy had deflated by the time I could look up. Nevertheless I got to my feet and went through the motions.

"Yeeeehaaaa!" Otto Hager yelled behind me as I got out of my harness. I ran around to the apex of my chute and pulled it straight preparatory to rolling it up when Otto bounded toward me, jumped on my back, and pulled me to the ground. "Yeeeehaaaa!" he yelled again, pummeling my back. "Nothing to it! Right, Gabel!"

"Goddamn, Otto," I said, getting off the ground. "Yeah, right." But I was thinking of the jump tomorrow, and the one after that, and the one after *that* . . . . I rolled up my parachute and stowed the main and reserve in the kit bag, put the load on my shoulder, and unenthusiastically double timed off the drop zone. Except for Otto's exuberance there was a strange lack of gaiety. Even though there had been no jump refusals, and only two men were hospitalized, it was a silent convoy that rolled back to the company area.

We ate our lunch in silence and answered questions of "How was it?" from the Dog KPs with a shrug and an "OK, I guess."

That afternoon in rigger Shed 1 we repacked our parachutes. They seemed more than simply pieces of equipment as we removed them from the hanging shed. We had shaken the dirt and branches from them and laid them out on the long rigger tables. Panels folded and kept in place with shot bags, suspension lines straight and smooth running down the length of the table, pack and harness neatly laid out, we waited for a rigger inspection prior to packing. It was a routine well learned, and this time we followed it with utter, serious concentration. Fold, pack, lace up, and stow. Only one reserve parachute had to be repacked; only one person had had to use his.

The next three jumps lacked the impact on us of the first one; not many of us slept well that Monday night. Jump stories the old hands had told us about the second jump being the worst of them all chased each other through my mind. Why would that be? "You know what to expect and that makes it worse," had been the explanation. But that seemed absurd. If you *know* . . . .

Dawn brought the familiar bugle call prior to reveille. "The one after that" was almost upon us.

The lights were still on in the battalion mess hall, for the sun had not really come up. I took my place in line and looked around. Here and there was a familiar face and we nodded to one another. Only a few men came in with their cliques or with a buddy. Most seemed to want to be by themselves, sitting with men of other companies where they would be unknown and could remain in their own little shells. The only sounds were the metallic sounds of trays and silverware. The usual murmur of human voices was notably absent.

"Want more than three?" a KP on the serving line asked. We had pancakes and the KP reached to steady my tray, which I had failed to put down on the tray rail.

"Sorry," I said. "No. Three is plenty, thanks."

I did not know that KP standing there in his pathetic blue denim, but I had seen him on the serving line before. As with the rest of the Dog Company KPs, I looked on him with a mixture of contempt, pity, and a strange emotion akin to fear. For here was a man who had been what I had been but who for one reason or another had washed out. The unthinkable thought, "Suppose I wash out and end up like you?" surfaced in my consciousness with increasing frequency and intensity as we progressed through the stages of the parachute school. And on this second day of D Stage I felt more akin to this man in blue denim fatigues than to the men in the jumpsuits called troopers. How proud I had been only a few weeks ago when we were issued those glamorous uniforms! This day they were simply work clothes; tonight they might no longer make a difference. Still, one thing I was certain of; I would not end up in blue denim. I shook myself out of this denim fixation but not before giving the KP a sad smile. I was sad for him, not sorry. There was no contempt today, just melancholy; my feeling embraced the whole battalion.

I walked toward one of the long tables where there was still room and asked no one in particular, "May I sit here?" Two men looked up and said in unison, "Sure," then lowered their heads again to their pancakes. We ate in complete silence and got up, one by one, to turn in our trays and return to our company areas.

The ominous prologue to the green light played itself out.

This time my stick was the second to jump; we had to watch while the other stick responded to the jump commands. Here and there a smile flashed across to us; but most of the faces were drawn, and some of the bodies were bent as though in pain.

"Is everybody happy?"

"Yeahhh," came the nervous reply. The green light flashed on.

"Go!"

"Go!"

"Go!"

Shuffling boots on the steel slats, the scraping, swishing sound of anchor-line snap fasteners on the cable overhead, the wide-eyed men pushing ahead toward the jump door—then all the bucket seats across from us were empty, the aisle cleared, the stick gone, its static lines outside the door pressed to the plane's fuselage by the propeller wash, like umbilical cords reaching after their babies out there in that cruel blast, to babies that no longer needed them.

The static jumpmaster and the Air Corps crew member strained out the door to haul in the static lines and pushed them out of the way into the interior of the plane. "Here we go," said Otto with that odd grin of his.

The plane banked as the jumpmaster turned toward us and cupped his hands around his mouth, megaphone fashion. "Get ready." I was weak. I was afraid I wouldn't be able to respond simply because I was weak. What if I couldn't get to my feet? What if I fell down once I was on my feet? Would they help me up? Would they unhook me and sit me back down? "Stand up!" Both my feet hit the steel rails beneath me simultaneously and I grasped the cable with my left hand as I rose. I was still weak and wondered how I had got to my feet. "Hook up!" I heard the clatter of anchor-line fasteners slamming home in unison and saw the cable rocking up and down. "Check equipment!" Weak hands flew over the pack in front of me, a slight tug on the top of my main pack on my back. "Sound off equipment check!" Will he hear my squeaky voice or will he have to come to me?

The engines roared their steady roar at one-hundred thirty miles an hour. I did not look out the window, only at the pack of the man in front of me.

"Stand in the door!" The snake of which I was a part wriggled forward. Then we heard the inevitable.

"Is everybody happy?"

"Yeahhh."

There was a slight change to the engine noise and a slight lift as the tail of the aircraft went into jump attitude.

"Go!"

"Go!"

"Go!"

My feet were heavy as lead. I had to drag myself aft. My left hand made it out the door. Did I pivot? Am I out of balance? The tap of the jumpmaster registered as though my right leg was anesthetized. Goodbye, all! I lurched forward and shut my eyes tightly, fear squeezing me like a vise. Even before the prop blast washed me down, I croaked through clenched teeth, "One thousand," but much faster than the day before. The huge wave of the propeller blast seemed to turn me, but I was too terrified to open my eyes to check my body position. "Two thousand." The washdown of the blast continued, but again there was no sensation of falling. "Three thou . . . ." The opening shock caught me in a teeth-rattling jerk as though a giant hand had just pulled up a yoyo—me—after it had hit bottom. The steel connector links of my risers had slammed into the rear of my helmet, jamming the front of it painfully over my eyes and onto my nose. A sharp pain coursed over my entire body as I struggled to push my helmet back and through the taut risers for a look at my canopy. I wondered briefly what that exit must have looked like from the ground.

Canopy OK. I forced my head forward and looked down. A trooper was immediately below me and I slipped right. Slightly above me two troopers were floating down. Rate of descent OK. We were oscillating and I was nervously preparing for landing. What if I clobbered in? What if I broke something? I would not be disqualified, but I would lose time in a hospital and could not complete jump training with my unit. Would I even stay in the regiment?

I hit the ground on my right side and felt a tugging on my shoulders. The canopy was still inflated and the parachute dragged me gently along the dusty ground. I pulled its skirt in to deflate it and got out of the harness.

"OK?" It was the inevitable Otto, not yelling or cheerfully knocking me down this time, lying to my left on his canopy, still in his harness.

"Yeah. How about you?"

"Yep."

We rolled up our parachutes and packed them in the kit bags carried under our reserve packs. There were no injuries in our plane load and we limped off the drop zone.

Again we rode back to Lawson Field in silence.

The third jump was a "mass jump." There were no individual tap-outs. At the command "Go!" the entire stick exited as fast as it took each man to make his proper pivot into the door and his proper exit. This was considerably easier on me than the preceding jump. Now we had a battalion total of six people in the hospital. One of my pressing questions was answered. We learned that they would complete jump training with regular classes of the PTR and rejoin us later. We were overjoyed. Sure as hell no other regiment would get them!

On the fourth day we made an "equipment jump." Its purpose was to give us the experience of exiting the aircraft and landing with the M-1 rifle disassembled into two parts and packed in a Griswold container (named after the paratroop officer who invented it) strapped to the left side of the soldier. Musette bag, bayonet, and ammunition completed the individual equipment. Preceding the first stick, two "door bundles" would be dropped with a simulated load of rations, ammunition, communications equipment, and other supplies needed to sustain a parachute infantry unit on the ground. Again, the new experience and the additional activities connected with this type of jump slightly mitigated the inevitable fear that was a part of D Stage.

As we hit the ground this time and assembled our weapons, a great weight lifted from us. "Haaa!" yelled Otto as he pounced on his canopy and stripped his harness off. "Done! Tomorrow don't make no rat's ass." I laughed for the first time in God knows how long. It was true. Tomorrow, no matter what happened, we would be qualified paratroopers because we would exit that airplane for the fifth time regardless of what happened at the moment of impact with the ground afterward. A dead man tomorrow would be a dead *paratrooper*.

There was an air of excitement, of subdued animation, in the barracks that night. There was talk and a feeling of unity again. We had made it because tomorrow we would jump even if they had repacked our backpack with bedsheets. It was to be our first night jump, with equipment, followed by a tactical assembly problem on the ground.

Most of us seemed to have had a good, sound sleep that night. There was no reveille the next morning. Breakfast was served from eight until ten o'clock. Our first formation wasn't until one in the afternoon, in the company area. It was like a Sunday! I woke up about 7:30 A.M. and luxuriated in my bunk as though I were in a fancy resort hotel with nothing to do except look forward to a day of swimming and tennis. After a half hour of basking in the knowledge that this was the last day of the most grueling sixteen weeks we had probably ever spent in our lives, I quietly got up to shower and shave. For the last time before it would go to the cleaners, I put on my jumpsuit. It was rumpled but, because most of the Georgia dust had been shaken out of it, it was still relatively clean after the past four days. Lovingly I laced up my paratrooper boots and thought of the line in our song that went, "They picked him up still in his chute and poured him from his boots," and I chuckled. So what? First of all, everything was going to be OK. Second of all, I was going to be a paratrooper, poured from boots or not. It was an entirely new feeling for me—not a feeling of abandon, nothing desperate about it at all; just a feeling of relief, accomplishment, and an immense pride.

Again I walked to breakfast alone; but this time I wanted to be alone with my joy, just as I had previously wanted to be alone with my fear. The mess hall was still nearly empty. The troops seemed determined to play banker and have breakfast as close to 10:00 A.M. as possible, so I found myself alone in the serving line.

"Last jump today, eh?" asked the KP in blue denim as he put a hot roll on my tray. This morning I felt absolutely no kinship with him. He was a dog. He had signed a quit slip. He was not one of us, and there should have been a rule about such vermin speaking to paratroopers. I tried to suppress these arrogant thoughts, but they persisted.

"Right, Jocko," I said. "What else you got besides these buns?"

The KP shrank back into his bedraggled shell and my superior attitude receded correspondingly; one does not kick servants and other prostrate creatures. "Eggs, any way you like them, french toast, pancakes . . . ," he mumbled obediently.

"Scramble me a couple of eggs. And let's have another hot bun," I said in a slightly more friendly voice.

The KP said, "Coming right up. Why don't you take your coffee and sit down? I'll bring the tray when the eggs are done. Not many people here yet."

Poor bastard! They should really ship these poor bastards out after they sign a quit slip. "OK. Thanks a hell of a lot," I said with a brief smile and walked to an empty table. The few men scattered about singly and in small groups waved and I waved back, proud to be one of them.

I sat and basked until the KP brought me a steaming tray of eggs and hot buns. Fresh eggs today! As I started to eat, Otto walked in and shouted through the mess hall, "Hey, you stuck-up son of a bitch, you vant to be alone?"

I lifted up my left arm, showing the fist with middle finger extended while continuing to eat my eggs.

"I love you, too!" Otto yelled.

One of the men near my table said, "Christ, Hager, you are the loudest son of a bitch in this whole goddamn outfit. Can't you say anything at all in a normal voice?"

Otto made the same sign I had and said, "How's that?" We laughed and continued our demolition work on that delicious breakfast. Otto lumbered over to me with his tray and asked, "OK to sit here, your majesty?"

"I got a choice?"

"No." Otto sat down and said "Haaa" before he dug into his eggs, french toast, and pancakes. He grabbed the syrup on the table and poured it over everything on his tray, including the eggs.

"I think I'm going to be sick," I said. "How the hell can you eat that way?"

"Gagay?" mumbled Otto, his mouth bulging with food. "Gungellooeen gagay? " He shoveled in his food while I tried to finish my breakfast without watching him.

After breakfast Otto announced that he was going back to bed and told me to wake him for lunch, which I promised to do. Then I went for a walk.

We were now allowed to wear the round blue and white parachute patch on the left side of our garrison caps centered over our left eyebrow. With the infantry-blue braid on the cap, dressed in our jumpsuits, we were indistinguishable from qualified paratroopers, since jump wings or other insignia were not allowed on the jump jacket. This was the psychological frosting on the cake that had been so expertly baked by some sharp military brass. Having once worn that parachute patch and the jumpsuit with boots, nobody could have endured going back to units that were not airborne. We were now considered "in," a part of that special group called parachute infantry. And the brains behind this delicate operation that had made parachute infantrymen out of football lettermen, campus Romeos, hot-rodding teenagers, and high school gang members knew that they had us now. They had the finest fighting instrument ever fielded by any army, including the German.

During my walk here and there I would meet an officer, his parachute patch on the right side of his cap, rank insignia on the left, the curved silver wings on his chest, and I would give a sharp salute with a "Good morning, sir!" It would be answered as snappily with a "Good morning, trooper!" and a grim, little smile speaking volumes. It was a very pleasant walk. Buildings that had looked gray and forbidding before now looked like home. Trees that had gone unnoticed were tall and straight with the lush brown and gold colors of autumn. The grass bordering Fort Benning's main boulevard was dark green and for the first time I noticed the many small daisies hunched among the well-trimmed blades of grass.

Our 1:00 P.M. formation was followed by a briefing from our company commander concerning the tactical problem following our final jump. "You're jumping at eight hundred feet tonight, so there'd better be no grab-ass in the air. When you land you roll up your chutes and put 'em in the kit bag and leave 'em right there on the drop zone. Riggers will pick 'em up. You get off the DZ on the double to your platoon assembly point." The captain showed us a spot on an aerial photo of a DZ in the Alabama area known as the "peanut patch." The captain continued, "There will be recognition lights at each platoon area. You guys have a green light and it'll flash three times at intervals of one minute. After assembly, your platoon moves to the company assembly point—and that's all. Not much of a tactical problem, so don't louse it up. You'll be graded. Fast assembly is what we're looking for."

"Now, one more thing. That road," he pointed it out on the photo, "looks like the Chattahoochee River from the air at night; so if you come near it when you descend, don't prepare for a water landing." We had heard stories about that—troopers over the road unbuckling their harnesses, thinking they were over the river, and dropping out of their harnesses at eighty feet.

The entire battalion was to be aloft. The exercise would terminate after the battalion was assembled and ready for its ground mission. Our next formation in Class D uniform was at 8:00 P.M. in the company area. After supper we had three hours to rest and to get ready.

Between the briefing and the formation, any prejump anxiety we felt was more like anticipatory excitement than fear. The mood of the day held. There was laughter and joking; we were almost festive. We polished boots, dusted our jumpsuits again, and cleaned weapons very sociably.

When we were formed at 8:00 P.M., it was dark, but the sky was star studded. "Square your helmets. Fix your chin straps. We're going to give Benning a little show tonight. We're going to march through the main post and we're going to sing! Fix bayonets!" *That* was something new; who had thought *that* one up? The night air was filled with the ominous sound of bayonets drawn from scabbards, followed by the clicks of metal against metal as the mean, nasty weapons closed on the rifle studs. "Sling arms! I want those bayonets straight up and lined up! That's the way!"

And then through the night, "Battalion . . . !" "Company . . . !" "Atten—*Hut*!" So help me, the last time I had heard the sound was on the Moorweide in Hamburg when the German garrison was drawn up for a ceremonial parade in honor of Hindenburg's birthday—the sound of a battalion slamming its heels together in absolute unison. A chill went down my spine.

We marched from the gravel of the company area to the asphalt road. I regretted that we did not have hobnailed boots. Our boots striking the pavement in unison seemed to shake the street; but, oh, what hobnails would have sounded like! We executed the left turn onto Fort Benning's main thoroughfare. Company A's first sergeant turned his head and growled, "OK, you guys, we're gonna sing 'Is Everybody Happy?' Now!" With the next right boot hitting the pavement, Company A bellowed the paratrooper song to the tune of "The Battle Hymn of the Republic." We called it "Blood on the Risers."

"Is everybody happy?" cried the sergeant, looking up.
Our hero feebly answered, "Yes," and then they stood him up.
He jumped into the icy blast; his static line unhooked,
And he ain't gonna jump no more!

Gory, gory, what a hell of a way to die!
Gory, gory, what a hell of a way to die!
Gory, gory, what a hell of a way to die!
And he ain't gonna jump no more!

The moonlight played over the steel helmets moving up and down. A wave of dully gleaming bayonets straight up next to the helmets bobbed toward the stars in chilling rhythm. With goose bumps on my arms and neck, I knew why we had fixed bayonets. There was no other place in the world I would rather have been than where I was at that moment: in the middle of a platoon of Company A.

Lights flashed on in the windows of the darkened barracks area. Windows opened and soldiers in T-shirts looked down onto the long column in wonder and envy. Surely the worst cynic among them was awed at the sight and sound of the First Battalion, 513th Parachute Infantry Regiment, marching toward Lawson Field for its qualifying jump.

> He counted loud, he counted long; he waited for the shock.
> He felt the wind, he felt the air, he felt the awful drop.
> The silk from his reserve spilled out and wrapped around his legs,
> And he ain't gonna jump no more!
>
> Gory, gory, what a hell of a way to die . . . .

The entire battalion had joined in and the lusty, defiant roar of the song announced our approach far ahead.

People were now coming out of the main post theater, and clusters of soldiers gathered in barracks doors. They had all seen well-drilled units marching and counting cadence. In the field they might even have heard us singing, "I've Been Working on the Railroad," as we marched back from a training exercise. But this they had not seen before. We did not look or sound like a unit made up of "good old boys from Brooklyn and Dubuque, givin' it their all for Mom and apple pie." Our audience watched in silence. We didn't know whether they approved or disapproved, and we didn't give a damn! Out of the corner of my eyes I could see some of them whispering to each other, but most stood stock still, perhaps mesmerized. They were all, no doubt, confirmed civilians at heart and must have wondered whether the time had really come when it was necessary for America to start producing its own elite military corps and whether its ability to do so was good or bad. They might have had mixed feelings about us, but they gave us their undivided attention.

> The ambulance was on the ground; the jeeps were running wild.
> The medics jumped and danced with glee, rolled up their sleeves, and smiled;
> For it had been a week or more since last a chute had failed—
> And he ain't gonna jump no more!

Gory, gory, what a hell of a way to die . . . ."

Although we all sang as loud as we could and the sound of six hundred young voices was a collective roar, I could hear Otto at the tail end of the platoon clearly over all the rest.

There was blood upon the risers; there were brains upon the chute.
Intestines were a-dangling from his paratrooper boots.
They picked him up still in his chute and poured him from his boots—
And he ain't gonna jump no more!

Gory, gory, what a hell of a way to die . . . .

The song had ended and the battalion continued its march toward Lawson Field. The road dipped slightly before we reached the Air Corps barracks area, and as we entered it we burst out in song once more:

Oh, hi-dee, di-dee, Christ almighty, who the hell are we?
Zim, zam, goddamn: The Parachute Infantry

The battalion was released to the PTR and our officers and senior NCOs got into jeeps headed for the drop zone. We were now cautiously defiant as we faced the PTR men for the last time.

"Hey, Jocko! Let's get the goddamn show on the road!"

"Ho, PTR! We ain't got all night!"

And the PTR NCOs growled back, "You're still with us and you're still subject to being graded, so settle down!" The routine of prejump activities went fast and smoothly.

At exactly 10:00 P.M., we were airborne and climbing. As we circled to get into the prescribed formation, the jumpmaster went up and down the aisle, looking us over. Otto started the paratrooper song again and we all joined in. As the aircraft leveled off and prepared to fly a straight course, the jumpmaster yelled, "All right, all right; quiet! When you guys go out this time I want you to holler 'Geronimo!' as loud as you can. But now keep the goddamn noise down and get your exit straight.

You're still being graded!" He lurched back toward the door just as the red light flashed on. "Get ready!"

My stick was first again. My fear, and I'm sure it was somewhere deep down, was almost totally submerged by my desire to get out the door. With each jump command in that so familiar sequence, the anticipation of the silver wings made me positively impatient.

"Is everybody happy?"

"Yeaaah; let's get the hell going! Move us out!" came the raucous replies.

And then at last came "Go!" and the scrape and clink of anchor line hooks.

Shuffling toward the jump door, I looked out the window as I came abreast of the port engine. It was a shock to see its exhaust flame, visible only at night. A long, ice-blue flame, it stabbed from the roaring engine toward the jump door where it turned red and seemed to shoot right past the exit like the fiery tongue of a dragon. I wondered unrealistically if it actually did that during the day, too. And why, I wondered, did it not catch the parachute canopy as it deployed and burn it to a crisp?

Benny was in front of me. I thought of him as an individual I did not particularly care for but still as an individual rather than a part of the stick. I heard his "Geronimo!" as he disappeared out the door, and I pivoted into the space where he had been. His canopy hadn't taken fire.

I felt good. I actually savored the moment and insolently grinned at the jumpmaster. Below me the blue and red exhaust flame licked threateningly along the fuselage, but the hell with it—I've got a reserve! Then my head was out, the skin of my cheek pulled back by the prop blast; I yelled, "Geronimo!" as I made a nearly perfect exit. In the starlight I could see the ground beneath my feet and only a very little horizon, so I knew there would be a minimum of shock. I didn't bother to count. I felt a gentle yoyo pull and checked my canopy. "Yaaaah!" I heard Benny just below me, and "Haaaah!" I heard Otto just above me as his chute opened. I was too happy to make any noise.

Rebel yells filled the air as the white chutes floated in the wind-still, starlit night. From below we could hear familiar voices through public address speakers: "Quiet in the air. This is a tactical exercise. There will be no noise!" But it did no good. For all their discipline, the troopers were free now and for just a few moments they exercised their freedom with joyful whooping. "Quiet! You are still being graded!" The noise subsided a bit. If there were the tiniest chance of disqualification at this late date, silence was the better part of freedom.

130 Training

Troopers of the 513th PIR in a mass practice jump in the Sandhills area of North Carolina

I hit the ground and could have made a forbidden standing landing but did not take a chance on it. Dutifully, I rolled into a front right PLF, my first one. The chute collapsed and gently fell on top of me.

"Yahoo! I'm a paratrooper!" someone yelled near me, and I said, "Amen."

As I disentangled myself from the canopy, Otto bounded over. "Shake, you son of a bitch!" he said, holding out his hand. "Shake the hand of a paratrooper!"

"You, too," I said solemnly; we shook hands.

The unseen PA set blared, "Move off the DZ on the double!" We got our M-1s out of the Griswold containers, quickly and automatically assembled them, rolled up our parachutes, and double timed toward the woods and the blinking lights.

"Hager, Benny, and Gabel," said the platoon sergeant as we came into the assembly area; someone made a note on a clipboard. Several people were already there and we shook hands all around. Our faces could have lighted the entire state of Alabama as we looked at one another. More of our gang came in; more handshakes.

"Seventy-five percent effective as of twenty-two forty-five," said the platoon sergeant into the mike of a PRC-300.

"Roger," crackled the reply. We kept on looking at each other and admiring each other.

There was a commotion on the field just outside the assembly area. "Let go o'me, you stupid bastard!" one of our men was yelling. Two men came into the assembly area, one hopping on his left leg and using his rifle as a crutch, the other a medic. "Hey, sarge," said our limping man, "tell this here goddamn medic to leave me alone."

"What's up?" asked the sergeant of the medic, who still had one hand on the hobbling trooper.

"This guy broke his leg. We tried to get him on a jeep, but he rolled off and headed in this direction. Wants to go back with you guys." More handshaking, laughing, and cursing.

"Put a splint on him and leave him with us. You'll get him back after the mess hall ruckus."

The final report read, "Fully effective. One walking casualty." The platoon was ordered to the company assembly area. In another half hour the exercise was over. Total casualties for the battalion jump were six broken limbs. Training grand total for the entire regiment was two killed, twelve in the hospital.

We loaded onto trucks and rolled away from the peanut patch, back toward the main post. There was singing, yelling, backslapping, cussing until we rolled into the Frying Pan and stopped in front of the battalion mess hall. We carried the trooper with the broken leg inside on our shoulders. "Gangway for the Second Platoon, Company A, you nonjumping bastards!" Benny yelled at a couple of KPs who were merely trying to hold open the door for us. Other trucks followed, disgorging their loads of brand-new paratroopers.

The mess hall was sheer pandemonium. Dusty, grinning troopers milled around two long tables laden with doughnuts. On smaller tables were steaming metal coffee urns. Mark Leverson, normally so conspicuous for his reserved and correct behavior, walked up to me, doughnut in one hand, cup of coffee in the other. "Congratulations," he grinned and then kicked me with his left knee, never spilling a drop. It was so uncharacteristic of the cool Leverson that my return kick came too late.

People who had been zombies at the beginning of the week hugged each other and slapped each other on the back. All were brothers and the whole battalion was one huge, unwieldy family. Here and there an officer or senior NCO surfaced, grinning as broadly and proudly as the "little brothers" and shaking all the hands they could reach, saying, "Congratulations," or "Good job," or, best of all, "Glad you're now really one of us." They were all here, sharing the happiness of the moment like fathers at a graduation—battalion commanders, staff officers, company commanders, and platoon leaders as well as the regimental commander and his executive officer. First sergeants, platoon sergeants, and squad leaders shouldered their way through us like roosters among a flock of chicks. They, too, had graduated, for now they were leaders of paratroopers. We would get our wings at formal exercises in battalion formation the next morning at ten.

Again there was no reveille and we awoke from sheer excitement. We went to breakfast in fatigues, not daring to put on the starched khakis we were to wear in the formation. After breakfast came the hour-long ritual of shining boots.

In a way, the formation itself was almost anticlimactic. We stood in starched perfection, awaiting the formalization of the fait accompli that had occurred last night when we jumped from the C-47 for the fifth time. The battalion adjutant read the qualification orders. Then each company commander, accompanied by his first sergeant, received the wings to be presented to the men in his unit.

The company was at parade rest. The company commander, first sergeant at his left, marched up to the acting squad leader of the First Squad, First Platoon. The acting squad leader snapped to attention. Inaudible words passed between the captain and the trooper. Then the captain took a set of wings from a box the first sergeant was carrying and pinned them over the trooper's left breast pocket. For a second the captain looked at his trooper. Then he shook his hand and said, "Congratulations, Johnson." In the precise movement customary during inspections, the company commander moved from man to man. The man approached snapped to attention. The man who had just received his wings returned to a stiff parade-rest position.

And now it was my turn. We both stood at attention, my commander and I. We were worlds apart. He had been a distant and somewhat mysterious authority figure whose age was immaterial, whose origin would be traceable no further than to the banks of the Hudson River, whose commands were transmitted by platoon leaders and platoon sergeants and unquestioningly accepted. He was a parachute infantry officer. Because of that, I believed with all my soul that he was honorable, he was wise, he was brave, and he was right at all times. Up to this point I had not considered him or any other officer as quite human.

And now his eyes were level with mine. His craggy, habitually grim face that, generally from a distance, always looked forbidding to me had an almost imperceptible smile around the eyes. Very quietly, he said, "I'm proud of you." I gulped and clamped down on my jaws as I felt my throat tighten. He turned and took a set of wings from the first sergeant. While he pinned them on me, he murmured, "You better check to see if I got 'em on straight," and then he held out his hand and said, "Congratulations, Gabel." Worlds apart—yet he was *my* commander and I was *his* trooper. As I snapped back into parade rest, glancing down at my wings, regulation straight over my left breast pocket, I knew I had come home.

9
England

The 513th Parachute Infantry Regiment now began a period of travel and training. It was not that our movements from the Alabama area to Fort Bragg and then to Camp Mackall, North Carolina, to Camp Forrest, Tennessee, and finally to embarkation at Boston were not also training. With each move we became a more responsive organization. Little by little we got rid of excess personal items. Pinups were left behind for others to admire. We stripped down to our field equipment, our weapons, and our duffel bags. Our most cherished possessions consisted of our snapshots and letters carefully tucked in our wallets. As we passed from one barracks to another or from one camp to the next, the only permanency grew to be the 513th itself—the human relationships and bonds of friendship welding us together. Little by little we all began to look upon the 513th as our family, as our home.

To those troopers who had never known a real home, the experience was at last an initiation; to the rest of us, the experience was of the gradual acceptance of an association, in a form we could see, feel, and understand, designed to defend all those elusive things that home now so dearly meant to us: family, friends, and country.

We had become part of the Seventeenth Airborne Division commanded by Major General William "Bud" Miley, one of the earliest American paratroopers. Though we participated in several minor skirmishes with local citizens along the way who mistook our gold and black "talon" patch for a chicken's foot, we soon earned the respect and admiration of our civilian neighbors.

The military skills that we perfected amidst sun, rain, snow, and mud were, of course, important and would be dispensable when we got into combat; but the intangible relationships we were developing were even more so. Morale and motivation continued to grow as our confidence increased. Since our officers and noncommissioned officers had been hand-picked, leadership was all but flawless. Finally, we were kept in superb physical condition by those prebreakfast runs invariably followed by many long hours in the field. And to give us the food we needed to fuel our energy, Baier and his mess crew kept close behind us with their steaming marmite cans.

By July 1944 we had received orders for the Taunton Staging Area near the port of Boston. There was a holiday atmosphere in the regiment. This was it! We were finally going overseas! All our movements were conducted with the utmost secrecy.

On the afternoon of July 29, 1944, the day before we were to leave Camp Forrest, Tennessee, for Taunton, I was told to report to the orderly room in Class A uniform. I counted my sins and got over there in a hurry. The sergeant motioned me with his head to the CO's office. Something was *very* wrong; he should have taken me to the door and announced me. In a panic I got myself into the captain's office, pulled myself erect, gave my snappiest salute, and in my loudest "command" voice announced, "Private Gabel reporting, sir!" Then I looked.

Seated behind the captain's desk was a WAC lieutenant.

I'd heard about soldiers in skirts, but this was the first one I'd actually seen.

Discipline and my salute held until she returned the latter. She said, "Ma'am."

Utterly flustered, I said, "Ma'am, sir!" in my command voice.

She said, "Oh, Christ," with a sigh.

I stood there, awaiting court martial.

She said, "Private Gabel, we're going to take a ride to Chattanooga." I didn't dare say a word, much less ask a question. I remembered to walk to her left and a little behind as we went through the sergeant's anteroom and out to the staff car. I opened the door for her, but the door on the wrong side. She wearily corrected me. We sorted ourselves out eventually; the driver started the engine, and we took off.

Why?

We pulled up in the parking lot of the Chattanooga courthouse. I had expected military discipline rather than trial by a civilian jury.

Inside I was photographed and vaguely wondered why I wasn't fingerprinted. I took some sort of oath. I filled out some forms. The final form was on heavy parchment, rolled into a typewriter. I told the typist I was five feet eight tall, although I was only five feet seven—might as well go for broke—and when she pulled the parchment out of her typewriter I signed it where she told me to.

It was a certificate of naturalization. I had just become a United States citizen.

I'd never really understood how a Hollywood High School student and a Harley-Davidson rider for the Bank of California could be classified as an enemy alien. But in the process of winning my wings I'd forgotten that, like anybody from the Hanseatic port of Hamburg on the North Sea, my first choice for military service had been the Navy, the V-12 program that lack of citizenship had precluded me from joining. I had become completely at home with my unit. And my unit remembered what I had forgotten; my unit saw to it that I became a citizen at the last possible moment before going overseas. I was now a paratrooper, American variety, legally as well as morally.

We were brought into Taunton near Boston at night. No leaves or passes were granted. When it was Company A's turn to embark, I discovered that we would sail on the U.S.S. *Washington*—the same liner I had come to the United States on before the war. But her interior was unrecognizable. The elegant lounges and staterooms had disappeared; they had been converted to accommodate as many troops as could physically be jammed inside.

This was certainly not to be a pleasure cruise. We were part of a large convoy forming out of New York, Boston, and even Halifax far to the north. Our route hugged the east coast until we left our air cover in Labrador and headed for Liverpool by way of Greenland, Iceland, and the Shetlands. It was reassuring to learn that we were being escorted by a dozen destroyers as well as by the old battleship *Texas*.

Sleeping and eating were staggered for three shifts. Temporary bunks were stacked three deep, and each bunk provided for three troopers in rotation. We were required to wear our life jackets at all times when not in our bunks. Frequent life raft drills were held. When we were not sleeping or eating, we formed small groups in any available part of the ship and practiced stripping and cleaning our weapons or reviewed those military subjects that could be covered under such cramped conditions.

On several occasions the alarms sounded, and evasive action was taken to throw off Nazi submarines lurking along our route. As we approached the Outer Hebrides, we were very happy to be met by escorting aircraft from the RAF's Coastal Command.

And what a contrast it was as we arrived in Liverpool on one of those beautiful English summer days in August! Dozens of barrage balloons ascended into the cloudless blue sky, and as we docked, signs greeted us, directing us to the local air raid shelters. This wasn't much like home. Women and older men predominated in the crowd on the docks. This we soon found to be normal throughout the United Kingdom.

Our first evening ashore found us in a tent camp on "Windmill Hill" at Tidworth Barracks on the famous Salisbury Plain. Target ranges of every description were available. We lost no time in zeroing our weapons and practicing our marksmanship. There were very few British troops about because, with the exception of recruit depots, the tactical units of the British Army were already deployed in a great arc extending through France to Italy and to the Middle and Far East.

There was a notable air of expectation among the local villagers upon our arrival; it was as though they were waiting for a cyclone to hit. When a few of our venturesome troopers engaged them in conversation, we soon understood their apprehension. It seemed that the Aussies had been stationed at Tidworth, and the place would never be quite the same again. The villagers assumed that American paratroopers would have the same impact as the Aussies. The fact that no untoward incidents occurred was a mark of our discipline and training. With obvious relief the local population soon took us into their homes and into their hearts.

There was little time off. We trained a full six days each week. Experience in Normandy and Italy dictated lots of night exercises, too, including several night jumps. I was delighted at how effectively our training was integrated into that beautiful English countryside. Tactical exercises progressed over hill and dale. The war was very close to those British who maintained the home front. They did not begrudge us swarming through their fields, climbing their fences, or driving our lumbering Army trucks over an occasional lawn or flower bed. They went all out to give us what they had and we reciprocated as best we could. Our offerings were usually in the form of food; for they were terribly short of rations, particularly meats and sweets.

The day First Sergeant Wade Allen handed me my transfer orders was a turning point in my short military life. The orders transferred me from Company A to Headquarters Company, First Battalion, for duty with the S-2 section. Finally S-2, I thought. It had taken them a long time to get around to giving me an intelligence assignment. I knew that it would be the lowest job at the lowest level of combat intelligence, but—by God—it was a start for a United States citizen.

It took me no time at all to find out just how low a job my first intelligence assignment would be. My records had already been screened at Headquarters Company, and the first sergeant simply said, as I walked into the orderly room tent, "Good to have you, Gabel. Come on, I'll take you to the CO and then to your section." After the one-minute ceremony of reporting to the headquarters company commander, a captain whose name was Rockett and who was an unknown quantity, the first sergeant took me to the S-2 tent. There behind a field table sat a young, blond first lieutenant who, even in his neat and well-fitting fatigue uniform, looked more like a high-society tennis player than a paratroop officer.

The first sergeant and I saluted. "Sir, this is Gabel, your new man."

The officer looked up and smiled, showing large, white, well-cared-for teeth. Society type, I thought again. Rich playboy. I would try not to like that man. "Good," he said and stood up, still smiling. He stuck out his hand and I shook it. "Glad you're here," he continued. "My name is White. We've been looking for you," and to the first sergeant, "Anything else you need from us right now?"

"No, sir. Thank you, sir." They saluted almost simultaneously, and the first sergeant left.

"Sit down, Gabel," the lieutenant said, indicating one of the three folding chairs in the tent. I sat. "You are now a scout."

"Yes, sir," I said, remembering the stories I had heard that battalion scouts are tactically used simply to draw fire and are replaced by new, live bodies every other day.

Lieutenant White looked at me and smiled his café-society smile. "The stories are not true," he said; I decided I was going to like him, playboy or not. "OK, let's go meet the section," he said and got up. We walked along the new duckboards to one of the hexagonal tents, and Lieutenant White stepped through the entrance flap. A voice called, "Attention!" and I heard the thump of boots on the wooden floor before I, too, stepped through the entrance. "At ease. I brought you our new man: Gabel." I glanced around quickly and felt at home almost at once. There was Frenchie, grinning behind yellow teeth, and Herrick the Horse, and two others I had seen around. The only one in the tent I had not seen before was the sergeant.

He was the one Lieutenant White steered me toward. "This is your section leader, Sergeant Dalton," he said. I shook hands with the sergeant, who grinned and said, "Welcome aboard." He was tall and lean, about my age, with greenish eyes that nearly closed into slits as he smiled, giving him a pixie appearance in spite of his tall frame. His light-brown hair was short and neat, and his uniform was every bit as immaculate as the lieutenant's. I liked him instantly. "OK, Jaycee," Lieutenant White said to the sergeant, "I leave Gabel to your tender mercies." He left quickly, before the section could be called to attention again.

"Well," said the sergeant as he took me around the tent, "you already know Herrick." We shook hands and continued our tour. "And Leo Beaulieu, known as Frenchie." More handshaking. The two men I didn't know were operations men who doubled as clerks. "Now, where are your things?"

"Still over at Company A."

1st Sgt. Joe Carter, Headquarters Company, 1st Battalion, 513th PIR (left); Sgt. J. C. Dalton, Headquarters Company, 1st Battalion, 513th PIR (right).

"Come on; I'll help you get 'em." Here was another indication of how things were going to be in the S-2 section of the First Battalion. The section leader had not said, "Go get your things." He had not told one of the men to help. He had not even asked whether help was needed.

We walked the short distance to Company A and, to the good-natured kidding of the men, I picked up my duffel bag and barracks bag while J.C. took my rifle, webb equipment, and musette bag with the steel helmet laced to it by its chin straps, and we trekked back to the S-2 tent. "Well, after all that hard work I think we ought to go get ourselves a cup of coffee," grinned the section leader.

"OK, sergeant," I said, and we took off toward the kitchen tent.

"The 'sergeant' is for formations and other formal occasions. Right now, I'm 'Jaycee.'"

"What's the 'J.C.' for, Jaycee?"

He grinned his pixie grin at me and said, "You'll never know." And although we eventually became closer than brothers ever could be, I have never found out for sure. But because we also called him "Jake," to which he never objected, I supposed that at least the "J" may have stood for "Jacob."

The kitchen tent was holy ground, and it was one of the unwritten but scrupulously observed laws that only officers and NCOs could walk into it unless, of course, one was on KP. I therefore had my first feeling of superiority over my KP peers when J.C. and I walked up to a large, stainless steel pot on one of the ranges and ladled coffee into our canteen cups. Sergeant Baier was there, as always.

Perhaps the ordinary mess sergeant warrants no particular attention, but Baier was not ordinary. He was fat—but that's not exceptional. He looked like a cartoon straight out of Julius Streicher's newspaper, *Der Stuermer*, and he was the only nonjumper in the battalion—that last *was* exceptional. On this occasion he looked up suspiciously and asked J.C. in his Brooklyn-Jewish accent, "So who's that with you?" Of course he knew perfectly well who I was. We had come into Company A at the same time, though it remained a mystery how Norman had got there in the first place. He had lamented that he had not volunteered for airborne training, that he shouldn't even be in the Army, much less in a parachute infantry regiment, that, as an orthodox Jew, he would not so much as lift a webb belt, much less a rifle, and that, besides, he was a sick man. Though he never admitted it, he had been given several opportunities to transfer since he was unacceptable for parachute training; but he had literally begged to stay, had actually become glider qualified, and had even tried to go on runs with the unit, though he was excused from PT. Unaccountably he had been permitted to stay on as a cook. From the very beginning there had been a silent understanding that Norman Baier was one of us, that no one was to be permitted to make fun of him, and that any outsider foolish enough to do so would be taken care of immediately.

Moreover, Norman was not just a "mascot" or a battalion good-luck charm; he was recognized as courageous and later, when he became a cook, as valuable a member of the unit as any rifleman. He had entered the service straight from high school; so either he had a natural talent for cooking or he had worked exceptionally hard. It wasn't long before he was promoted to first cook. By now he was indisputably the best mess sergeant in the regiment, and we considered him indispensable. He ran a tight ship and put out such superior food that rumor had it he was frequently and surreptitiously contacted by other battalions and offered bribes to take over their messes.

"Meet our new battalion scout," said J.C.

"Oy veyh," Baier replied, looking heavenward. "Poor battalion."

We took our steaming canteen cups and retreated to a corner of the tent where it was both warm and well out of the way of the busy cooks. The space heaters in the large mess tent would not be fired until lunch time.

J.C. began his informal interview. "Whitey says you speak German. How well?"

"Better than English," I said. "I've been speaking it much longer."

J.C. whistled. "And you've been to the corps intelligence school. What did you get there?"

"Oh, the usual. Map reading, scouting and patroling, camouflage, a little IPW, a lot of OB . . . you know."

"How did you do?"

"Lousy in map reading but pretty well in OB and that sort of thing." We sipped our coffee, taking care not to maintain prolonged contact with the rounded edges of our cups. I made a mental note for the umpteenth time to get a new canteen cup, one that did not have those confounded round edges that became so hot they blistered the lips.

"How about scouting and patroling?"

I remembered the blackened faces, the socks wrapped around stacking swivels, the wool knit caps, the creeping, the crawling, the eternal avoid-dry-twigs admonitions. "A Kit Carson I'm not," I admitted.

J.C. laughed softly. There was something warm and very reassuring in that laugh. It terminated the interview. "OK, we'll go turn in your rifle and get you a Thompson submachine gun. Then you get a pair of binoculars and a compass, and that'll make you official."

After Jake and I had settled into a double-decker, with Jake as the ranking person naturally taking the lower bunk, he led me to the S-3 side of the tent to introduce me. Though I had seen the S-3 men often, I had never had occasion to talk to them. They were NCOs and had a superior aura that discouraged outside approach. First I was introduced to the section leader, Staff Sergeant Tony Mora. He was a Spaniard with dark brown hair, brown eyes, a slightly hooked nose, and a prominent chin that made him look a little like a bulldog. He smiled as he shook my hand and said, "Welcome to the ivory tower."

The chief clerk was his exact opposite, a tall, slender, blond Scandinavian with frosty blue eyes and a like manner. Something about him was familiar. Finally I remembered the battalion mess hall at Fort Benning after our qualifying night jump; I remembered Mark Leverson's knee and his unspilled coffee as he kicked me, and I grinned. "Hello," he said coolly as we shook hands.

"OK," said Jake, "now I'll take you to my buddy in the machine gun platoon." We walked past the mortar platoon tent to the machine gunners' tent. "Joe Cooley," said Jake, pointing to the number one gunner sitting on his lower bunk lovingly cleaning his .45 and who, as we were introduced, stuck out his elbow for me to shake since he was holding an oily barrel in one hand and a ramrod in the other. Joe Cooley's gangling frame was sandwiched low between his and the upper bunk in the same space in which I could sit upright. He looked like an eighteen-year-old Gregory Peck with a shorn head, having only brown bristles on it. He had large, blue, intelligent eyes and a wide mouth. All of Joe seemed to be one big constant smile that would envelop him no matter what he or anyone or anything did to suppress it. He tried to simulate a frown and failed as he looked at the disassembled .45 on a rag at the foot of his bunk, saying cheerfully, "The hell with it." Then he started to assemble the weapon.

"What say we go to Andover tonight?" asked Jake, and it was clear he meant the three of us.

"To eat?" asked Joe, still, it seemed to me, simulating an intent frown for the benefit of the rest of the world that would surely resent the thoroughly imperturbable, good-humored, almost mocking soul that peeped out of his eyes.

"No. The English have food problems enough without your appetite," said Jake. "We'll go have a beer and see a movie or something."

"OK, smart ass," said Joe. Then to me, "How'd you get hooked up with something like that?"

"Orders," I said, and Joe snorted a short laugh.

Jake growled, "Watch it, Gabe, or you'll be on my shit list and get transferred to the machine gun platoon, Cooley's section."

I was glad the three of us would be going to Andover that evening. My treasured privacy, my jealously guarded loner status, had now either been demolished or, more likely, had taken on a new dimension. The three of us, Jake, Joe, and I, became more than friends, more than buddies. We became an entity. There were many entities in our close-knit organization. Groups of threes and fours, usually from the same squads or sections, core elements within the families that were the small units, were readily recognized as entities. "You seen Jake, Joe, or Gabe?" This sharing of loner status was a one-time experience. It had evolved never to be relinquished, never to be repeated. Often three such entities would make up a squad, with incredible results in combat. They would literally insist on going hungry for one another, freezing for one another, dying for one another. And the squad would try to protect them or bail them out without the slightest regard to consequences, cussing them all the way for making it necessary. Such a rifle squad, machine gun section, scout-observer section, pathfinder section was a mystical concoction, delicately brewed from many ingredients, its quality enhanced by time like a rare vintage. But sooner or later, the Great Connoisseur would

Joe Cooley, Headquarters Company, 1st Battalion, 513th PIR

partake of this vintage, would drain the goblet. And never again would the goblet be filled by just that kind of heady brew; all the vintner could do was to remember exactly what it was that produced it, treasure the formula, and try again.

Since in our case only Jake and I were in the same section, our triumvirate had to have a slightly reinforced cohesive ingredient. Whatever it was, we had it. Wherever Joe was, we knew he was doing a superior job, not only because we would be told so or would hear stories but because we simply expected it to be so, just as Joe had a right to expect the best from us. No one, of course, ever remotely articulated these expectations. It was simply unthinkable that one part of this entity would do anything that would in any way be contrary to its collective character. The same spirit in necessarily different forms permeated the platoons, companies, and battalions and gave the regiment its unique essence. We cared for the regiment. The cohesive ingredient binding us at the human level took on shape at the regimental level. Any one of us, perhaps injured in a parachute jump and unable to participate in a division review but watching from the sidelines, would say as our regiment passed the division review stand at "eyes right": "That's us!" That's us. The men, the squads, the platoons, the companies . . . expecting the regiment to manifest its collective character, just as long ago the regiment had expected them to do it with honor.

Here in the regiment lived the spirit of the armies.

If we were ever conscious of it, we could not have explicated it. There wasn't time or leisure for military philosophy, not even on off-duty time. After some weeks on Windmill Hill, we moved to Camp Barton-Stacey, where we continued our training. Below us was one of the best trout streams I had ever seen; unfortunately, we were too busy to make much use of it. And on the banks of the stream was the picturesque little village of Fortan in Longparish. All the houses had thatched roofs in a sylvan setting far removed from the war.

The training schedule of the S-2 section was not greatly different from the one our command school had used except that there was less classroom instruction and more field training, mostly scouting and patroling. The pace was leisurely compared with that of the rifle companies; even the battalion details were few and light. I for one had never seen an S-2 man on KP or ration breakdown or any of the other onerous housekeeping duties soldiers are usually detailed to at least one day a week. And scouting and patroling was notoriously susceptible to the application of the "eyewash" principle. It looked demanding enough on paper; but once a scout had reached his objective in the field, faraway from the section, he could spend hours "observing" activities in the environs of Tidworth and Barton-Stacey that had very little to do with his mission. Jake would catch us goofing off by his spot checks. He would ask for an observer report that he would then demolish by saying things like "Yes, there *was* a jeep driving down that road at fourteen-thirty hours because I was driving it. Shape up, you guys." Such low-key admonitions were effective. They conveyed disappointment, bringing the personal element to bear. The scout had gratuitously shafted the section leader, and no one wanted to do that. In general, we appreciated our status as a semi-independent element of the battalion and, lest we spoil a good deal, we usually worked earnestly at our training.

On Sundays we broke the regular routine. Church services were held in the open above the wandering stream. And on Sundays, passes could be obtained for the nearby cities of Andover or Winchester. Both cities had canteens, the British version of our United Service Organization (USO). Here tea was served by local women volunteers and we had a chance to relax for a few hours.

A pass to London was not impossible to get. However, since a Sunday pass expired at midnight, it was necessary to leave London by 10:00 P.M.

Nevertheless, everybody wanted to go; and since no more than one fifth of any unit could be that faraway from camp at any one time, it took a while for all of us to make the trip. Eventually we all did.

Jake, Joe, and I were determined to get the most from our London passes; so we got up at 4:00 A.M. to catch a ride into Andover where we could take the express into the city. I didn't see a single civilian aboard; the United States Army had taken over in Class A uniforms. We arrived absolutely starved for breakfast.

"Let's eat here in the station," Joe proposed.

"Oh, no we *don't*," I said definitely. "According to my mother, there's only one place to eat in London. Come on; we're catching a cab." Well, we found one and settled in. I told the driver, "To the Savoy." Jake and Joe gasped, but I glared them into silence.

We paid off the cab, and as it pulled away Jake and Joe found their voices. "Gabe, we can't go in there. Have you lost your goddamn mind? We don't *belong* in the Savoy. They'll kick us out. We'll create an international incident. *Gabe* . . . ." I was walking to the entrance, and they scrambled after me. The door was opened by a most dignified and portly doorman, who looked us up and down and did not smile.

"What can I do for you young gentlemen?" he eventually asked.

"Is breakfast being served?" I countered.

"Indeed it is."

"We would like to have breakfast."

The doorman looked us over again, considering. It was a tense moment. Finally, but still without a smile, he said, "Step right this way," and we were in, the three of us the only customers in uniform, the only customers under fifty years old. We were considerably more perturbed than the British, who peered at us for only a moment before returning phlegmatically to their tea and crumpets. It is difficult to create an international incident involving the imperturbable British as one of the parties.

When we ordered four eggs apiece and coffee, the hovering waiter said, "We don't have fresh eggs. It's the war, you know. Can you eat powdered eggs?" And powdered scrambled eggs was what we were served in the elegant, soothing, beautifully decorated dining room of the Savoy. None of us ever forgot the experience.

The rest of the day remains kaleidoscopic in my mind. Joe insisted that we visit Madame Tussaud's Wax Museum; he was particularly interested in grinning at the criminal figures. I insisted on a trip to the British Museum. This was toward evening, and we were interrupted by a V-1 that shook the three of us up until we noticed that the custodians could not get the British users of the museum to leave for the nearby bomb shelter. The three of us were scared but were determined not to show it for the sake of our national honor. It wasn't easy, but we managed. We saw the changing of the guard and momentarily envied the colorful uniforms until we realized that the busbys would sadly interfere with hooking up to the static line. We walked and we took cabs and we wandered about absorbing London through our pores. Somehow or other we managed to catch the last train back to camp. That was Jake's doing—a real accomplishment.

And we were immediately immersed in more training.

On the training schedule, the subject "combat in towns and cities" evoked memories of the Army's stateside replicas of towns, one-street wooden façades, like cheaply constructed movie sets for a western, found in every infantry training center across the country. We had worked our way through them at Fort Benning, Fort Bragg, and Camp Mackall, using blank ammunition and dummy grenades. Even with the remarks "Southhampton" and "live fire" on the schedule, we saw ourselves merely shooting up one more movie set except that we were going to put holes through it this time.

The train ride to Southhampton was pleasant and relaxing, the obligatory dirty jokes generated the usual raucous laughter, card players yelled at one another, and groups of men sang the newest songs picked up from the limeys. But the noise suddenly died down as we entered Southhampton and rolled slowly through its working-class residential area. For the first time, we were face to face with the results of mass destruction from the air.

It was different from London. Most of the London any of us had seen had been either undamaged or was under repair. In Piccadilly or Kensington we had not seen so much as a broken window; the random destruction of the V-1s and V-2s had seemed merely interesting as the subject of an "explosive effects" study or had provided a vicarious sense of war participation to those curious enough to go to the district where "last night's" buzz bomb had come down.

But Southhampton had been systematically destroyed by large formations of bombers. Air raids here had truly *struck home*. Row after row, street after street of gutted two-story houses and the remains of ugly, red-brick tenements told of the suffering of their former occupants. I looked at the burned-out shells and tried to imagine the people who once lived there, poor working people who had never had much and finally, in one night, lost the few possessions they had managed to accumulate. If they were still alive, where would they have gone? Where would they be now? If their sons came home on furlough they would find this . . . . We were all silent, thinking the same thing: Suppose it happened in America and we came home to devastation?

The train stopped; as we assembled on the platform and waited for instructions, "combat in towns and cities" had suddenly become the gateway to war that it was fully intended to be.

The British had laid out the combat course for us, and quite a few British officers and NCOs were at the station watching us. At a square that had been cleared of rubble, British officers were conferring with our battalion commander, the S-3, and the company commanders. The units were moved to their exercise areas. Staff sections had been broken up for this training, and I had been assigned to go with one of the rifle squads of Company A.

The overall exercise was simple enough. From the square in front of the train station, several streets ran generally parallel to the northwest. Each was about five hundred yards long, and they all terminated at a main thoroughfare. Each company was assigned three streets, one platoon per street. Each house was presumed occupied by enemy troops. Two assault squads would clear the house by "mouse holing" or by a direct assault when covered by fire from the opposite side of the street. Mouse holing consisted of making an entry breach in the brick walls large enough to crawl through. Before crawling through, we were taught to toss a grenade in to clear out any enemy.

The third rifle squad would initially be in platoon reserve. The weapons squad with its attached machine gun would be in general support. Command control was effected by radio; movement to the company objective (the dead end at the main thoroughfare) would be closely coordinated by the company commander. The company would carry and fire its basic load of live ammunition. Special medical teams, in addition to the regular medics, would follow the companies.

We were thoroughly acquainted with the tactics involved. Clear the houses, cover the houses across the street for the other squad, and then move while the squad across the street covered our squad. Any major problem and the weapons squad with its 60-mm mortar, 2.5 rocket launcher, and machine gun would lend a hand. What was new was the live ammunition and grenades we were to use at such close quarters and under conditions simply begging for ricochets, short mortar rounds and rockets landing on us rather than on the "enemy," and hand grenade errors. The presence of several ambulances and the extra medics did nothing to contradict our particular assessments of the dangers of the exercise.

We were issued basic loads and instructed on the "enemy" situation, which included a short review of the mechanics involved in clearing an individual house. It was old hat. Either get to the roof and clear it, or mouse hole. Toss a hand grenade into each room and enter after the explosion. Machine gunners and weapons squads would take care of anyone flushed out at street level. They would also provide street security and general support. Then came a reminder of safety precautions. The instructions on that subject were unusually short. After all, we could see the perils for ourselves.

Machine guns and rocket launchers opened the action. Tracer rounds from the rifles of NCOs marked the targets; our machine gunners, the best anywhere, fired precise bursts—every tenth round a tracer—into the window or door or pile of rubble designated. Rockets crashed into "strong points" and the cacophony of street fighting forced each man to peer intently at the leaders for hand signals.

As the tracer arc shifted up and to the right, our squad sprinted forward to the first house and up a British storm ladder to the roof. Two houses up the street, our machine gunner and a BAR raked the second story of a burned-out tenement, ricochets whining off the brickwork and tracer rounds changing direction so as to make me wince and wonder how in the hell we were supposed to make it all the way to the end of the street. But make it we did. It was indeed realistic training, and we learned from it.

During one of our tactical exercises we were visited by two great airborne soldiers, Major General Matthew B. Ridgeway, recently commanding the Eighty-second Airborne Division and then heading the American XVIII Airborne Corps, and Major General F. A. M. Browning, the commander of the British airborne forces, whose novelist wife, Daphne Du Maurier, was responsible for introducing the wine-red beret as a distinctive badge for Allied airborne troops. Both generals wasted little time, saw a lot, and were obviously pleased with what they saw.

We thought that we were honed and ready for combat, but did we move? No. Only selected officers and NCOs from each platoon left on one occasion for nearby airfields to join with the 101st Airborne Division in a great airborne thrust into Holland near Eindhoven (the Eighty-second Airborne and the British First Airborne divisions were also to be involved at Nijmegen and Arnhem). A substantial cadre from the 513th was being attached to the 101st to obtain battle experience. Most, though not all, returned a few weeks later, dog-tired but battlewise. They increased our fighting potential. So did a sprinkling of paratroop veterans who had joined us at home while recuperating from wounds. Among these was Major William Moir, our regimental surgeon, who had been awarded the coveted Distinguished Service Cross. As the battalion surgeon of the 509th Battalion, Major Moir had taken over and commanded the critical attack upon a Vichy French airfield in North Africa after a nonstop flight from Britain in September 1943.

The war was coming closer.

The culmination of our training was to be a free-play field training exercise parachuting the 513th and its supporting elements in attack against a defending 507th. Of significance to me personally was the experimental introduction of a then fashionable accoutrement: the Cushman motorscooter.

This military precursor of the civilian scooter so popular on city streets shortly after the war was then still more motorcycle than its later progeny, the sole attribute mitigating its totally ridiculous appearance. As a former knight of the Harley-Davidson order, I looked upon this quixotic steed with amusement and contempt. It was to be tested for use by scout sections and reconnaissance platoons, and one of the ugly little things was assigned to me. At full throttle it would go all of forty-five miles per hour, but it could go all day on one gallon of gas. It was said to be indestructible, so it would be parachute-delivered by the heavy drop serial. For reconnaissance purposes its one-cylinder racket, uninhibited by any civilian refinements such as a muffler, would make it as inconspicuous as a P-51 buzzing a Sunday-school picnic.

So we jumped, and I located my scooter. Unfortunately, it worked just fine. Crushed, I mounted it, checked my map, and, Thompson submachine gun and all, set out down a charming country lane. The Cushman made much more noise than the machine gun would have, and I was utterly disgusted. I rode it and rode it. Oddly enough, I saw nobody about. I should have joined up with my outfit in a half-hour's travel, even considering the pitiful amount of power Rosinante's engine delivered; I'd been going for a fantastically noisy hour. But it was a beautiful day so I rode some more. Still no troopers showed up.

However, just about tea time I came across a delightful country inn. At full throttle I swooped to its entrance (not very dramatically) and shut off the miserable engine. Troops have to be fed, even if they must scavenge off the countryside. An army travels on its stomach. And here was a most civilized opportunity to scavenge. So in I clattered, into a most crowded dining room, boots thudding, carrying my Thompson submachine gun. I was annoyed at the Cushman; I was annoyed at getting lost; I was hungry. When a waiter approached me to ask that I park the Thompson somewhere, I remembered Fort Benning and explained that a soldier and his weapon are never parted . . . . Patiently he told me that some of his patrons were afraid of the gun. This flattered me, so I took it back to the entrance and stuck it in the umbrella stand. Then I had my high tea.

Afterward I got around to showing the waiter my map. He said I'd apparently read it upside down and pointed me back the way I had come. Much later, when Jake and Joe asked where in the hell I'd been, I lied through my teeth and told them I'd had to fix the engine on the Cushman after the jump. I never did tell them where I'd been. I doubt if I could have found the inn again anyway. Somehow Jake and Joe never did believe me.

At last history beckoned to us; it was our turn now. On December 16, 1944, Adolph Hitler took his last desperate gamble with the commencement of the Battle of the Bulge. We were immediately alerted. This time the alert was no drill. To our delight, on December 19, the 513th departed from the RAF airfield at Chilboton on our way to France. We couldn't have been happier to face the ultimate test of our training. We knew we were ready.

Part Two
Combat

10
France and Belgium, December 1944–January 1945

Landing at airfields in northern France near Rheims came as something of a shock. We had exchanged the peaceful, pastoral English countryside for a landscape that bore the visible scars of warfare. In trucks and on foot we assembled at an old French Army casern at Mourmelon-le-Grand. The barracks offered little comfort, for they, too, were scarred; they were without heat and without windows, and the latrines had to be seen and smelled to be believed. Still, our morale was exceedingly high. We were on the move. On Christmas Day we took up defensive positions on the Meuse River, the scene of heavy fighting by the American Expeditionary Force in World War I.

Baier and his crew outdid themselves on Christmas Day. Turkey, sweet potatoes, cranberry sauce, and all the rest had caught up with him on December 24. He set up shop in a gutted building and with herculean effort provided our feast. Kicking bits of rubble, we filed through the serving line and discovered that the flavors of home did much to compensate for the sights of destruction.

After the war I found out that the 513th had been ordered to hold the line of the Meuse from Saint-Mihiel through Verdun to Stenay in order to channel von Rundstedt's thrust to the north of the river. At the time we knew only that names familiar to us from history books were taking on flesh. It was eerie to dig in on those famous battlefields where so much blood had been spilt twenty-seven years before when America had made the world safe for democracy. None of us commented much. I for one, though, could hear the echo of old bombardments and could see the earth exploding around me to make shell holes. Apparently history was going to repeat itself. Well, that was nothing new except that this time I was going to lend a personal hand to the reenactment.

Nobody said much. Jake and I found ourselves one day in the enormous, beautiful American Meuse-Argonne cemetery, which had been meticulously cared for by the Germans during their occupation. What were Jake and I doing? We were digging a fox hole between two long rows of white marble headstones, and so were others of our unit. Not even the dead could rest in peace when history was in command.

Jake said, "All quiet on the western front."

"Yeah. So far."

"I'm reminded of all quiet on the western front."

"You're talking as funny as Frenchie. Besides, how can its being quiet here *remind* you of its being quiet here when you haven't *been* here before?"

Jake glanced around at me. "Don't you read remark?"

"Does anybody? I *listen* to remark. Are you practicing for a psycho discharge?"

"You illiterate bastard! I'm talking about a book by a Kraut named R-E-M-A-R-Q-U-E. How come you haven't read it?"

I stared. "Was it about a German soldier in 1917 and 1918 that got killed just before the armistice?" Jake nodded. "What was its name again?" Jake patiently repeated it.

I went back to digging. Somebody had lent me the book as Remarque had written it, in German, very shortly after I'd come to the United States. Its title in German was *Im Westen Nichts Neues* (There Is Nothing New in the West) and I brooded for a moment on the inanities of translators. I remembered the book well, and I remembered my reaction to it. No wonder we Germans had lost the First World War when the seasoned soldier (the narrator) was such a sniveler. If I were a recruit, I'd never foul my pants during my first combat experience. I'd never do anything so disgusting. Of course I'd be scared; it seemed that everybody was. But I'd master my fear—that's what bravery is all about. Now we Germans had Hitler. If the British and Americans ever came up against soldiers trained under Hitler, the results would be different. Soldiers trained under Hitler weren't snivelers. They'd gladly die for the *Vaterland* . . . .

I shook my head, trying to clear it of the strange double vision of me as an imagined German soldier under Hitler and me as a real American paratrooper beside Jake.

Jake and I were dedicated; the Germans were fanatics.

Somehow the formula didn't seem quite right. I shook my head again, hard. Mercifully the icy cold brought me back to our task—digging a foxhole among the graves of our predecessors, a foxhole that might become our grave.

That eventuality never came to pass. On December 29, new orders arrived; we were to take over the western sector of the Bastogne perimeter held by the 101st Airborne Division with elements of the Eleventh Armored Division. Of course we didn't know that then. We didn't lose much time in checking weapons and equipment, which was just as well. Very shortly orders came to entruck on the double. We were leaving our defensive position on the Meuse to make contact with the Germans. It was New Year's Day, 1945. Good soldier that I was, once aboard the truck I promptly went to sleep—and not because I was recovering from a New Year's Eve hangover.

I woke up when the convoy slithered to a halt. Tailgates banged down and there were shouts of "OK, hit it, you guys. Chow time." I had no idea how long I had slept. Compared with the trip from Mourmelon-le-Grand to the Meuse in cattle trucks, these deuce-and-a-halfs with seats for everybody were like first-class pullmans; sleep, though once interrupted by that strafing Kraut at midnight, had instantly returned.

Groggily I jumped from the truck and blinked my eyes against the brilliant sun on a snow-covered expanse of field. The battalion started to form on the field; it seemed in the middle of nowhere. The truck drivers had kept their engines running and were hurriedly and noisily slamming tailgates shut. Once back in their cabs, they impatiently gunned their engines.

"Where the hell are we?" I asked Jake.

"Beats me," he said. Much later I learned that we were in the environs of Bois de Fragette, Belgium. Jake turned toward the trucks and shouted at our driver, "What's goin' on? You guys leaving?"

"Hell, yes, sarge! This ain't no place for us!"

Puzzled, we watched as their lieutenant jumped into his jeep, gave a double-time signal to his drivers, and moved the empty convoy in a giant U-turn back in the direction we had just come from. All that remained were two of our own battalion trucks and the CO's jeep. From one of the trucks Baier and his cooks were unloading C-rations and a field range.

We watched the convoy disappear through a half-demolished village in the distance, not knowing whether the vehicles traveled east, west, north, or south. Toward the horizon in the other directions were gently sloping hills and woods. It was cold and silent except for the few orders passed along the formation by NCOs.

"Settle down. Make yourselves comfortable," said our first sergeant as he walked past our section.

"Where are we, sergeant?" asked Horseface Herrick.

The sergeant shrugged. "Don't know. All I know is we'll be here for chow and then move out on foot."

We sat in the snow, propped up against our musette bags and helmets, wool knit caps pulled as far down as they would stretch over our ears. From our left, the machine gun platoon was walking in a column of ducks past us. When Joe's lanky frame came abreast he grinned and waved, his left hand indolently draped over the receiver of his machine gun on his left shoulder. "See you guys later," he called.

"Where're you goin'?" Jake yelled.

"To the companies. I'm goin' over to Company C."

"What the hell for?"

"Jesus Christ, how should I know?"

It made no sense. Machine gun sections weren't detached to the companies unless . . . .

"Hey, Gabel," said Lieutenant White, appearing from somewhere along the line, "while you're waiting for the C-rations to get hot, how about looking over those Krauts and see what you can find."

"What Krauts, sir?" I said, wondering what kind of stupid exercise this whole thing would turn out to be.

"Goddamn," White said with some exasperation. "*Those* Krauts. What kind of a scout-observer are you, anyway?" He pointed into the field. Some two hundred yards away were five or six small mounds. I walked toward them. My first dead Germans. My first dead *anybodies*.

I had a feeling like the one I had had before my second jump, only more so—the elevator feeling with an additional quality of dread tacked on. I walked fast to get the job over with and then stood in the midst of the little group and carefully inspected each figure. The dread was instantly gone. They didn't seem real; they were like the wax figures we'd seen at Madame Tussaud's in London. They sprawled where they fell; two of them still had their helmets on, chin straps down. All had their leather ammunition pouches, their gas masks, and the knapsacks called *Brotbeutel* with canteens attached. Their K-98 rifles lay nearby. On first inspection, I could see no wounds, which made the whole scene look even more like a wax museum tableau. To reassure myself, I bent over the nearest one and touched his shoulder. It was hard as rock. I took off my gloves and touched his hands, trying to move the arms. Frozen stiff; hard as stone; nothing human. I was mightily relieved.

I walked over to the ranking body, a corporal, and began to search him. In his left breast pocket was a worn leather wallet and I opened it. There was a letter dated November 1944. In its fold were snapshots of a brown-haired young woman with a small blond child, a picture of the same woman close up, and a group picture of the woman beside a blond soldier holding the little blond girl in his arms. I looked down at the blond soldier, then I read what was written on the back of the photos, then I read the letter. I dropped to one knee, the letter and snapshots clutched in my left hand resting on his chest. Life in my left hand was resting on death. And she didn't even know, and the little blond child didn't know that I was here with their dead husband and father. And his mother wouldn't know, either. Or his father, the grandfather of that little girl. Only I knew . . . only I knew that he would never come back, would never be photographed again on a summer day in front of a little Black Forest inn . . . . I sobbed as I had not sobbed since I was a child, a child in Germany, and the blond soldier mercifully swam away in my tears.

I felt a hand gently pressing my shoulder. Lieutenant White said softly, "Kurt, that's not the way to do it."

"Goddamn it," I gasped, still clutching the photos and the letter. "Goddamn it," I bit my lip and snorted mightily to clear the awful tears away.

The lieutenant bent down, took my head in his hands, and pressed it gently against his chest as though I really were a little child and again softly said, "Now, you know, this really is not the way to go about business. Come on; let's go eat."

I stood up. The tears were gone. I looked down at the German who had betrayed me and now I was angry. I said, unable to look the lieutenant in the face, "Thank you, sir. I'm OK. I'll just finish my job here and be back in a couple of minutes."

"Sure?" he asked.

"Yes, sir," I said and then turned to look him in the eyes. "This is never going to happen again."

He nodded and walked away. I continued my search. Paybook, identification tags, unit marking, the letter again (for possible slips the field censor might have missed). On to the next body and its inventory. By the time I was finished, I knew what unit had been here, that they were partially mechanized, and that half its personnel had come from the eastern front. With contempt I thought, "You bastards are about as security conscious as a ladies' bridge club," and then I walked back to make my report and to gripe about cold C-rations.

Other soldiers were curious about the dead Germans and wandered over to the bodies to look at *their* first dead, to believe that *they* were invulnerable and would never end up sprawled frozen in the snow, to make brave and demonstratively callous remarks like "Look at those bastards. Must have had heart attacks. Not a scratch on 'em." But their bravado fooled no one, not even themselves.

There was movement in the battalion. "OK, let's get the show on the road! Column of twos. Five-yard intervals. Company A, Battalion Headquarters, with S-2 and S-3; Company B, mortar platoon; Company C . . . ." The sky clouded over; it became gray, and the grayness seemed to make it colder as we walked, somewhat faster than is usual in a tactical formation, along both sides of a snow-covered farm road that showed no tracks or other evidence of recent use.

My feet were cold despite the fairly rapid marching of the column. The submachine gun was heavy, dragging on my left shoulder, and I moved it to my right; but then I thought about Joe carrying the machine gun and about Otto carrying the 81-mm mortar base plate, and the Thompson somehow seemed lighter.

It wasn't a difficult march. The land was fairly level, the snow not too deep. Ordinarily we would be talking on a march like this, but no one talked. The only sounds were the crunching of boots on snow and the clinking of weapons and equipment.

I thought about my current favorite movie star, Gloria De Haven, and of how she sang that song to what's-his-name. "Some other time, I might have kissed you—yes, some other time . . . not now . . . ." It came off very well in my mind and I began to feel better. I imagined myself home on furlough, going to the Mocambo or the Trocadero and suddenly running into Gloria. I would say . . . .

"Hold it up. Both sides of the road. Sit down. Take a break. Don't bunch up." Had it been an hour already? And what was this "don't bunch up" bullshit? We sat back and took our break silently. Still I did not know in what direction we were moving or where we were going. And why the hell walk when we had those trucks? Alongside the road and in the woods was a column of tanks, their crews sitting on the hulls or standing about. A few derisive remarks, inevitable whenever paratroopers and tankers met, flew back and forth between the two units.

"How about a ride on your tin can?"

"We ain't goin' where you're goin'. We been there and TS for you!"

"All right, let's go!" The break was over. March an hour, break ten minutes; march an hour, break ten minutes. Maybe that was the war. We'd been strafed once by Bedcheck Charley in that little burg near the Meuse and once more on the road yesterday (or was it the day before?) and maybe that's all the war there was. We hadn't even seen any artillery positions, though we had heard firing far off by Neufchateau. Oh, well . . . I could tell them at home that, yes, sure, I was shot at. It was rough walking all over France and Belgium with those German planes. I decided to go back to Gloria De Haven and she started singing again. "Some other time . . . ."

"Spread it out more, you guys. Company A, speed it up!" That was the battalion exec. What the hell was bothering him?

Just ahead were some woods. Kind of scrawny, I thought. Company

A started to pull ahead slightly. I could hear the machine gunners and the 60-mm mortar men cussing up a storm.

"Off the road! Over this way!" It was Major Kies again, our battalion executive officer. We made what looked like a totally screwed up left oblique toward the edge of the woods and I thought we were going to take a premature break.

"On the double! Move! Move!" What in the goddamn hell had gotten into that exec, I thought, and at that moment a deafening noise erupted. It sounded like the rifle range after the command "Commence firing!" has been given, but with machine guns and explosions mixed in. Tracers were going in all directions, looking like a moving, illuminated net being cast over us. We ran into it and I had the incongruous impression that this was some kind of a live-fire exercise some weirdo had dreamed up, like the one in Southhampton.

Explosions burst all around. Snow flew up; tracers whanged against trees and changed direction in sharp angles. "Over here," yelled Jake, and I followed him. He made for a large, funnel-shaped hole. Out of it scrambled two Germans with their hands high in the air. I was amazed. "So this is combat," I managed to think. The Germans ran past us toward the road and I flopped into the hole after Jake. Over the rim of the hole I could see some of the men of Company A running in one direction and a squad of Germans with their hands up running in the opposite direction. Nobody seemed to pay any attention to the Germans. "Am I supposed to do anything?" I asked Jake stupidly.

"Let's find out what the hell's going on first," Jake said.

"Well, anyway, I'm now ready to go to that school in Paris they wanted me to go to," I said. "Go tell the CO."

Jake grinned. "TS," he said, shoving his helmet back and carefully hoisting himself up for a look around.

None of the stories I had read or been told about war, particularly World War I, had prepared me for this. I had imagined the move to "the front" as an approach toward an evil, enchanted forest or castle where several distinctly recognizable phenomena had to be encountered before one's arrival at that place of mystery where Death dwelt. Of course we were on trucks a good deal of the time, and most of us were asleep or dozing, so I may have missed some of the portents; but on an approach march I surely expected to see the silent, bombed-out villages where the quartermaster and ordnance people had established themselves; then, farther forward, the artillery positions of our division. Certainly the landscape would change as the distant rumble of "the front" grew ever nearer and ever more ominous. The charred trees, the craters, the abandoned dugouts, the torn barbed wire . . . and all we saw were our own tanks and those tired crewmen, and we had no idea that we were relieving an armored division, elements of our own Eleventh, along the southwest perimeter of the city of Bastogne. We had simply taken another truck ride, made another march in tactical column. No rear echelon, no artillery, no warning murmur of "the front." Just a fouled-up left oblique and that murderous pyrotechnic display that I did not even recognize as murderous.

The noise overhead seemed to be slackening off or moving toward one side or another. "Company B, on the double! Get that second platoon over this way! 81-mm mortars!" That was Lieutenant Obley's voice. Then Captain Rockett: "Headquarters, over here!" Finally a sign of something understandable. Jake and I both peered out of our hole, then jumped out and ran toward where we thought Rockett must be. We saw other holes, other soldiers in them, a platoon of Company A disappearing through a gully in the woods, some soldiers on the ground with a medic sprinting from one to another. We heard belching noises to our left rear and hissing overhead. We fell flat. Ahead were explosions, louder than before. We ran; more belching; we hit the ground again. More hissing. It took two tries to remember that those were our guns—tank guns or pack howitzers. Then we saw the road again. Captain Rockett was standing there with Tony Mora and Leverson. "Dig in right here," he said. Then to me: "Get over to Lieutenant White back down the road. There's a bunch of Kraut prisoners over there."

"Yes, sir," I said and looked over at Jake happily.

"Trust Gabel to find a way out of digging a hole," he said; then, "Run along, dear. Mother will build you a little nest. Don't be late for supper." I double timed down the road toward the edge of the woods we had entered in another time, in another world.

Lieutenant White and three riflemen stood near a dejected and frightened group of Germans, some twenty of them. "See what you can do," White said; I picked the oldest and most frightened-looking, who was wounded and bleeding from the left thigh. He started pleading with me before I had a chance to ask questions and I had to calm him to prevent hysteria. He gave me his unit, its approximate strength, and its mission so far as he knew it. In quick succession other prisoners confirmed the information and added to it. "OK, Kurt. Good enough. I'll get the dope to regiment. Take this old guy to the battalion aid station. You guys," he said to the riflemen, "take the rest down the road till you run into regiment. I'll let your CO know where you are. We want to get these guys exploited as soon as possible," then he was off.

From two walking wounded I got directions to the aid station and we, the German limping beside me, walked along a path in the woods, generally parallel to the road, where the medics were supposed to be setting up.

"Are you going to shoot me now?" asked the elderly German pathetically.

I looked at him in wonder. He was remarkably like Jerry Colonna, mustache and all. I laughed as I thought of the Bob Hope movies in which Colonna, bug-eyed and mouth wide open, would make hilarious high-pitched noises sustained for an interminable time. "What makes you think I'm going to shoot you?" I asked.

"Ihr seid doch Fallschirmjäger," he whined: "Well, you are paratroopers."

"Is that what they told you we'd do?" I asked him, wondering why we hadn't been given that information. But then, hell, we hadn't even known that we were going into the line today. Goddamn, screwed-up Army...

"They said paratroopers never take prisoners...."

"What else?" I prodded. Then, seeing the panic in his bugeyes, I talked in fast German, laced with northern dialect, just as though I were in his own unit: "Don't be idiotic. Hell, man, I'm taking you to the aid station to get a bandage on you. Who told you all this garbage? The NSFO?"

"Yes," he replied, not even wondering that I knew that since the twentieth of July all units had a National Socialist leadership officer attached. "He said American paratroop units were made up of convicted murderers who had been given a choice either to die or to go into the paratroops and that they always killed prisoners."

"And you believed him?"

"I don't know...."

We had reached the aid station. The medics had set up their tent. A field ambulance was just lumbering off and another one was arriving; men on stretchers were lined up in front of the tent; bandaged troopers were sitting, leaning against trees—the place was a beehive, and I wondered at the number of casualties we had sustained in such a short time. Time? How long ago had we entered these woods? I felt as though we had been here forever.

"Where's the doc?" I asked one of the medics.

"Inside."

The little tent was crowded with wounded, half of them on stretchers, the other half sitting or standing, fidgeting with blood-soaked bandages they had put on awkwardly from their first aid kits, looking as though they expected to be chewed out by the doc for not having listened in first aid class.

I waved at the ones I knew. "Short war . . . ."

They waved and grinned apologetically. The doc, a young captain, was standing over one of them, unraveling his filthy, twisted bandage. He said, "Oh shit!" and called a medic.

As he turned back, I said, "Doc, could you look at this Kraut when you get a chance?"

He glanced around. "Hell, I got other things to worry about."

I pleaded, "Doc, I just want to leave him here. Can you evacuate him through your channels? I've got to get back."

"All right, all right. Put him in that chair. Greg!" he called to one of the medics, "Get that bandage off that Kraut."

"Thanks, Doc," I said and started to leave. The medic Greg, annoyed at this additional bit of work, wheeled around at the German and at the same time drew his knife from the scabbard laced paratrooper-style to his right leg above the boot. The German screamed, leaped from his chair, fell, and tried to scramble out the door after me.

"Help, help," he screamed, absolutely the spitting image of Jerry Colonna.

"Get back in the chair," I said sternly. "The medic is trying to cut your bandage off and look at your wound."

"What the hell's the matter with that guy?" asked the medic, still pointing his knife in the direction of the German now writhing in the chair, blood rapidly soaking through the cheap ersatz bandage the Germans issued.

"No, no, please, please . . . ," he whined in his high-pitched Colonna voice.

"They told him we bad-assed paratroopers kill all prisoners," I explained. By now the giggling that had started when the German had leaped from the chair had turned into general hilarity. Only the medics, the doctor, and I were not amused.

"Goddamn it," roared the doctor, "I've got stomach wounds in here. No laughing! Get that goddamn Kraut processed and out of here!" I made my way from the tent as fast as I could before that hopping-mad doctor could hand the prisoner back to me, then went to look for White at the CP area to tell him that we were all brutal killers.

By the time I got back to our area, all foxholes had been dug, commo wire had been strung, and Baier was seeing to setting up the chow line. I saw marmite cans. Much to everyone's amazement, we were going to have a hot meal on the eve of our first action. After peering into several foxholes, I found ours, distinguishable by my musette bag and our binculars. Jake was not in sight. The hole was covered by a shelter half, and some sturdy branches over it provided at least a semblance of cover against shrapnel and splinters. I lifted the flap and crawled inside. The hole was rather shallow, no more than three feet deep, but it was wide enough for the two of us. Both our sleeping bags had been rolled on its floor side by side.

"Well, how do you like your new home?" Jake's voice called down from above.

"Pretty shallow. Could also have been a little wider. When are you going to dig yours?"

"You ungrateful, lazy son of a bitch! Get outa there and cut some more branches for cover!" Jake yelled at me. Then, "Never mind. Get our mess kits. They're serving."

A line was forming near the marmite cans, a chow line like all the other chow lines from Fort Benning to Neufchateau. Men stood, mess kit in left hand, thumb holding the open cover down on the kit handle, right hand holding the canteen cup, feet stamping the snow against the cold. At least Benning didn't have this kind of weather, I thought, longing (to my surprise) to be back in the Alabama area. Otherwise it was the same old chow line. The only reminder that we were on the line was the gurgling of our 155s overhead. DivArty or somebody was shooting at the Krauts in the next woods, maybe just to let them know we had lots of ammunition. They were a little late with it, I thought, but better late than not at all—though the men at the aid station probably had a different opinion.

The cooks opened the lids of the cans and we moved up. "Get those men spread out," Lieutenant Treppendahl, the signal officer who was also mess officer, yelled at one of his NCOs. Before the latter could move, we heard a hissing sound, high and thin at first, then lower, a pronounced whoosh that blended into an explosion accompanied by whining and whirling about. The explosion was followed instantly by another hissing, whooshing sound; in the split-second interval between, we had thrown ourselves onto the ground—not fast enough for two or three men. Cries of "Medic!" sounded, and we heard the command, "Back to your holes. Take cover!" On the way to our holes four more rounds landed; by the time we slithered home, the sound of an 88 had forever embedded itself in our brains, and our bodies would forever react to it.

"All right, let's try again! Three men at a time, you goddamn dummies! Mortar platoon first by sections. Get the lead out!" That was the first sergeant.

"This," said Jake indignantly, "is no way for civilized human beings to dine." I agreed. I remembered our training at Benning in "tactical feeding" and very nearly whinnied; only animals feed. But that would not have been proper behavior for a person stretched out on a sleeping bag face down with helmet on in a very human foxhole. There was now no need of these precautions. The Germans, having lost their lucrative target, could not afford to waste precious artillery ammunition on groups of only three men. I wondered briefly how their forward observer could see into our woods, how he could see our chow line, but then turned my attention back to our hole as I cumbersomely turned around, jabbing Jake with my elbow. "And another thing, deary," said Jake; "if you thrash around like this habitually, you'll simply have to sleep in the guest room."

That struck me as particularly funny and set the tone for all our foxhole-dwelling days. "Calm down, dear," I replied; "we'll be moving out of here before long and I just know you'll find us a much nicer and larger place. Now let's kiss and make up, and I'll take you to a fantastic little place for dinner."

In the dim light filtering through the branch-covered shelter half I could see Jake grinning his pixie grin. He scrambled out of the hole. "I'll find out from Treppendahl what the feeding sequence is," he said. "Then I'll reserve us a table. Stay in the hole. Be right back."

I stretched out as far as I could. The hole wasn't quite long enough and I had to bend my knees a little. Otherwise it seemed almost cozy on the sleeping bag with my head resting on my musette bag and a roof over my head. I pretended that it was warm, wriggled my ice-cold toes inside my boots, and cursed the cold that was the real bother. Life wouldn't be half bad if only it were a little warmer. Overhead our 155s seemed to gurgle at a faster pace; then they slowed down again to their former routine, almost monotonous exhibition of America's inexhaustible arsenal, a constant, arrogant display of abundance.

"S-2 and -3, chow! Three at a time!" Jake finally yelled, and I got out of the hole to wait my turn. As section leader, Jake would eat last and so, in order to join him, I would have to wait until the others got through the line.

By the time dusk crept in to make the trees look ghostly and the men indistinguishable from each other, the front line had become home. There seemed to be a small gap between two of the line companies, and the S-2 and S-3 sections were told to furnish men for the night on the perimeter.

"Better let Frenchie and Gabel stay in and sleep," Lieutenant White had told Jake. "They're going to be moving around first thing in the morning."

"The little darlings," Jake said over his shoulder in our direction. "Go to bed and forgive mother for not tucking you in. Be back soon's I get the working people set up."

I crawled into our hole and struggled into the sleeping bag, wearing everything including boots, and zipped the bag all the way up. Stories I had heard about Germans bayoneting people in zipped-up bags would not apply here. This was the 513th on line. Besides, it was too cold to sleep unzipped. I slept immediately and did not wake up even when Jake came back from the perimeter.

There was no work for me the next morning. I had gotten a free sleep. There had been some commotion on line. There had been some fire on our position; two people had been wounded and evacuated; and I had slept through it all. That was hard to believe.

After breakfast we moved to a new position, not too faraway across the logging road to slightly higher ground, and again we were told to dig in. "You," said Jake sternly, "are going to do your full share of the work this time." And he sat down on a stump to watch me try to loosen the hard ground with my entrenching tool.

I folded the spade part perpendicular to the short handle and secured the lock nut against the spade, making the tool into a pick. Then I knelt in the snow, hacking away at the frozen ground. I heard rifle fire behind me and stopped working to look around. Who in the hell would fire a rifle in the CP area, I wondered. There was some yelling; it sounded like, "OK, over here. I got the son of a bitch," and then some more rifle fire. Men were running back and forth between the trees and I said to Jake, who had not changed his position on the stump, "What are those idiots doing?"

"Hell, I don't know. If someone wants us to know, we'll be told. You just keep on working."

As I hacked again, two litter bearers angled past with Lieutenant William Obley, the mortar platoon leader, on the stretcher. "What got him?" Jake asked.

"Sniper. Through the chest," one of the men answered.

"What the hell's a sniper doin' here?"

"There were a couple in the trees. Ain't here no more," the trooper grinned. Obley made a "thumbs up" sign and the little procession disappeared.

"Shouldn't we go look for some more snipers?" I asked Jake.

"Never mind the snipers, Gabe; you just keep working."

"OK, sergeant, your majesty. If I get shot, you can just see who the hell is gonna do your slave labor for you."

"You should be so lucky," said Jake. "Now quit yakking and work!"

I hacked and scraped at the ground again. Now and then someone galloped by, but each time I looked up Jake said, "Work!" Someone brought over a couple of sets of German enlisted shoulder loops and showed them to Jake, asking, "Can you tell anything from these?"

Jake shook his head and said, "Infantry private, that's all. What was on his sleeve?"

"Nothing."

"How about the paybook?"

"Nothing in the pockets."

"Hey," I said, "I'm supposed to be the expert on all that stuff. Maybe I better go see what else there might be."

Jake pointed his finger at me and said, "Goddamn it, Gabe! If you don't finish breaking up that ground pretty quick you're gonna find yourself on permanent KP!" I continued my work. Soon everything settled down to normal.

High above, the 155 shells of Division Artillery made their way to the far woods, their impact barely audible in the snowy distance. Here and there the gurgling of an 8-inch howitzer from Corps Artillery mingled in. There was no reply from the Germans. All in all, things were quite tolerable if only the ground hadn't been so hard. Finally Jake seemed satisfied and said, "OK. Try digging that stuff out, now."

"And just what the hell will you be doing while I slave away here?"

"I'm going to use my exalted rank to get us an engineer shovel." With that Jake walked toward the CP area. I folded my spade into the digging position and shoveled dirt, too tired to curse.

Jake came back with a full-sized shovel and told me to take a break. I sat and watched him making great strides in the construction of our home with that civilian-type shovel until the platoon sergeant of the mortar platoon came along. "All right, Dalton," he growled. "Let's have that shovel back, goddamn it. Or else go dig the mortars in!"

"Petty bureaucrat," said Jake and handed over the shovel, got out his entrenching tool, and went to work like other ordinary mortals.

"Still," I said, "your exalted rank got it almost half done."

"Take over, smart-ass," said Jake, and he climbed out of the hole which was now respectably deep.

Either the German forward observer had found a target of sufficient scope or the Germans were feeling embarrassed just sitting there taking our steady stream of artillery rounds without answering, because the sharp hiss of an 88 sent us flat into our new hole, face down. There was the now familiar explosion and the whining steel fragments of a treeburst. "Close," said Jake just as another one came in, crashing slightly farther away. "That's all they can spare," Jake said. "Let's get this hole dug!" We went to work with a vengeance and the hole got deeper and deeper. "Strange what a little artillery can do toward the construction of field fortifications," Jake said archly. "I must remember that for a lecture to basic trainees when I'm shipped home with a case of battle fatigue. Now incidentally," he continued in the tone of a lecturing professor, "I know what they mean by battle fatigue. Could you spare a few more rounds?" I did not find that particularly funny, but I increased my shoveling pace anyway.

By the time Baier set up his chow line that evening, our hole was completed. It was deep and wide, a good eight feet long with room to spare for our equipment, and the walls of its lower portion were lined with wood from ammunition crates. It had a sturdy cover of thick branches over which we had draped our two shelter halfs and on top of them we had piled dirt and snow. One shelter-half flap at the entrance served as a door to our underground abode. It was a lovely home and it was universally envied. After supper we moved our sleeping bags in and stowed our equipment. If we had had air mattresses in 1944, we would probably have become Belgian citizens and be living there still.

I put our musette bags under the heads of the sleeping bags and called up to Jake for our weapons. He handed me my Thompson sub and his M-1, saying, "Are you sure there's no need for that talented interior decorator from Sloane's?"

"No, dear," I said, "but I'm not sure I like the Steinway where it is now."

Jake laughed. "I told you this house was just not right for a grand piano; but no, you had to keep up with the van Cleefs!"

Herrick the Horse, watching from his hole next door, said, "You guys are stark, raving mad. They oughtta evacuate the both of you!"

That night I pulled guard, luckily just on the CP perimeter. There was a rifle platoon out ahead and I didn't see how I could be of any use in this rear echelon position. Well, we had diligently practiced how to be miserable so that part of our training came in handy during the ice-cold two hours that followed. Time dragged on uneventfully until Frenchie relieved me in a flurry of password and countersign. The whole thing had the feel of a particularly miserable night problem with realism added in the form of live artillery.

In front of our hole, our lovely little home, I got out of my equipment, glowingly anticipating the warm sleeping bag under safe cover. I dropped my webbing and submachine gun in the space we had left for it at the foot of our sleeping bags and then climbed down, dragging my overcoat behind me. Big as the hole was, I still bumped Jake and mumbled unanswered apologies. After I got into the bag, again with my boots on, I spread my overcoat over all and zipped myself in. Inside that bag, wearing practically everything I owned, with the overcoat draped over the whole bundle, I slowly got warm and comfortable.

The luminous dial of my S-2 watch showed that it was past midnight. I almost woke Jake to ask him what day it was. Well, I thought, it is probably a week day. And right now, at this very moment, Ruth would be getting ready to eat dinner.

Just imagine! At this very time, on the same planet, there is that comfortable house in Hollywood, California, with the thick carpets and the white overstuffed chairs and couches and a mahogany dining table under the crystal chandelier in the softly carpeted, warm dining room. And charming, blond Mrs. Walton is setting the table and there is a roast in the oven in the soft-green, sparkling warm kitchen. And Ruth is standing on a thick, soft bathroom carpet in front of her mirror in her warm, clean bathroom, combing her hair, that soft, honey-blond hair falling onto her shoulders. And at this very moment her mother is calling from that elegant, warm dining room, "Ruth, ask your father if he wants a martini!"

And now, at this very moment, Ruth is saying, "Just a second, mother. Soon's I finish combing my hair."

And now she's done and is walking into that silver-gray and white living room toward the fireplace with its roaring fire spreading its warmth and pine scent into the room, and she says to her father, "Daddy, Mother wants to know if you want a martini."

And her father, sitting in that deep, soft, white overstuffed chair looks up from the paper and smiles and says, "Hey, great! Yes, please. Ruth, it says here that the Seventeenth Airborne is chasing Runstedt somewhere in the Ardennes."

And Ruth, almost back in the study where the bar is, wheels around and runs to him and says, "Let me see!" And her father hands her the paper, just now, on the same planet . . . .

I was thoroughly warm now. Overhead, the 155s of DivArty and the 8-inch howitzers of Corps softly gurgled their lullaby. And just before I drifted into sleep, Ruth was saying to her father, "I wonder where Kurt is right now, at this very moment . . . ."

11
Mande St. Etienne (Bastogne)

"Over here, 81-mm mortars!" someone yelled. "Commo section, let's move out!" Then Jake's voice sounded from somewhere in the trees: "S-2, let's go!" I scrambled out of our foxhole, which had been such a comfortable little home to us and bid it a sad goodbye, slung my Thompson sub, barrel down, over my left shoulder, and headed toward the depth of the woods. I had taken only a few steps when I heard the short, whining hiss an 88 mm makes over its target, that unmistakable sound that would end in a "dzzooop" before the crash of the explosion.

It came as a complete surprise and I did not react instantly. There was no "dzzooop" sound; in its stead came a high, metallic crash with the whir and hum of steel splinters that meant a proximity fuse and tree-burst. The splinters were whapping into the trees, and more whining hisses filled the air before I dove into the nearest hole from which someone seemed to be coming out but then changed his mind and slithered back.

"Move over," I said. The hole was a two-man foxhole, almost as nice as ours, but the trooper in it was stretched across it diagonally, taking up all the room. I was on top of him and said again, impatiently, "Hey, come on. Move it!" There was no response and I realized that he was dead. I knew it wasn't Jake, and Joe had moved out with Company C, so I didn't bother to look at the face. I wriggled against the side of the hole, carefully keeping my submachine gun on my chest away from the dirt and snow, and drew the trooper's body over me as best I could. I felt safe and almost comfortable. It was like being in a house with rain pelting outside the window. I even had time to reflect that the German FO must have been glued to his artillery scope all this time and that our little woods must have been well registered.

The whining, whirring, whapping and crashing stopped overhead. There were more explosions, but they were farther to the right. The fire had shifted. I clambered out of the hole. There were some black craters where proximity fuses must have failed; tree branches were dark on the white snow; here and there huddled a still, dark figure. There were cries of "Medic!" To my left, just above the little road we had walked on so long ago, half sat, half lay one of the mortar men, his back against a tree. One of his legs was gone and he held the stump with both hands. His overcoat was open and so was the field jacket under it. I took his belt off his field pants and started to make a tourniquet.

"Don't bother," he said.

"Bullshit," I replied and screamed, "Medic!" I worked as fast as I could and wondered why I didn't get blood all over me. "Medic, goddamn it!" I yelled. A stretcher team was walking on the road and the men looked up. "Well, get up here, goddamn it!" I yelled, and they sprinted up the embankment.

"Don't bother," said the mortar man. "I'm about done."

"Shut your goddamn mouth," I said. "You're going to Paris. Say hello to Obley."

The stretcher team started to work on him and I waved and walked back toward our old holes. Except for some dead and wounded, no one was there. I angled back toward the road and bounced down the embankment at a point where a trail from the woods to our left entered the road. Firing had now stopped completely. I stood alone in the silence at that little intersection and was afraid. Enviously I glanced back toward the wounded and glumly wondered why, with all those splinters around, I couldn't have gotten a nice clean one in the shoulder or leg.

In the weird, sickening silence I heard the crunching of many feet in the dry snow before I could see the troops rounding a gentle curve on the trail. They entered the road, one column on each side, one soldier every five yards. It seemed like a long column, but I knew it was only one platoon. They walked as we all walked—silent, looking only at the man in front, until something else besides walking was called for. I ran up to the platoon leader and, saluting, said, "Gabel, Headquarters First, sir. I've lost my unit. May I go with you?"

The young lieutenant looked at me without slowing his pace. "This is Second Platoon, F Company, Second Battalion. We're the assault platoon."

No one in our unit had mentioned attack. We had assumed we were going forward but hadn't considered the implications. After all, they only "attack" in the movies. We real troopers just seemed to go from one place to another. The words "assault platoon" were new to me. And not only had I lost my own platoon and my own company, but I'd managed to lose my battalion. So I repeated, "Sir, may I go along?"

"How much ammo you got?"

The lieutenant seemed interested in the Thompson sub. I hoped he wouldn't asked me what my job was. I surely was the only scout in the whole United States Army who had ever lost his own unit, and I did not care to discuss the matter. "Two magazines besides this one."

He could see by the K-ration bag tied over the muzzle of the Thompson sub that I had not fired any rounds of the magazine in the weapon. "OK. You're with the bazooka team."

"Thank you, sir."

I drifted back and let the column walk by. No one looked at me and I looked at no one. I wished it could have been a platoon of Company A or at least some outfit from the First Battalion, but it was a fleeting thought. They were of the 513th, and that was good enough.

The bazooka team was somewhere in the middle of the column and I speeded up my pace as the gunner carrying the tube came abreast. "Lieutenant said to go with you," I said. "Gabel. First Bat." He nodded and gave me his name. I wedged into the column behind the second ammo bearer. "Where you guys goin'?" I asked.

"Hell, I don't know. I ain't no officer," replied the trooper without so much as moving his head. All was silent again as we walked on.

We walked rapidly and I wondered briefly what the rush was. I knew nothing of the importance of time, did not know of "axis of advance" or "boundaries" or "line of departure" or "assault position," of fire coordination or tank support, of final objectives or organization of terrain. I didn't know we were headed for Mande St. Etienne, closer to Bastogne than the Bois de Fragette from which we had begun our advance. None of these things were my business. What I needed to know, the squad leader or the platoon leader would tell me. So I walked rapidly, getting warm on this cold January day, concentrating on the man in front of me. At least I was no longer alone, and that was the main thing.

After a while, something in my peripheral vision changed and I looked up. We were out of the woods and seemed to be on what once must have been cultivated land, some farmer's field that had not been planted recently. "OK, spread out!" The lieutenant was walking backward, facing his column, arms extended. Smoothly the platoon spread into a wedge, the bazooka team at the extreme right.

My heart pounded. There was no longer a man in front of me whose boots I could watch from the safety of the column. I had changed from passenger to driver and now had to watch traffic.

Snow was everywhere, and all was a huge white blanket except for the forest falling behind to our left and right. Ahead were hillocks here and there, and the white fields disappeared in the dull gray distance. I watched the platoon leader and adjusted my walk to the speed of the platoon. The lieutenant was unsatisfied with the formation and signaled us to spread out more. He signaled for the bazooka team to get closer to him, and a rifle squad now overlapped our right flank. The platoon leader's pace had increased and I found myself running short distances to maintain my position in the formation. Ahead there was a slight rise in the ground, not much more than a ditch across a farmer's field, and we seemed to be aiming for it.

Suddenly the air directly above us was alive with sounds I had not heard before. The noise was akin to some very expensive fireworks a professional pyrotechnician might use on the Fourth of July, something that would make a screeching sound as it went down to explode. The screeches above were generally of the same tone but came from many projectiles. And those projectiles seemed to stay in the air quite some time. It was my first experience with what we later called "screaming meemies" and what the Germans called *Nebelwerfer* or fog thrower, the latest in multiple rockets.

The first salvo crashed into our formation as the next sounds already howled above us. The platoon leader spread his arms and yelled, "Hit it!" I hit the snow, face first, and felt multiple concussions as the rockets pounded down. They howled and burst, and I clawed the ground and saw nothing but snow just below the gash my helmet had made in the earth. I whimpered inside, now knowing that this, too, was carefully preregistered concentration, a fire trap that the Germans had waited for us to walk into and lie down in.

Between the explosions and over the screeching I heard a yell, "Move!" It was unbelievable that anyone would be able to yell, and the word "move" seemed incongruous. I turned my head to the right with some effort, scraping the rim of my helmet along the snow. From the extreme right, where I had seen no troops, a captain was running toward the rifle squad that had spread to the right of the bazooka team. "Get up!" he yelled, his face contorted with rage. "Get up, you stupid bastards. You'll die here. There's no cover. Move, move!" He grabbed one soldier by the shoulder and kicked another. I had never heard an officer yell like that, had never seen that kind of rage. "Get 'em up, goddamn it!" he bellowed toward the platoon leader, thrusting his fist up and down in the signal for double time.

The rockets seemed to lose their terror next to that captain. I did not know who he was and did not care. Under no circumstances would I let him come near me and yell at me. I almost forgot about the howling rockets, the explosions, the cries of "Medic!" I jumped up and stumbled forward in the direction of my fall. Left and right I could see others jumping up and running toward the long ditch in front of us. Suddenly the screeching stopped. I kept my eyes on the ditch and ran. The platoon leader and the platoon sergeant had reached the ditch and were kneeling at its bank, spreading their arms, palms down. The platoon literally crashed up against the ditch and lay exhausted.

I turned over on my side and watched the lieutenant for further signals. The bazooka gunner and his ammo bearers were next to me. I searched for the captain, but he was no longer there. Must be with the rest of the company, I figured. But where was the rest of the company?

Ahead—it seemed like a mile—was a road, slightly elevated above the white fields. A group of farmhouses, not quite a village, straddled it. I didn't know that it was the Bastogne Road; I didn't know we were attacking the Flamierge sector; I only suspected, from the darker indentations on the slope of the elevated road facing us, that the Germans were over there. Nothing moved. The white-gray snow blanket seemed to stifle all sound.

Through the weird silence rang the command: "Fix bayonets!" I felt the shock of it jerk my body. Surely this was some kind of psychological game they played in Company F! Fix bayonets? That's World War I stuff. Bayonets were for opening C-ration cans. Sometimes you threw them at trees while imitating Errol Flynn or John Wayne, and of course in basic training you had to pretend how fierce you were as you thrust them into sandbag dummies. But here? I searched for the lieutenant, expecting to see a big grin on his face as he enjoyed this stupid joke. He knelt at the center of the long line of troops, the platoon sergeant beside him. His face was hidden from me by his helmet.

There was the blood-freezing sound of fourteen bayonets drawn from scabbards and clicking home on their studs under the rifle barrels. I had never liked those short, wicked bayonet knives paratroopers were issued, and I was glad that I was armed with a submachine gun where there was no place to fix one.

Still there was no movement on the other side. Perhaps our artillery had wiped out the position. It was a comforting thought. Company F was just going to put on a nice little show. The platoon sergeant moved over toward the left of the line of troops and the lieutenant came toward us. "Take the bazooka team about a hundred yards up. Right there where you see that crater. Cover us." He was addressing me and, although I wasn't sure why he chose me or exactly what I was to do, I felt a sudden surge of pride.

"Yes, sir," I said. I seemed to be in charge of the bazooka team.

"Go," said the lieutenant and, bent low to the ground, loped off to the left and the center of the line again.

Lt. Samuel Calhoun, 2d Platoon, Company F, 2d Battalion, 513th PIR. He led the bayonet charge near Mande St. Etienne.

"Let's go," I said and started to run toward the crater. I could hear the cumbersome movements of the gunner and his two ammo bearers as they scrambled up. The extra rifleman assigned to the team was running close to me at my right. I ran toward the depression in the ground that seemed quite faraway, looking at nothing but that crater, wanting to make absolutely sure that I did exactly as I had been ordered. What I would do after I got there, I would figure out later. But the order to get to that crater was clear and comforting.

From the road and the cluster of houses came a long burst of MG 42 fire. As always, it sounded like a motorcycle in low gear; but now it was accompanied by whipping, cracking sounds nearby. Rifle fire joined the MG 42. I kept looking at the crater and running toward it, only vaguely aware that our little group was the target of the MG 42 and the rifles. Reaching the crater was now the most important thing to me only because that goal had been assigned by the platoon leader. Unreasoningly I was enraged by the MG 42 gunner, who must surely know that I had been told to get our little group to the crater and who therefore should leave us alone.

I reached the crater and jumped in. With a thud the rifleman flopped in next to me. The crater was not as deep as I thought it would be and as I looked back I could see the bazooka gunner and the two ammo bearers over its rim before they stumbled down to join us. Two more short bursts sounded from the 42, then silence.

The road still seemed faraway although, peering over the rim of the old crater, I could see the houses more clearly. The machine gunner wasn't visible, but the odd-looking holes stretched along the embankment of the road seemed to have forms in them. They looked like dirty potato sacks and I thought it was a neat trick of the Germans to put potato sacks in those holes.

"Let's go!" I heard the lieutenant's voice, and it sounded like a jump command. It was supposed to. I looked around, still totally unprepared for what I saw and heard. The second platoon of Company F was jumping out of the irrigation ditch in one long line of skirmishers, rifles at high port with the short bayonet knives clearly visible against the snow; the platoon was roaring "Geronimo!" In a wave from its left to its right and back again came the chilling yell of "Geronimo-o-o! Geronimo-o-o!" over and over, and all the *Banzais* or *Sieg Heils* of all the fanatics in the so-called civilized world would have sounded like whimpers in comparison.

The platoon was storming over the ground my bazooka team had just covered and for a moment I was afraid of them, afraid they would storm over our crater and butcher us. Then a great surge of pride went through me like none I've experienced before or since.

I don't know what the Germans must have thought, but for the longest time there was no fire from the road and the houses. Then the MG 42 rattled, and a slower automatic weapon sounded, presumably an MG 39, and rifles. And there was the belching sound of a PAK. "Sniper!" yelled the rifleman next to me and pointed to a tree on the right of the group of houses. He fired several times in succession and the two ammo bearers fired their pistols. There was a potato sack in the tree branches. It was in the sight of my submachine gun and it fell out of the tree. Another at the base of the tree took some steps and also tumbled down. Inexplicably, two men ran from our right diagonally in front of our crater. The PAK, or two of them, belched repeatedly and one of the men was suddenly half gone. Only his legs were there and then fell.

"Geronimo-o-o!" The sound was above me and to my left. I sprang out of the crater and screamed "Geronimo!" To my right ran the bazooka gunner, the rifleman with his fixed bayonet, the ammo bearer, and another rifleman who had gotten mixed up in the formation. I jumped over the two legs and briefly looked for the rest of the man. His upper half was nowhere in sight. "Geronimo-o-o!" now came from the left and right of me. We scrambled up the embankment and five Germans came from the houses with their hands high over their heads. I had no idea what to do next. "Runter von der Strasse und hinlegen!" I yelled at them. They tumbled off the embankment and lay face down in the snow, arms still spread above their heads.

From the holes in the embankment the Germans, still looking like potato sacks in their dirty-white camouflage suits, capes draped over their helmets, tried to burrow out and lift their hands at the same time. For three or four whom I could see, it was too late. Troopers, still yelling, were thrusting bayonets into them, shooting, and yelling again. "Stupid Krauts," I thought, "why did they wait so long?" The machine guns and PAK had stopped firing. Only rifle fire continued and, from the sound of ejecting clips, I surmised that most of it was ours. A line of perhaps fifteen Germans was forming outside one of the houses. Our platoon leader was yelling something and pointed to the left, then he shouted to nobody in particular, "Get those Krauts off the road!"

"Runter von der Strasse!" I yelled again and pointed to the Germans lying in the snow. "Los! Zu denen!" They were wide-eyed with terror and half ran, half fell down the embankment to flop spread-eagled next to their comrades. Neither the lieutenant nor I noticed that I was speaking German.

The yelling had stopped. Here and there several rifle shots rang out in rapid succession. The lieutenant disappeared behind the house on the far left of the cluster. A machine gun team attached to the platoon slowly and deliberately placed tripod and gun into position by a barn in front of me. To the left, more Germans were trudging out of a barnyard. "Column of ducks, you bastards," someone yelled; two troopers manipulated them into the desired formation with rifle butts. "First squad, over here," came a command from the same direction. All firing had stopped. "Third squad!" More commands sounded through the area.

The platoon sergeant came toward our little group. "What's your name again?" he asked me.

"Gabel, sergeant."

"Thanks, Gabel," he said, and I felt as though I had just been given a medal. "OK, you guys," he said to the bazooka team, "Good job. Now get over next to the machine gun and stay there till we know what's goin' on. Keep an eye on the field back there." Then he turned to me again. "Gabel, come with me. Lieutenant wants ya." I waved at the bazooka team and trudged off behind the platoon sergeant.

The platoon leader was sitting on a heap of rubble that had once been a garden wall. "You speak German, eh?" he asked. And I'd thought he hadn't noticed!

"Yes, sir."

"Find out what we got here."

"Yes, sir." I went back to the spot at the bottom of the embankment that had by now become a sizeable prisoner collection point and looked over the epaulets on the Germans' shoulders for rank. There were no officers and only one *Portepée-unter-offizier* ("first-three-grader"). I kicked him in the ribs and said, "Mitkommen." He scrambled up, keeping his hands high, and stumbled in front of me until I said, "Halt. Hinsetzen." He flopped down and I stood over him, the muzzle of my Thompson submachine gun yawning its .45 caliber opening into his utterly terrified face. "Got a piece of paper and a pencil?" I asked the platoon sergeant, who had followed me. He got out a crumpled map, turned it over, and handed me a grease pencil. "Would you hold this?" I handed him my Thompson sub. Then to the German, "Division?"

"2. PD."

That was an SS panzer division, but these soldiers were not SS. "Und Ihre Einheit?" He gave me the number of a panzer grenadier regiment and quickly explained that it had been attached to the division only recently; he did not know why. "Was liegt in diesem Abschnitt?" The first battalion. I said that I meant what unit had been holding the sector we had just attacked, the little group of houses on the road. He repeated, "Das erste Battalion." I was taken aback. Surely the Second Platoon, Company F, had not attacked a German battalion! The battalion, the German continued under further questioning, consisted of two understrength companies and an attached battery of *Nebelwerfer*. All officers had withdrawn. He did not know what elements or how many people withdrew with them. Yes, there were heavy Panzers somewhere in the area, "*Tiger und Koenigstiger*." Many of the units in the Second Panzer Division were from the Army. He did not know any of the SS units. He did not know where his unit was supposed to go. I folded the map and took my weapon back from the platoon sergeant. "That's it," I said.

We walked back to the platoon leader, taking the German NCO with us. Firing had started again to the east of our position, firing from the MG 42. Four or five times it hissed its long bursts over the road. Our machine gun from the barn answered. The lieutenant, his field glasses under the rim of his helmet, was leaning in the direction of the fire as if to pinpoint it by the force of his body. The gunner on the .30 caliber machine gun turned on his side and yelled to the platoon leader, "I can't make out where that son of a bitch is!"

The platoon sergeant handed the map with my scribbling to the lieutenant, who glanced at it and said, "Give it to somebody to take to S-Two as soon as we reestablish contact."

The sergeant stuffed the map into his jacket. "What's this crap now?" he asked, moving his head in the direction of the firing.

"Well, look!" the lieutenant rasped. "That Kraut bastard is firing on the medics!"

I gazed straight down the road and to the field on its right, the field we had just come over—how many years ago? Three or four dark figures and several light ones lay on the snow. One of the dark ones got up and started to run toward our group of houses. On his left arm was a Red Cross arm band. A burst of the MG 42 whipped across the road and the medic went down.

One of our riflemen started toward him and again the German machine gun opened up. The rifleman hit the snow. "You hurt?" he called to the medic.

"Arm!" was the response.

Two troopers of the squad with the attached machine gun near the barn jumped up, literally crazed by an unspeakable rage. "You goddamn bastards!" one of them screamed, his voice cracking, "They were trying to get *your* wounded, too!" The pair yelled and fired across the ghostly, empty white field toward the phantom MG 42. They were still firing when the German machine gun lashed its string of bullets toward them, and they took cover only after their clips ejected with an empty "ping." Furiously our machine gunner raked the field on the other side of the road.

"Hold it! Goddamn it, *hold* it!" the lieutenant yelled over the noise. "I can't see where the hell they are!" Somewhere in the folds of that ghostly white blanket north of the road was the expertly camouflaged German machine gun, its sound distorted by distance and the way the gunner traversed the barrel. No muzzle flash was visible, no matter how hard I strained to see. No figures moved. "We can't get to them," the lieutenant said and put his field glasses down.

"Yes, we can," I said to no one in particular.

The platoon sergeant asked, "What you got in mind?" and then called to the medic on the field, "Just hold it right there, Charley. We'll get to you in a minute. All you guys out there stay down!"

Now the lieutenant looked at me, too. "Well," I explained, "we'll just take the Kraut prisoners and line 'em up between the MG and the wounded. Simple."

The platoon sergeant nodded. "Not bad," he said.

"Can't do that," said the lieutenant. "That's about as far against the Geneva Conventions as you can go."

"Geneva Conventions shit, sir!" the platoon sergeant hissed at his officer, without in any way being disrespectful. "What do you suppose that bastard over there is doing to the Geneva Conventions when he shoots at medics and wounded?" The young sergeant was deeply outraged but was trying to control his fury, trying simply to advise his officer on a course of action he found to be practicable in getting his men to safety. That was all that mattered to the sergeant at this time, and that was all that really mattered to his platoon leader as well.

"Go," said the officer and put his binoculars back to his eyes.

"Thank you, sir," I said and then felt a little embarrassed. By now, those men out there, those men I hadn't even met a few hours before, had become buddies almost like Jake and Joe. For Joe I would have done what those two troopers near the barn had just done. For Jake I would have gone out there, like the trooper who went for the medic. During the attack I never thought of stopping for anyone; but here, watching the wounded medic, I knew that sooner or later his buddy would try rescuing him again and then we all would have to go, with or without orders. And we would get hurt. The "thank you" was for letting us have the easy way out of the inevitable.

The platoon sergeant, the German, and I went back to the prisoners. On the way, I asked the German, "Kennen Sie den MG Schützen da draussen?" He replied that he did know the gunner of the MG 42, and I figured that this little exercise would go smoothly. When we got to the prisoners, I commanded, "Aufstehen. In einem Glied Antreten!" They got up and fell in as though they were on a drill field. "Rechts—um!" I commanded, and they executed a flawless right face. I was beginning to have fun. "Ohne Tritt—Vorwärtz—Marsch!" I was proud of myself for remembering the command for "route step" and equally pleased to remember the appropriate command for halting a body of men that was not a part of an identifiable unit with "Das Ganze—Halt!" I had suddenly turned into a German NCO. "Links—um!" I shouted snappily and then gave them "at ease," snarling, "Rührt Euch." I lectured them on the problem of the MG-42 gunner. I pointed to our machine gun covering the road and the field to the north, to the rifle squad near the barn, and to my Thompson sub. I explained carefully that their lives depended on following instructions to the letter, that if even one of them attempted to run or to take cover, all would be ripped to pieces. Finally I said that I was certain all would go well and that we would all be safely back in a few minutes. Then I marched my little formation, in route step and with hands high above their heads, up on the road and out toward the medic and the wounded and the dead.

"Get the Germans, too," shouted the lieutenant, and I nodded. It would help him to have peace of mind about the Geneva Conventions and, after all, we might get additional information from more prisoners.

We walked past the barn, the machine gunner grinning broadly as he brought the barrel around and gave me a "thumbs up." I placed myself off the road at the center of the line of Germans, crouching low with the submachine gun pointed chest level at the Germans, a sheepdog herding a small flock. There were two short, tentative bursts from the MG 42. The prisoners glanced at me and I yelled, "Weitergehen. Hände schön hochhalten!" They continued walking, crawfish fashion, turning their bodies toward the German lines and waving their hands.

"Nicht schiessen, Helmuth. Wir sind's. Nicht schiessen!" Their plea was loud and clear, echoing over the white field.

The words "Scheisse—Mistvieher—" whipped over from the other side, and there was no more firing. We halted near our medic and waited until troopers dashed out to gather up the wounded, first ours, then the German. It went fast and smoothly.

I walked the Germans back toward our machine gunner, who said, "Hey . . . ," with a gesture of his head, and the sound and gesture made me feel good.

After I got rid of the prisoners, I went to the lieutenant and asked, "Sir, can I go back to my outfit now?"

"You know where it is?"

"No, sir."

"The colonel came up with the company. Ask him."

"What colonel, sir?"

The platoon leader pointed to a group of three figures sitting on the road at the left of the houses. One had a PRC-300 radio and the smaller figure was holding the transmitter. The third was sitting to one side of the group, apparently resting. Another PRC-300 was near him. "The little one is the commander of the Second Battalion," said the platoon leader.

"Thank you, sir," I said and started for the group.

"Good going," shouted the platoon leader after me, and again I felt as though I had just been decorated.

The company had come up; that's what the lieutenant had said. But I still couldn't see any more men than those of the platoon. Maybe they had moved through to the other side of the road; but if they had, I hadn't seen them. Then I heard artillery fire. Ours. Actually the firing had been going on for some time; but just as the high trajectory of rounds not meant for us used to whistle their lullaby to us in those nice, snug holes back at the Bois de Fragette, so this artillery fire got itself submerged after the first few rounds had come over. I became conscious of it again only after I had approached the little command group.

The battalion commander was sitting in the snow, his spread legs framing a map over which his body was straining in utmost concentration. Even though he would alternately look from the map to the terrain in front of him, I could not see his face; it was completely concealed by his helmet. Later, when I learned that one of his nicknames was "Boots and Helmet," I would remember that the first thing I thought of in my initial encounter with him was a turtle.

"I want a sensing on that last round," the colonel was saying impatiently into the instrument as though the poor forward observer he was talking to stood in front of him. Although he had a rather high-pitched voice, the tone made me glad I wasn't at the other end of that transmission. But the very fact that a battalion commander was talking on a radio to someone who must be forward of where I was made me feel practically in the rear echelon. Things were looking up.

Static hissed through the transmitter and a human voice was discernible somewhere within that noise. It became silent when the colonel clamped down on the push-to-talk button. "I want an accounting of what you get out there. Give me a sensing on that last round. No more fire until I know where it goes!" It didn't seem reasonable to me, but then I didn't know that in the attack we had sustained casualties from our own artillery fire. The firing stopped. I guessed that if the FO wanted it to continue, he'd either have to get the information from somebody who saw the last round hit or else invent something. Only static came through the receiver.

"Sir," I said, and the colonel shifted slightly and looked up. I still couldn't see his face clearly, only blue eyes that blinked a couple of times, a longish nose, and a slash of a mouth that still had the annoyance of unaccounted-for artillery rounds on it. Gone was the turtle impression. In its stead was something else that I couldn't immediately identify. I saluted and said, "PFC Gabel, First Battalion. Sir, I'd like permission to go back to my outfit." Again I was careful not to mention that I was a battalion scout.

For a moment I thought the colonel smiled. "You won't be able to do that, son," he said. "Germans are between us and them." Although I had become quite comfortable with Company F, the prospect of being away from my own people for any length of time was a very unhappy one for me. It must have shown because the colonel said, not unkindly,

Lt. Col. A. C. Miller II, commanding officer, 2d Battalion, 513th PIR

"Tell you what. You stay with me till we establish contact. You can be my bodyguard. How much ammo have you got for that Thompson?"

It was the second time someone was interested in my submachine gun. "Magazine is half full, and I've got two more clips, sir."

"Good. Stay over there with Calloway." The colonel waved his hand toward the third soldier in the little group, who was now sprawled out in the snow, and I walked over to him.

Things were indeed looking up. Being bodyguard to a battalion commander would be a snap. A high-ranking officer like that would be in nice, safe places. In addition, his being here must mean that the other companies of the battalion were somewhere around. So far as I was concerned, the situation was restored to normal. I started thinking of food and warmth.

"Howdy," said Calloway without moving a muscle as I sat down next to him.

"Hello," I replied and introduced myself. I fished a can of K-ration cheese out of one of my oversized patch pockets and opened it. It was easier to break open the K-ration boxes and to stow individual items like cheese or meat, crackers, powdered coffee, and such in various pockets rather than drag a bulky box around. "Colonel wants me to stick with him till we get contact over on the left, I guess. What's his name, anyway?"

"Miller. Acey-Deucey Miller."

"Why Acey-Deucey?"

"Well, his initials are A.C. The big wheels call him Ace. We call him Acey-Deucey. Sometimes Boots-and-Helmet."

I laughed; they *would* call him that. "Want a piece of cheese?" I asked Calloway, hoping he wouldn't.

"Naah," he said. "Just had some. Thanks."

I started to eat my cheese, then searched my pockets for some crackers. "What's he like?" I asked, thinking I might as well get briefed on my new temporary CO.

"Son of a bitch," said Calloway. "That little fart is gonna run your ass off."

I took a closer look at Calloway. He was still stretched out on the snow, and even though he was bundled up in field jacket, field pants with bulging pockets, and an overcoat, his six-foot frame looked wiry. His helmet was off; his hair was a dark-brown matted bird's nest. He had a rugged face and large, good-humored brown eyes. I liked him. "What do you do?" I asked.

"I'm his driver."

I had visions of me sitting in the back of a jeep after the rifle companies got back on the road, luxuriating as we drove past the long lines of marching infantry toward the First Battalion. "Where's your vehicle?" I inquired hopefully.

Calloway laughed. "Shee-it, I don't know. Back there somewhere. I don't guess I'll ever see the goddamn thing again."

I wasn't sure what a driver did when he no longer had a vehicle, but I thought that he would at least stay with the battalion rear command post and I said so.

"You kiddin'?" he asked scornfully. "That little bastard don't waste nothin'. I'm an extra rifle and radio man. He ain't about to be keepin' anyone sitting around." I thought of the colonel boring after that unaccounted-for artillery round, and it dawned on me that it might have been easier simply to stay with the Second Platoon for the next few days.

Now, too, I dimly remembered having heard the name "Acey-Deucey" before. Was it in England? Was it back in the Alabama area? Yes, of course. He was the executive officer of the 513th when it was first activated in 1943 and later had taken command of the Second Battalion. Not knowing him was, of course, perfectly natural. I barely knew my own First Battalion commander, Alton Taylor, and that only because I was in the S-2 section. I would see him on the march sometimes, and once or twice Lieutenant White had taken me to the CP where I would see him. He was a craggy old man in his mid-thirties and didn't talk much, and that was all I knew of him.

The artillery fire had started again. It seemed heavier than before. Someone out there must have satisfied old Acey-Deucey. I took my helmet off, stretched out on the ground, and propped the helmet under my head. But now, completely at rest, I had leisure to feel the cold seeping into my body. I pulled my wool knit cap deep over my ears and onto my face, and I tried to make myself small as though I could thereby crawl deeper into my overcoat; but it did no good. My feet were so cold I almost didn't feel them.

"Let's see what that house over there looks like." It was Colonel Miller's voice above me and I started up from what must have been a snooze. By now I had completely lost track of time. My watch was somewhere in my pants pocket, and digging it out presented a small problem in rigging. Though the sky seemed to have changed little from its gray of early morning, the passage of time was evident from the change in artillery fire, which was slow now and seemed to come from only one tube, and also from the absence of the German prisoners. Calloway was already on his feet with a radio awkwardly strapped on his back. It was the one for the battalion net, and he must have carried it ever since he left the jeep because the regular radio operator was also carrying one. I got to my feet. "Let me carry your rifle," I said to Calloway, feeling as though someone was doing my job for me.

"Hah," he grinned. "You wanna carry somethin', carry the radio."

"That'll take a direct order from higher up," I informed him primly and we ambled over to the farmhouse from which Company F had flushed those frightened German soldiers.

It was a two-story stone house and looked much like the ancestral farmhouses of the North German plains I had known in my youth. Except for the roof, the house seemed fairly well intact.

There was a typically dark entry and a long corridor with stark, whitewashed walls. On the right was a huge kitchen with an iron coal-burning range almost as big as the one my grandmother had had. Two troopers were putting coal scraps and some wood in it, and several others were standing around it anticipating warmth soon to come. They were less than happy at the sight of Acey-Deucey. "Sir, the lieutenant said it was OK," one of them said sheepishly, and the colonel replied, "Looks good to me. Go right ahead." We walked on and looked into all the rooms. They were sparsely furnished and it was hard to tell whether the family had originally had little furniture or had loaded much of it onto their wagons when they left. The smell of milk permeated the whole house.

At the far end of the hall was a fairly large room that could have been the parlor. Against one wall between two windows stood a massive secretary with its heavy lid open as a desk. Against the other walls were three German field beds with straw sacks for mattresses. The colonel walked over to one of the beds, took off his helmet and webbing, and sat down. He looked around, blinked a couple of times as he turned his head, and said, "Good." With his hands gripping the bed frame and his brown hair sticking up here and there, the eyes blinking with each turn of the head as he took in the room, he looked like a little eagle. That was it! An eaglet. Perched there in temporary repose before pouncing on the next FO. "Settle down," he said to us, and we promptly did just that.

I piled my equipment in one corner of the room, propped my musette bag on top of the pile, leaned against it, and dozed off. The colonel would do whatever colonels do; Calloway and the radio operator would have to work the radios; but I had no mission. So I would sleep, and after that I would look for some hot chow or at least for some heat.

I awoke to the cussing of two people who had tripped over my legs. They were communications men and were reeling out wire and hooking up EE8 telephones. "How about movin' your ass against the wall," one of them growled, and I figured I might as well get up. The room looked like Grand Central Station. Dusk was approaching, and two soldiers were hanging blankets over the windows for blackout. Another soldier was working on a Coleman lantern. Two more were moving tables into the room. My new boss was talking to a captain I had seen somewhere before but could not place. And over all this mass of humanity crawled the commo men with their EE8 field phones and wire. A full-fledged command post was growing around the battalion commander.

"LP one," said one of the commo men after cranking the EE8. "LP one, are you in?"

"LP one," came the answer.

"Commo check." The trooper cranked another phone. "LP two."

Three LPs responded. On either side of the secretary, the two AN/PRC-300 radios sat propped up on boxes, their antennas rigged out the windows. Three more telephones, their leather cases marked "D," "E," and "F," were sitting in a neat row on a small table against the wall opposite the colonel's bed. Those would be the lines to the rifle companies.

Two officers walked into the room. One was a tall, young major. "Exec," Calloway explained. "Name is Edwards." I watched with some admiration as each man did his assigned job silently and efficiently, and I watched the officers talking softly, nodding, leaving the room. It was dark now and a Coleman lantern hissed and sputtered into light. It was warmer in the room and I started to unbutton my overcoat. All the comforts of home, I thought.

"Come on, son," said Ace. "What did you say your name was?"

"Gabel, sir."

"OK, Gabel. Let's see what it looks like out there." For the first time in I didn't know how long, I was about to get warm, and just then this Ace character wanted to go for a walk. I gritted my teeth, buttoned my coat, put my webb equipment on, and grabbed my weapon. Ace, as I had now started to call him to myself, was already in the dark hall on his way out. As I passed the kitchen, I could see the glow of the stove and smell K-ration beef heating in a pan. Happy murmuring came from that place and I cursed the moment that the platoon leader had pointed me in the direction of Acey-Deucey and his rage for work.

After the warmth of the farmhouse and the promise of the friendly kitchen, the cold outside was doubly cruel. Ace took off toward a little wood north of the road, unceremoniously hopping down the road embankment and moving at a fast pace through knee-deep snow. I hopped along behind him, trying to stay close not so much like a bodyguard trying to protect his charge but rather like the child afraid of being separated from his father in the dark. I had no idea what Ace was looking for; but I was sure that wherever he was, that place would be safe.

He stopped abruptly and I almost bumped into him. He bent down and talked to someone. Curiously I peered around him. There was a double foxhole with two troopers in it who were telling Ace what direction they were covering. Briefly I wondered how they got there and how Ace knew that they were in this spot, and then we started off again. We came to another foxhole and next to it a slightly larger one—a machine gun position. Here we stopped a little longer because Ace seemed to be interested in fields of fire. On we went, this time curving around the front of the woods, circling to the east. Ace made a slight jog toward the south and stopped at still another hole. The two troopers in it had an EE8 telephone and Ace hunkered down next to them.

Up to now, this little exercise had seemed like field training in England. That was where last I had seen officers bending over foxholes, sighting over machine gun barrels, pointing out quadrants. But we had just made a jog back in the direction of the woods and were talking to someone in a listening post (LP). That crazy little colonel had therefore walked us over German territory; he had not even bothered to give a password as he approached our holes and for some reason had not been challenged. Was this SOP here? I had been on LP a few times and the only person I had ever seen out there was Jake, and even he would never have approached me from the direction of the enemy. What was with this colonel? What was with this Second Battalion?

When we left the LP, I paid attention to direction and to our situation. Over the strain of this new concentration, I forgot the cold and my physical misery. The perimeter of what was left of the Second Battalion started slowly to take shape in my mind—Companies D, E, and F positioned along the curve of the woods.

From foxhole to foxhole we went, almost always approaching from the front, rarely getting challenged and then only, it seemed to me, by a trooper who wanted to show the battalion commander how much on the ball he was.

The moon had come out, and the curve of the woods line, lifting and dipping over hill and dale, stood out sharply against the snow. This is what the Germans are looking at, I thought, resigned to my fate. I was now silently preparing the speech I would make to any German patrol that was, sooner or later, bound to come across the two of us. I would tell them that we were glad to be bumping into them because we had a message for the German commander, namely that Ace Miller expected him to surrender and that we wanted to know where the Germans would like the ceremony to be held. By the time we reached the interior of the woods, I was convinced that my strategy would have worked. Still I felt a little better when we started to look at mortar positions deep within the safe folds of the forest.

We left the forest and it was again safe enough for me to concentrate on my misery. I was bone tired and my legs were about to give out. I struggled to keep up with Ace as we crossed the fields between the woods and the road back toward the plateau that had become the battalion forward CP. There was no change of pace; I wondered truculently how an old man over thirty could totally ignore time and space, rushing through deep snow for hours without rest, without so much as breathing hard. I thought of Calloway and his warning. It must have been Ace Miller who came up with the idea of the Alabama area run from the barracks to the Chattahoochee ferry and back.

When we walked into the farmhouse I was too tired to enjoy the lingering smell of heated K-rations or even the warmth of the dimly lit operations area.

"Get some sleep, Gabel," Ace said, with a wave toward a bed.

"That's your bed, sir," I said, looking at it longingly.

"I won't need it now. I've got to do some work." What the hell had he just been doing, I wondered, and was almost annoyed, though I could not say exactly why.

I sat on the bed, carefully stretched out on it, and thought how nice it would be if I could take my boots off. That was, of course, out of the question; but it was a nice thought. Ace had removed his webb equipment and was now peeling off his green officer's overcoat with the nice woolen lining. He walked over to me and spread the coat over me like a blanket. "Go to sleep, son," he said, and I felt myself turning to jelly. I couldn't say thanks because I knew that if I as much as opened my mouth I would bawl like a baby. Ace looked down at me briefly, blinked his eagle eyes once, and walked over to the desk. I closed my eyes and thought, "Ace and Major Edwards and the company commanders will now work their alchemy at that desk; they will make calls on the PRC-300 and EE8s, and in the morning there will be no more Germans." I fell asleep.

12
Bois de Fragette

A palpable change in the routine of the command post woke me. No one had raised his voice. There was no increase in radio traffic. Yet everything was different from what it had been before. "Do you think it could be something else?" Ace was talking softly on one of the EE8s. Two of the runners were shouldering their rifles and had started toward the door. Calloway was cramming things into his musette bag. The company commanders were no longer in the room; neither was the exec. "All right, son," Ace said. "How many tanks do you think?" I whipped the overcoat off me and got out of bed wide awake. Slowly, so as not to make a distracting movement, I put on my webb belt and harness, pulled my gas mask over my shoulder, and reached for my helmet and weapon. "LP two! LP two!" Ace turned around to one of the commo men. "Check that line. Seems to be out." The trooper left the room. One of the company's EE8s whirred. Ace took the receiver out of its leather sheath and turned the butterfly switch. To another trooper he said, "Get those blankets off the windows." Then into the instrument, "Six." An unintelligible voice made a report that seemed long in comparison to the normal traffic. "Infantry with them?" Ace asked with a slight edge to his voice. I put my helmet on and shouldered my weapon. "How far did they move through?" To Calloway, Ace said, "Open the window."

Gray daylight peeped into the room with the damp, cold, snow-laden air. Ace cocked his eagle head and listened to the phone and to the gray cold outside. I could hear nothing and did not dare to move toward the window, which must now be kept clear for the commander. "All right. Move to battalion CP. Further orders from here. Six out."

Ace turned the crank on the EE8 marked "D" and said into the room, "Get the radios outside and stand by. Commo, break it down when I'm through here!" There was no switchboard at the forward CP, so Ace must have meant the field phones. As the radio operator, Calloway, and I left the room, the communications trooper was already disconnecting the LP phones. We had established his CP in minutes and we seemed to move out of it within seconds of a given order. I again wondered if this is what all forward CPs looked liked and why there were no staff officers except the exec. Or had they appeared in the night and been sent to other places on mysterious missions while I was asleep? Had all this been anticipated? Would Ace, after he got off the last phone, come strolling outside to us and say, "Well, let's have breakfast while we're waiting for things to get squared away out there"?

The three of us stood in the cobblestone yard of the farmhouse and listened, the white condensation of our breaths puffing into the biting cold air and betraying our heartbeats. I concentrated on motor noises, on tracks, on the squeaking of bogey wheels and could not say what kind of firing was going on. We had checked two antitank guns during the night, guns attached to the battalion from another outfit. We had checked the 81- and the 60-mm mortars and the bazooka positions. I assumed the weapons were all firing without really hearing them, only listening selectively for the roaring, clanking, squeaking sounds of panzers. But I could hear only engines I was sure belonged to our deuce-and-a-halfs laboring up the hills. There! I had been right all along! Ace would simply not permit a German panzer attack; that's what the staff officers had been about last night. The S-1, well, he would be at the rear CP getting replacements. The S-2—who knows? If he's as good as Peter White, he'd probably be at the German CP, screwing up their maps. And the S-3 was undoubtedly getting air support, or Corps Artillery, or whatever else an S-3 does. But the S-4! I knew just exactly what he was doing. First he had found those deuce-and-a-halfs that were roaring up the hills so that we could load up and ride northeast to Houffalize. He had gotten his directions a little fouled up, but that happens. Then he had hot chow waiting for us along the way. He had set up a QM shower unit . . . .

The motor noises shifted, as though gears had been shifted. And now I could hear the squeaking of bogey wheels.

Ace came out of the house and walked rapidly across the small courtyard to the front of the little farm complex. We followed. Ace held up his left hand, palm up like a waiter holding an invisible tray, and the radio man put the transceiver into it. Ace talked while we were walking, the three of us close on his heels. Troops from the rifle companies were on the road. Some were half walking, half double timing from the woods toward the houses along the road. They looked as though they were in squad formation, but they were the remnants of platoons.

The Ace walked back to the street of the little village. It was crowded with what was left of the Second Battalion, and we stood in a vortex of troops swirling left and right around us. From out of nowhere the tall, powerful frame of the executive officer had appeared next to Ace. The pair were looking at a map.

Three or four gurgling hisses of flat-trajectory 88s sent us down on our bellies before the explosions crashed into the little cluster of houses and men. Ace and Major Edwards jumped up and sprinted toward one of the houses. I took cover next to a barn on the other side of the street, feeling faraway from the safety of Ace. Calloway was lying near Ace, but I could not see the radio operator. There were more explosions, the rounds seeming to come in from different directions. I watched amazed as Ace and the major got to their feet and continued studying the map. Ace pointed in a southerly direction and Major Edwards nodded, then saluted—saluted, without seeming to be aware of the holocaust around him. "All right, D Company!" he roared and galloped toward the east end of the tiny village. He was a magnet as he ran, drawing troops toward himself from all directions. Ace, still holding the map, started walking in the same direction as his executive officer, who was no longer in sight. I slithered along my side of the street parallel to Ace and stopped in the doorway of a house.

The movement of troops was beginning to take on a pattern—from left to right in a fairly steady stream. Ace stood in the middle of the road like a policeman and even made traffic direction movements with his left arm. "Follow Company D," he shouted. "Over to those woods. We'll assemble there!"

I could neither see the woods Ace was talking about nor had I noticed any in the direction Ace was pointing; but I knew they would be there and that we would assemble in them and that then we would be safe. All I had to do was to be sure I could see Ace and understand his orders and follow them exactly, and everything would be well.

The 88 fire stopped and I could hear the engine noises again. My little fantasy about the trucks, the hot chow, and the shower units had been washed away as sandcastles are washed away by the tide. I knew they had been sandcastles when they first appeared, just as I knew they would be washed away. Still, the engine noises were just that: noises. I had not seen the vehicles that made the noises nor had I seen any Germans—just felt their imminent presence. Except for Ace's pointing out the direction he wanted the troops to go in, I was no longer sure of the direction from which the Germans seemed to be approaching. That was, in any event, officers' business; I was intent on putting the motor noises, and the occasional hand grenade and mortar explosions, out of my mind. The hand grenades were ours; the mortars I wasn't sure of. After the flat-trajectory 88s, they didn't much matter anyhow.

The panorama of troops moving from left to right in front of me had changed. On both sides of the street two squads, the remains of platoons, had stopped and were flattened on the ground against buildings and garden walls. There seemed to be no officers with them. In fact, I had not seen any officers except Ace and the exec; I thought that if they all walked around the way Ace and the exec had done, perhaps they had all been killed.

Ace, in his policeman's role, told the two platoons to move as though they were parked in a "no parking" zone. The men got up and eased forward, hugging the buildings for cover. Across the cobblestoned street about fifty yards to my right a Royal Tiger rounded the corner, its right track grinding a brick wall and shattering it as the tank lurched into its turn. A shower of brick fell onto the hull of the tank, bouncing off like so many raindrops. The Royal Tiger stopped and at the same time its turret moved and the long 88 gun started to depress. The gun was being aimed at me or at the building where I crouched. The second during which I looked past the muzzle brake down into the black hole of the 88 as the turret came to a halt seemed like a whole minute during which I seemed to lose control over every one of my muscles. Not even my eyes could blink. There was an immense yellow flash, the recoil of the gun, and a slight rocking motion of the hull before my eyes would close tightly. A high, metallic, belching sound, of such intensity that the brain could not translate what the ear was trying to tell it, accompanied the flash and the rocking motion of the tank. Instantaneously there was a crashing as though hundreds of trash cans had been dropped onto the cobblestones from a great height and were bursting into a million brittle pieces.

The entire portion of the house above the doorway in which I was crouched disintegrated in that sound. I could see nothing but felt as though I was lifted and pummeled by huge fists and flung onto the pavement and pummeled some more. I could feel no pain and was only interested in getting across the street. I briefly noted that I was covered with a pile of bricks and that brick dust was running down my neck as I scrabbled forward and upward like a burrowing animal. As I scrambled across the street I could see the turret move further to the right, tracking me. Even under these extreme circumstances and utterly terrified, I could not account for an 88 being aimed at me and kept wondering just what it was really being aimed at. The gun suddenly stopped, then traversed to the left, still generally pointing in my direction, and again I saw the yellow flash, the recoil, and the rocking of the hull. This time the sounds merged and seemed not so loud as before. A large brick barn to the right of the demolished house from which I had just emerged seemed to collapse in slow motion. I felt some of the pounding, almost familiar now, and noted a crunching, scraping clangor against my helmet as my head slammed into the icy slush. Unaccountably, I was lying flat against the side of a wrecked building parallel to the panzer. Another Royal Tiger, bogey wheels screeching, now hulked into view next to the first one. It fired, but I could hear the firing and impact only as though I had dense cotton in my ears. Three troopers ran toward the tanks from the far side of the demolished barn, and my numbed brain dimly registered that three paratroopers were attacking two Royal Tiger tanks.

Through the cotton barrier in my ears, I heard Ace yelling, "Over here, goddamn it!" and saw that he meant me. I was told to do something and the order reassured me that the world had not yet collapsed. Almost happily I scrambled across the street. "We're ready to move," Ace said, and I nodded stupidly. Ace, Calloway, a machine gun team, a bazooka man, and I seemed to be the only people left in the tiny village. The tanks were no longer where I had seen them moments before. No German infantry were visible anywhere, though they should have been close to the panzers. Everything seemed strangely quiet, giving rise to another of my fantasies that the Germans had changed their minds.

"Calloway, get us some curtains or something else white for camouflage out of that house," Ace said, indicating his former CP. "Yes, sir," said Calloway, and I noticed that he no longer had the radio. He trotted off and I thought, as my latest fantasy was duly washed away, that this was one hell of a time to be getting material for camouflage so that we could get dressed up like the Germans in their snowsuits. At the same time I thought that the Ace must know exactly how much time we had and what was going to happen and that there must be a good reason for hanging around.

Calloway came out of the house and ambled over to us, his dirty, stubbled face in a wide grin. He had two white curtains of Belgian lace that would have cost a fortune back in the States. "Here you are, sir," he said to the colonel as he handed him one of them, and "Here, Gabel," as he handed me the other. I watched as Ace cut a hole in his curtain and stuck his head through it, draping the rest over his body. He was completely covered by the thing and looked like a kid on Halloween dressed up as a steel-helmeted ghost. I did the same thing and felt a little silly.

"Sir," said Calloway, "May I go back and get me one, too?"

"Go ahead, but hurry. We're moving out," Ace said. He turned to the machine gunner. "Set up the gun and the bazooka over there and fire as soon as you see 'em. Don't let 'em come through!"

"Yes, sir," the gunner replied. His response fastened itself to my vitals never to leave.

"Let's go, Gabel," said Ace and turned.

For the first time since the tanks started to fire I felt something akin to anger. And for the first time I was going to disagree with an officer. "Sir, we can't leave them here!" I was surprised to hear those words coming quite imperiously from my throat.

Ace stopped briefly and looked at me. I thought he smiled wanly. "It's all right, son," he said almost sadly. "They'll be fine."

Ahead, the highway that was also the main street of this little village was empty. The remains of the Second Battalion were slithering down the embankment and walking rapidly, in widely dispersed formations, over the snowy expanse of fields and meadows, single black dots on that awful gray-white sheet that stretched into infinity, blending with a gray-white nothing in the distance, a nothing that was supposed to hold those woods that were supposed to be our haven. There was no cover in sight. And as I glanced back fearfully, angrily, I saw the machine gun team (the man who had said, "Yes, sir," carrying the gun, another the tripod, an ammunition bearer, and the bazooka man) walking to the edge of the first house. When Ace and I were about to leave the road, I glanced back once more and saw them on the ground in position, as though they were in training exercise and about to be checked for proper action. I had never known them, but I was awed by them. I was and I remained awed. They would fire and they would die and there would never be anyone who could ever redeem that "Yes, sir."

"Calloway, sir!" I yelled at Ace as we jumped down the embankment.

"He'll catch up," Ace said, and we broke into a trot to shorten the distance between us and the troops ahead.

The snow was deep and it was difficult to run in it. In a very few minutes I started to get warm. Briefly the engine noises fluttered behind us but seemed to dim out into a different direction. Two or three explosions—mortars, I thought—broke the general silence behind us. Then came the hammering of a 30-caliber machine gun, our gun. The sound of it went to the same place where that "Yes, sir," had lodged itself and it churned around there, tearing at my soul. An MG 42 answered and there were more explosions. Then the firing stopped.

I stumbled and fell, got up, tripped over my camouflage curtain and fell again. Furiously I tore the curtain off and ran to catch up with Ace. The effort of running was now beginning to make itself felt. It was still a downhill run, but the white fields dipped and rose in deceptively gentle waves, a dead-white, soft, undulating sea whose shrouded shore became more elusive with each step I took.

Ace maintained his position in the center and back of his battalion, its few remaining men trudging like dark sheep before their shepherd. His curtain billowed like a tattered sail, and I thought he was about as much camouflaged as Hollywood and Vine on Saturday night. I remained a few steps behind him, dimly remembering that I was his "bodyguard," though in actuality his immediate vicinity represented safety to me, an area I would try hard not to leave.

The fields leveled and walking grew harder as I pulled one leg out of knee-deep snow, laboriously planted it ahead, and pulled the other leg behind it. The snow wanted to keep a hold on my legs, and it was a struggle to free them. My equipment weighed a ton and further impeded every move. I unsnapped my gas mask and dropped it to the ground, feeling a brief moment of respite.

The snow did not seem to bother Ace, who, shepherd fashion, swept his head right and left over his formation, pointing a direction to men who would occasionally turn around. Once or twice troopers, company runners, would drop back and approach Ace. There would be a short exchange of words and the runners would go on again at a trot. I could not understand how they could run in this cloying, pulling, God-awful snow, and I was annoyed at their display of superiority.

The direction of march changed slightly and we were headed toward what appeared to be gently rising ground. By now my breath was coming hard and my body, especially my legs, ached. Almost desperately I unbuckled my webb belt and shrugged my harness off. Canteen, entrenching tool, compass, first aid packet, the musette bag with underwear and socks in it—all plopped into the snow. Though I was now more maneuverable, the leaden feeling was hardly abated. Up to this point I had not reflected on exactly what we were doing. To me it had been simply another move, albeit a more urgent move than usual. There had been orders, and we had moved. That the order directed us to withdraw, to fall back, had not occurred to me. The act of dropping my equipment brought with it the realization that we were withdrawing, that we were retreating. It was a new experience, but I was too tired to give it much thought. Nor was I really aware of the absurd odds involved: heavy German armor and mechanized infantry, well supported by the most sophisticated artillery, against light infantry without artillery support. That was beyond my ken. I only knew that we had to move to be saved and that in order to be saved, I had to keep up, and to do that, I had to drop equipment I had no use for at the moment. By the time we had climbed over the rise that seemed to go on and on, the snow was littered with canteens and webbing and musette bags and gas masks.

As gently as it had risen, the ground sloped down; but the going was no easier. Still, one leg struggled to get out of the snow only to plunge deeper into it again as the body, pushed slightly forward by the terrain, supplied the extra weight. And the other leg still had to drag itself out of the wet, clinging hole that seemed deeper than the one before. I ripped off my overcoat, that cumbersome, olive-drab contraption that never really seemed to keep the biting cold out, and as it dropped I remembered with a pang that my two magazines full of ammunition were still in its pockets. Again I had a reprieve from the leaden weight on me. For a while it was easier to walk. I even looked up now and again to see Ace in front of me, the curtain forms of our men, who seemed to have come closer together. It looked like many close-in squad diamond formations.

Through the silence, the tearing bursts of fire from the two or three MG 42s ripped over us, slashing into the battalion like steel whips. It came as no surprise, but it made me forget the snow. "Spread 'em out! Move, on the double!" The commands were repeated ahead and the squad diamonds spread wider over the gray-white landscape. But dark forms remained on the ground, looking like so many discarded olive-drab overcoats.

Except for that brief flurry of movement that spread the formations out, the battalion did not seem to increase its pace significantly. Were they all as bone tired as I was? Did they, too, think it perfectly normal for those 42s to rip into us? Was it all going according to some preconceived plan?

Ace fell. I stopped, dropped to my knee, and rolled onto my side. My first thought was that he had tripped over his curtain. Then I thought, what if he's been hit? What do I do with him? Ace looked around past me, then at me, and said in an annoyed tone, "How about firing your weapon once in a while?" Firing meant that I would have to turn around and face the Germans, something I did not want to do because I was sure that to look around would mean that I would turn to stone.

I came up with various reasons why I would not fire my weapon. First of all, Ace had merely asked a rhetorical question; he had certainly not ordered me to fire. Second, the Germans would be out of range. After all, a submachine gun wasn't much better than a pistol. Most important of all, I would have to clean my weapon again. And I had done that once already in the last two or three days back at the house. It was a decided pain in the ass to clean the thing in the cold and snow . . . . But in my secret heart of hearts I knew that I would not fire because I was afraid. When Ace fell, I realized that Ace was the last man behind his battalion, and I was behind him. His billowing white capelike curtain, the only one among the dark figures trudging over the snow, surely made him special. Worse still, an automatic weapon would invite immediate counterfire of the MG 42 closest to us and of God knows what else. Neither one of us would ever be able to get off this cold piece of Belgian soil. Unless I received an unmistakable order, I would not draw any more attention to ourselves than we already had.

Snakelike, I finished slithering my body in a turn and forced myself to look back.

Down the gentle slope we had just come up were two or three V-shaped formations of Germans in the familiar white snowsuits—no longer like potato sacks but like menacing ghosts. How far—how near—I could not have said; but, as on a movie screen in slow motion, I saw three of them at the head of the V closest to us come to a slithering halt. One reached in back as though to lift off a pack but instead threw forward and over his head an ugly contraption that looked like a giant praying mantis. Its front legs planted themselves in the snow while the German, still holding it by its shorter rear legs, bent to place those down, too. At the same time, the white figure slightly behind and to the left of the object planted the receiver group and barrel of that most formidable of German infantry weapons onto the quadrupod. In a fraction of a second, I marveled in spite of my fear, a superbly trained crew had brought an MG 42 into action. Belted ammunition was already in the receiver, and the third man in this group, the ammo bearer, stood ready to feed the insatiable reaper. The entire crew stood upright, as though they were on a firing range, their gun high up on the telescoped quadrupod.

The whole monstrous scene was before me like one of the more elaborate tableaus in Madame Tussaud's Wax Museum. Movement seemed to have stopped. Was I imagining that they stopped? Or was it just the machine gun team? On the far right, white forms were still moving—some walking, some running—but they seemed to slow down as they came abreast of the MG team. Much farther on the right, it seemed almost at the horizon, four or five tracked vehicles of theirs lumbered away from the road, almost parallel with the left flank of the battalion. I did not dwell on the significance of these formations, these movements. My whole being was riveted on the tableau of the MG 42. To fire at it would be sheer folly, I knew. One of the gunners was the German equivalent of Jake, one was Joe, and one was me.

Suppose I were behind that gun? And a Kraut let go at us with his Schmeisser and hit Jake or Joe? That Kraut would be a dead man. He could jump up with his hands raised, waving a picture of his wife and children, and I would kill him. He could scream that he was my long-lost father or brother, and I would kill him.

I did not shoot. In a cold sweat I waited for Ace to shout "Fire!" and at the command I would of course empty my magazine at the tableau and wait to die.

The awful seconds passed. Why didn't the Germans fire? Why didn't they storm over us? It never occurred to me that they might not have wanted to engage us in close combat. I didn't consider that they might have been the same soldiers who fled before our attack—or that those who fled might have spread stories about the American paratroopers who attacked with bayonet knives and their spine-chilling roar of "Geronimo-o-o!" and that these, their replacements, were content to fire at the paratroopers from a safe distance. Those were the stories we heard later. But at this dreadful point in time I was simply afraid of hearing the command "Fire."

There was no command. With immense relief I heard the clatter of Ace's equipment as he recovered and got up to move. Still the Germans did not shoot. I rolled over and got to my feet, turning away from the white, silent figures. Ahead was the reassuring billow of Ace's curtain—the *Mayflower* in full sail—and I struggled to catch up. A rifleman had gotten between Ace and me and I was going to ream his ass, no matter how tired I was, as soon as I caught up. How dare he get between the commander and his "bodyguard"? It seemed very important to get to that guy and send him the hell back to his own outfit.

The MG 42 fired a long burst. Well, *finally*, I thought as I struggled on to catch that interloper ahead of me. Some officer must have finally made the German fire. I had almost caught up with the soldier, cumbersomely lifting his legs out of the snow and planting them just like everybody else. There was a short burst—the crackling and whistling steel whip of the 42—and the man in front of me pitched forward and lay still on his face. I stepped over him wondering just how in the hell that could have happened without me being hit—certainly I didn't feel anything. Now Ace was directly in front of me, unobstructed by whoever was back there. The thought of stopping for the fallen trooper never entered my mind. He was out of it. He was lucky. He was either dead or the German medics would get him. There were only three men in the whole world I would have stopped for at that moment: Jake, Joe, and the little lieutenant colonel in front of me.

The fight to reduce the gap between me and Ace became unbearable. I no longer felt the individual limbs of my body, only the body as one clump of unmaneuverable lead with the heavy submachine gun bouncing back and forth on my chest, its carrying strap sawing into the right side of my neck. Forever, it seemed, that cumbersome weapon had been a part of my body; even with its magazine empty and no prospect of ammunition resupply, I would have been incapable of giving it up. It would be like giving up a leg or an arm. Only a dead or wounded trooper had the right to be parted from it, though I had seen wounded on stretchers clutching their M-2s, and medics who would automatically pick up a fallen weapon and place it on the stretcher with the unconscious soldier much as he would place a nearly severed, dangling arm close to the body of its owner. That had never been remarkable; only much later, when I heard stories of leg-division soldiers throwing away weapons as they fled Luxembourg, did I reflect with wondrous disgust on such an unthinkably obscene act.

The gap between me and Ace was all I was capable of concentrating on. The firing behind me had become meaningless except for the hope that I would be hit. Then I could lie down and would not have to get up again. There seemed to be very little rifle fire, and only the MG 42s and 39s and *Sturmgewehre* rattled sporadically, each burst holding out the promise of salvation, each silence punctuating a dull disappointment, a resentment at having to propel this leaden body forward into the all-encompassing whiteness to no purpose I could fathom. Stupid bastards can't hit anything, I thought. My most fervent wish now was a bullet or two—anywhere—to take me out of it.

What did not brush my mind was that the Germans must have been as weary as we, even though they had only recently dismounted from their half-tracks and from the tanks they were attacking with. I didn't know that they were reluctant to fire and had to be ordered on and on. I didn't consider that the line of skirmishers could go only as far as the machine gun sections; no matter how superbly those sections were trained, it took maximum effort to move guns, mounts, and ammunition over long distances in knee-deep snow. Even firing their 42s and 39s while they walked, which is what the Germans had been doing after their brief stop at the slope, made for frequent firing stoppages because of feed mechanism and ammunition belt defects that would bog them down. I didn't know that there were only a limited number of tanks and mechanized vehicles that the Germans carefully husbanded—vehicles and fuel were not expendable to the Germans. I didn't realize that the Germans commanding the dismounted *Panzergrenadiere* must be very nervous about being separated from their armored vehicles—perhaps unaware of new missions that might have been assigned the armor. I didn't consider that they must be apprehensive about the woods looming in the distance, the woods toward which they were being drawn by the paratroopers they were pursuing . . . .

Though from time to time the beginnings of a mosaic of our frontline enemy would form in my mind from talking to prisoners and to the civilians in the battle area, the shape would last only long enough for a report to Peter White or to Jake; then it would be wiped clear by the misery of living in the cold, of walking in the snow, of diarrhea, of night patrols, of 88s . . . and now it was completely wiped clear, as was everything else except the white gap in front of me and the resentment of not being hit after each burst from the German guns.

With no interest I heard a new, vaguely familiar sound that seemed to alter or obliterate the German fire. Explosions. Well, good. They can't miss with those . . . . But there was no whine, no whistling sound; just dry explosions, and they were behind me. I kept staring at the white gap in front of me, the gap that seemed not to get smaller, although something dark now swam into it. I bounced against something very hard and noticed, without interest, that it was a tree. A dark shape, not Ace, was crouched down and said, "Close, buddy. Ve-e-ery close." There were other trees, other people lying and crouching down, facing the direction I had just come from, men of our sister regiment, the 507th Parachute Infantry. We were in the woods, back in the Bois de Fragette, though I didn't recognize it. Farther in, the figures of the one hundred fifty or so men of the Second Battalion, 513th Parachute Infantry Regiment, sank to the ground and sprawled motionless where they lay. Next to me Ace ripped off his white, bullet-riddled curtain. "Good work, Gabel," I thought I heard him say. "I think you can make it back to your outfit a little later." My eyes couldn't focus on anything; everything swam in darks and lights. "Take a break," said Ace.

I tried to salute, but my right arm would not move. Ace strode into the woods and I felt as though I was balancing on a huge pile of feathers that was giving way. Like an open concertina placed on one end without support, I folded into myself but managed to fall on my back to keep my weapon from plowing into snow, dirt, and pine needles. Without interest I waited for the Germans to storm over us and plunge a bayonet into me. Without interest, without understanding, my open eyes saw two 60-mm mortars close by, close together, piles of mortar rounds between them, the gunners adjusting—the assistant gunners placing round after round into the tubes, barely waiting for the thump of the preceding round as it hurtled aloft.

A sergeant stood over me. "You hit?" he asked.

"Don't think so," I rasped, fighting to get the words out. "What do you want me to do?"

"Stay there. Move in when you can." He left. My eyes closed. Left and right I could hear rifle fire, 30-caliber machine gun fire, bazooka explosions. Overhead came the soft gurgling of 105 howitzers. DivArty was firing . . . and I thought that Ace was somewhere demanding an accounting of each round. There were shouts and I opened my eyes with some effort. Men were moving, but I wasn't interested. At last there was silence except for an occasional rifle shot and the gurgling of the 105s overhead.

I turned my head to the left and saw the mortar crews sitting on the ground, smoking. "Why don't you get some chow?" one of them said in my direction. I sat up, using a tree trunk for support, then used my legs to stem my back against the tree and hoisted myself up. I could feel my body ache and, although I still felt no interest in my situation, I was reassured by the aching, by the quiver in my legs, by the cold that was again asserting itself. "What are you guys?" I asked. "Five hundred and seventh," the trooper who had talked to me replied. "Go get some chow," he said again. "Company CP is about one hundred fifty yards that-away. Chow is close by." I nodded and stumbled off.

The stillness of the woods except for the steady burbling of the artillery rounds overhead seemed strangely comforting. Troopers of the 513th were lying singly or in clumps of twos and threes in the snow between the foxholes of the 507th. Their attitudes of almost unconscious exhaustion differentiated them from the men of the 507th as much as their lack of foxholes.

A hundred yards farther into the woods was the oversized hole of the company CP, the nest from where the collective mother hen—the company commander, executive officer, and first sergeant—could watch over the cold, miserable, thinned-out chicks of the rifle platoons on their semicircular perimeter. To the left of the command post, on stretchers and on the ground, were the wounded, waiting for evacuation. Next to them were eight or ten figures in white snowsuits—all that remained of the panzer grenadier group with those superb machine gun crews. White clumps of misery lay next to dark clumps of misery, neither caring who won or who lost.

I looked at them without interest and felt the meaning of the stillness without knowing. Even had I known that we had not suffered defeat because it is considered nearly impossible to disengage a unit that had been overrun by superior forces; even had I known that Ace calculated the German error of not having infantry on or close to their armor and never considered giving an order to surrender, though he could have done so with a clear conscience after the panzers had breached the line; even had I known that we had drawn the Germans into a fire trap where they were completely destroyed, I would not have had the energy to care.

13

Toward the Our River

The First Battalion seemed to be in reserve. At least the relative silence and an inactivity bordering on lethargy among the men made me think so. It had taken me the better part of a day and a lot of questions to find the battalion's sector, but I finally reported in to Peter White. He wasn't sure what day it was either.

When I started to explain where I had been for the past few days, Lieutenant White interrupted with a "Yeah, yeah—Jesus Christ! Nothing new in *your* getting lost. Now go get some sack time. We'll manage a little while longer without you." In spite of his words, though, White seemed glad to see me.

Jake had dug us a hole. It was not as fancy as our usual holes, and it had no cover except the shelter halfs for protection against snow and rain. "You dumb son of a bitch," Jake greeted me, "you'd lose your way in a phone booth. They had you MIA till we heard from the Second Bat S-2. We just managed to hold up the report. What the hell good are you, anyway?" I grinned. Jake was obviously relieved and very happy that I was back. He told me about the section and when I asked about Joe, he told me that Joe had been captured along with nearly one hundred of the battalion. Jake said that two rifle companies had been overrun, and he told me about Rosen.

Major David Rosen was the regimental S-3. I had only seen the man a few times, and what I saw of him I didn't like. He was a big wheel and he acted like one, but that didn't affect us because we were much too unimportant to ever get too close to the Godlike operations officer. Rosen, so the story went, had formally surrendered Companies B and C, or what was left of them. (I supposed if he had suggested that Company A surrender, John Spears would have blown his brains out, or at least placed him under arrest for court martial later.) He went into captivity, so the story went, with a jeep and trailer; in his trailer was, among other civilized accoutrements, his valpack with a Class A uniform. Most of the story I didn't believe, but the fact was that the two companies had been decimated, overrun, and many taken prisoner. I briefly remembered the Second Battalion being overrun—I did not remember anyone being taken prisoner and I wondered about that since I'd thought all of the 513th were of the same quality. But I was too tired to figure it out. Anyway, Joe had gone to Germany. Some of the men who had managed to get away had seen him taken. And now we were just supposed to sit here, wait for replacements, and help out Company A with some recon patrols now and then. But there wasn't much going on out there—and Company A wasn't much more than a platoon.

Chow on my first night back was strange. We waited in some large shell craters while Baier set up the marmite cans. So we were back to hot chow, which made Baier as happy as a Jewish grandmother serving chicken soup to the family on Friday night.

No one talked. Not even Otto, sitting in the crater with us. There were no more 81-mm mortars, and Otto, armed with one of the new M-3 submachine guns, had been out on patrols without rest. The stories were that Otto, ever since he lost his mortar, had been volunteering for patrols and had gone out even when he was finally told to sit down, shut up, and rest. From two of the patrols he had come back alone. He had been wounded, but he beat up the medic who tried to get him to the aid station. These stories I believed unreservedly. Otto and I shook hands and for the first time I saw Otto look sad and tired. Everyone looked sad and tired, even the wire men, who used to be pretty jaunty.

"Chow!" yelled Cohen, and three men got out of a crater.

"Aren't we supposed to be in reserve?" I asked.

Jake said, "I guess; I'm not really sure. But the Krauts can see us and they've been shooting, so we just act normal." The three men returned with their mess kits; three more went up. After our turn had come, we went to the S-2 hole, and Peter White held a little conference. This was another of his energy-saving ploys, combining chow with talks so we would not have to make an extra trip from our holes. And even this he tried to do as infrequently as possible.

Our lieutenant didn't know much more than Jake and began his "conference" with that revelation. In fact, he said, he knew less because he didn't even have any rumors. All he knew was that we were supposed to be screening the area in front of us so the Krauts wouldn't move in all of a sudden. He would scrape the patrols together and one of us would go out with them. He would scrape as few as he possibly could—but we had already figured that out. If it weren't for regimental S-2, there would probably be no patrols at all since we could pretty well see everything there was to see out there from our OPs.

The night passed without incident. Only Corps Artillery was firing its monotonous missions. As usual I slept like a log.

Morning chow was late and so we slept late. With the mess truck came a few more trucks with replacements.

We all sat in that nice big crater again—Otto, Frenchie, a couple of machine gunners, Jake, and I. We noticed a new man, a lieutenant in a brand-new field uniform. An officer replacement. An officer who looked very, *very* familiar. He examined us, who were in comparison just so many Willies and Joes out of a Mauldin cartoon, and he said, "Stay seated, men." That is what he said! We looked at one another to be sure we had heard right. White had said the same thing once when he dived into an S-2 hole where Jake and I were huddled during an artillery fracas. We nearly laughed ourselves sick while the rounds crashed into the CP. He had sounded exactly like Jake. But this now wasn't really an occasion for that kind of joke. "My name is Galicki," he said. "I'm the new machine gun platoon leader."

We were speechless. Galicki! The Great Galicki of C Stage fame. But who would have dreamed back there at the towers that we would meet him out here! We nodded to him, still speechless. "Any machine gunners here?" he asked snappily. The two gunners put up their hands as though they were back at C Stage, sitting in a circle around the Great Galicki, who had just asked them a question about a fine point in hand-to-hand combat during concurrent training at the towers. He nodded to them fraternally. Obviously he was groping for just the right form. He had been a superior instructor at the parachute school, and he was going to be a superior unit commander out here; but how to begin? "How're you people doin'?" he asked.

"All right, sir," someone said.

"I mean, what's going on? Is there any action?"

The word "action" sounded odd. "No, sir," said one of the machine gunners when no one else seemed to have a reply. Well, he's *their* officer so they might as well be the ones to talk to him, I thought.

Galicki began to get his stride. "Well, what do you *do* here?" he wanted to know.

"Oh, we just sort of lie around, I guess," said the gunner.

"Combat patrols?" Galicki asked, keen-eyed.

"Oh, no. No, sir." The gunner seemed horrified at the very question.

"You mean you don't go out and harass the Krauts?" The men became a little restless. No one answered because the question made no sense. Some people from other craters and holes started for chow in the customary groups of three. Galicki shifted his position, having fully adjusted to being on "the line" by now. He said, "Doesn't sound like the airborne I know!"

Jake and I got up to go back to our hole. We sat at its edge, leaning against a tree, and waited our turn for chow. Then an incredible thing happened. A man had climbed out of the "Galicki" crater and had made a gesture like a maitre d' in an expensive restaurant. He was followed by Galicki—and Galicki was followed by everyone else in the crater. Now Otto graciously waved the group to the chow line. The cooks stood transfixed as the group milled around the marmite cans. Eight men now stood by the chow containers. We grabbed our helmets and jumped into our hole. The cooks faded back into the trees as though the eight men were lepers.

The group stood around Galicki and we watched them, fascinated like cobras by a fakir's flute. Otto, holding his mess kit, cocked his head. There was not the slightest doubt in my mind that he was timing the sequence of German observation reports and fire commands. After minutes that seemed like hours, the little group in front of the marmite cans sprinted apart, each man toward his foxhole or a crater. Galicki, who had filled his mess kit, stood alone and utterly bewildered, balancing his kit in his left hand and his steaming canteen cup in his right. The whole fantastic scene had looked like something out of a Disney cartoon—the group materializing there and then suddenly vanishing, leaving Pluto or Donald Duck standing bewildered all by himself in an empty space.

At that instant the hissing whoosh of an 88 pressed us down into our hole. In the fraction of a second between explosion and the arrival of a second round—in that fraction of a second before our eyes disappeared below the rim of our foxhole—I saw Galicki's mess kit and canteen cup fly high in the air, eggs, pancakes, and coffee clear against a gray sky, and Galicki himself sliding along the ground, presumably toward a crater. It was the last time I ever saw that lieutenant.

The baffled German forward observer ceased fire instantly. He would have great difficulty with his battery commander explaining his hallucination.

Only once afterward was this incident ever alluded to. When we were back in our comfortable mess tent in Châlons-sur-Marne, all of us now NCOs, sitting around for a midmorning "discussion" over coffee, Captain Rockett joined us and made a conversational reference to it. When no one seemed to be able to remember the incident, the subject was closed permanently.

It had snowed and the sun came out. The tall, thick pines of the Ardennes, heavily laden with snow and glistening in the sun, looked like a scene from a particularly artistic Christmas card. We were told during breakfast that sunny day that the snow blanket also covered the fields south of the Bastogne-Marche Road in the area of Flamierge, an area now completely under the control of Patton's Third Army and well in the rear of the new front line. The heavy snow blanket on those fields had covered up all the bodies. QM Graves Registration was unable to find them. And so Graves Registration had asked the 513th to lend them some of the survivors to point out where those bodies were and to help with recovery. I was supposed to go with Company F and others of the Second Battalion.

The recovery detail for the Second Battalion sector climbed into two deuce-and-a-halfs. Ten other trucks—empty except for the driver and his assistant—followed behind as our convoy moved out. I sat next to the four men from Company F. They seemed to be the only survivors able to work. There were two or three others I dimly remembered from Headquarters Second, some from other line companies, and two Graves Registration men. Even at that we had plenty of room to lounge or curl up on the truck benches. No one spoke. I tried to sleep, but the trip was not long enough, or the trucks were too noisy in the deep snow, or I had had more sleep than usual the night before, or something. Sleep did not come to anyone on this ride.

We stopped and as we dismounted I saw that we were almost at the exact spot where I had joined the Second Platoon of Company F. A feeling of dread came over me. To my right was the rise in the ground where Jake and I had built that masterpiece of a foxhole. It must still be there, I thought, and was tempted to walk over to it. "OK, you guys; over here!" shouted a platoon sergeant who had been on the other truck. He was the only NCO from the 513th, and I had never seen him before. We gathered around him.

"We're gonna drop you guys off in the same general area you were in during the Flamierge thing and you help these people from the QM to find everybody. They'll tell you what they want done." The sergeant seemed tired. He looked around and said, "I'll be with their NCO, sort of in the middle of the line; in case you want me. Just do what they tell you." Then, to the QM people, "All right. You take charge." It made no difference to us who was in charge. It seemed to me, though, that we were somehow glad that our own sergeant was out of it.

"This Company F sector?" asked one of the QM men; when someone nodded, the QM man shouted, "OK, those men from Company F over here." As the five of us gathered around him, the convoy moved on, leaving three trucks behind with us. "OK," the QM man began again. "I'm gonna spread you guys out and you just walk over the ground you been on before and where you remember you saw somebody fall or you recognize anything else that tells you where the bodies are, shake 'em loose from the snow. Kinda move 'em together, your buddies in one pile and the Krauts in another. We'll have the trucks pick 'em up after you get 'em stacked. You get half an hour for noon chow. OK, move out."

We could have told him that we hadn't come under fire until we were almost a mile out, but no one seemed to have the energy to mention it. So we walked.

I don't remember much of my walk except my feeling of dread. There weren't too many bodies, not even where the *Nebelwerfer* had gotten us, until we changed direction to take the track where we had gone toward the wood with the 507th in it. I don't remember the way the recovery was organized except that we seemed to cross the terrain at different angles, the trucks widely dispersed and slowly moving with us in one line, dark against the brilliant white snow. I saw a rifle stuck in the snow, barrel down, and seemed to remember it. Beyond, toward the next man on the detail, were other rifles stuck in the snow. Then I saw the little white mounds that were the bodies, and I scraped the snow from them before moving them. I did that with a few others—maneuvered them into a neat row, found a rifle or a stack of equipment to mark the spot, and went on to the next group, not exactly knowing how I knew where they would be.

But then I found a large group, and things became very strange. The feeling of dread was suddenly gone. I moved from man to man, scraped the snow off each, moved them by dragging them by their frozen legs or arms—and I talked to them. I griped at them. I complained that they made very hard work for me. I explained to them that they should not have frozen in such awkward positions, making it difficult to move them and even more difficult to stack them neatly. I worked and worked, laying them out side by side. I propped my weapon, webbing, and helmet next to one, leaving a space there for me. I worked on and was particularly angry when I found three or four Germans that had to be stacked on a separate pile. Then I came to a trooper I thought I had seen falling. He was on his elbows and knees, his rifle and helmet next to him. I tipped him over and he fell to his side with a thump, elbows and knees drawn up like a fetus. He was big and blond, and I remembered his face from somewhere. The Milestone Club in London? Right? He was the guy who wouldn't get out of the shower and just kept me waiting there. And time in London was at a premium. "Just hold your goddamn horses, little trooper," he had said. He was one hell of a big man. Should have been a mortar man. I worked and worked to drag him toward my pile, and I called him all sorts of names. Then a whistle shrilled across the field and a faraway voice shouted, "Chow. Take a break!"

I stopped dragging the big trooper, walked to the space I had left for myself in the middle of my pile, and lay down on it. I carefully looked into the face of the man on my left and then into the face of the man on my right. I didn't know either of them. Their eyes were open, lids partially down, and they looked as if they would doze off any time now, like good infantrymen on a break. I wasn't sad, but I was puzzled. Why them? Why not me? Why should they lie here and not get up, and why should I lie here and be able to get up? It was baffling. I griped at them some more as I dug my K-ration cheese out of my pocket. "Half-an-hour break for noon chow after all that work," I griped. By now I was pretty sure that I was really dead—but able to talk and move because I was in charge of all these men and had to baby them along for a time. I took a bite of my cheese and out of habit offered it first to the man on my left and then to the man on my right before I remembered that their status was somewhat different from mine. I snorted and continued eating my cheese, selfishly grateful that no one wanted any. The feeling was exactly the same as when I had offered my cheese to Calloway right here in this general area and he hadn't needed any.

I propped my head and shoulders against the pile of my webbing on top of which rested my helmet. The back of my head was resting against the helmet, and I should have felt its camouflage netting through my wool knit cap. I should have felt the cold seeping in. But I didn't.

From my slightly elevated position I looked again from left to right along the row of men from the 513th. I resented their status. They had fallen and remained on the ground while I had had to continue struggling through the goddamn snow with that goddamn Ace driving everyone on and on. Now I had to work and work, babying the same guys who were lying there not doing a goddamn thing. Well, the hell with it! I wasn't going to have any more of this crap. I would simply stay right here after chow and not get up. Let someone else be in charge of this group. I was already covered with snow; I looked exactly like everyone else, and no one would know the difference. I settled back and closed my eyes.

It was rather nice to be dead. I felt that this was the exact spot in all the world where I really belonged—a feeling not unlike the one I had had when on the last evening of D Stage at Fort Benning, the First Battalion marched to Lawson Field for its qualifying night jump, bayonets fixed, singing the paratrooper song. Then I was in the middle of my Company A rifle platoon, not wanting to be anywhere else in the world.

The only difference was that then I was inordinately proud, and now I was dead.

The whistle shrilled again, and the faraway voice echoed across the white expanse, "OK, on your feet! Back to work!" A command to be obeyed by those who could.

The habit of obedience got my body on its feet, cursing the whistle and the command. The bastards just couldn't leave well enough alone!

I worked some more until I was finally done. There was almost a platoon of them in a more or less tight formation. Most of them were stacked two rows high, and only those frozen in excessively awkward positions were in a single row—all except the goddamn character from the Milestone Club and me.

Some QM trucks lumbered up and the troopers from Company F jumped down from one of them. The trucks had apparently gone from left to right, picking up the troopers and their piles as they went. It seemed to me there were bodies on two of the trucks. The Company F troopers stood next to me and looked at my pile. It must have been much bigger than any they had been working on. They looked at faces and said nothing.

Two QM men came over to us and one of them asked, "Dog tags on all of 'em?" I nodded, though I wasn't really sure. The QM men seemed impressed by my pile. The one who had spoken to me addressed the five of us. "You guys take a break now. We'll load 'em for you." He looked at the two other QM men above him on the truck bed and said, "OK; comin' up."

The two QM men on the ground grabbed the first of my men from the top of the stack by shoulders and legs and swung him three times to gain momentum, chanting, "One—two—three—*heave*," and on the last word let go of the man who flew through the air and landed on top of the other bodies on the truck. The two QM men above dragged him to the far end, stacked him, and got ready for the next. "One—two—three—*heave*," said the QM men on the ground; this time I could see me flying through the air and landing on top of the bodies in the truck.

We of the 513th had put our webb equipment back on, our weapons at their customary places dangling from our shoulders as we stood and watched. I don't know which one of us spoke, but one of us said in a very matter-of-fact voice, "You do that once more and I'll blow your goddamn heads off."

For a moment no one moved. Then the two QM men on the truck slowly climbed down and together with their two buddies on the ground carefully lifted the next man up and placed him gently on the truck. Each man in turn was gently lifted and placed on the truck. It was going to take a long time and so we helped after all. When we finally finished, we got on the truck for the ride back.

It was dusk when the convoy halted, and from one of the trucks came the command, "All Five-thirteenth dismount." Those of us alive climbed down, and the trucks carried the rest away.

It was dark when I reported in. I hit the sack and slept long and deep and without dreams.

After another day or two we moved again. It had become increasingly easier to tear ourselves away from dug-in positions because our foxholes had finally become just that—holes. Although Jake and I still carried on our verbal parody of suburbia, the exercise had become perfunctory. The old banter was gone. Even Gloria De Haven had lost her appeal, and Hollywood had faded into indistinct impressions of a long-ago experience. The bubbling letters from my mother still reached me, although in bunches and sporadically. So did letters from Ruth. But their power to reassure me that there were really people like that going to places like Mocambo or Trocadero or the Farmers Market and returning to pearl-gray luxury to sleep in warm bedrooms—that power had been dissipated.

I grabbed my gear and submachine gun and tacked onto the tail end of the machine gun platoon, or what was left of it. There were only two guns and for some reason they were not attached to the companies. The battalion moved out in single file, each man keeping his five-yard interval. Gloria De Haven was gone; Ruth was gone. There was no song and there were no images, just the tall machine gunner in front of me and snow in the five-yard space between us.

We moved out of the woods and over a field. The snow stifled all sound except the soft clink of belt grommets against trigger housings, mess kits inside musette bags, ammunition belts shifting in the boxes carried by the ammo bearers, pistol butts rubbing against canteens—the soft sounds of a tactical infantry column on the move.

Faraway on the right the rattling of a half-truck intruded and came nearer, finally into my peripheral vision. It pulled ahead to where I could see it without turning my head and I watched it, though with little interest. It stopped and three men got out. I recognized the tallest as the assistant division commander, Brigadier General John L. Whitelaw. He said something to the others and then walked alone toward our column. I had seen him only once before, after a jump on maneuvers in England when he had stopped me and asked what my mission was. Now he seemed to be coming straight for me. Without interest, I wondered what the hell he wanted this time.

But he walked next to the gunner ahead of me. He was wearing a parka of the kind I had seen tankers wear except that his was fur-lined. He said to the gunner in a kindly voice, "How're you doing, son?"

Without moving his head, without looking around, the machine gunner clearly and sharply spat out, "Fuck you."

The malevolence and contempt packed into those two words took my breath away. The general stopped as though he had been hit between the eyes by a sledgehammer, and for a second I expected him to fall down like an ox in a slaughterhouse. But he turned and walked rapidly back to his half-track, got in, and was driven away. It took all that time before I could rasp to the gunner in front of me, "Do you know who that was?"

"Hell, yes," he replied. After a pause he asked, "What's the bastard gonna do—shoot me? Put me in a nice warm jail?"

I have never been able to consider this incident a breach of discipline. No general, no prince, no king, no president has any business walking next to a tactical column of infantry under those circumstances. Any effort on the part of an outsider to "inspire the troops" at any place and any time where combat infantry treads its bloody path calls onto itself the fury and disdain of those infantrymen. In two words, the machine gunner had told the general to mind his own business, which was, is, and will be the exercise of his intellect within the framework of his mission. His job is to exercise his intellect to make absolutely certain that his assigned mission is carried out without spilling one more drop of blood than the mission requires, even at the risk of not getting a medal, a star, or his picture on the cover of *Time*. His is the same as the duty that infantry officers like Ace Miller, Morris Anderson, Irwin Edwards, John Spears, and Peter White live by and die by.

I was a little sorry to see this well-meaning but misguided assistant division commander receive the infantryman's cold contempt usually reserved for the heroic posturing of military egomaniacs. He was, after all, imitating a type, and much less so than many who affect the pearl-handled revolvers, hand-grenades-on-harness, and steely looks of the headliners they emulate. But in the 513th Parachute Infantry Regiment we were spoiled by the type of officer whom Clausewitz described as ideal. Lesser men were well advised to stay away from us.

Like a sick, olive-drab centipede, the remnants of the First Battalion continued to plod along an obscure trail, pounding the new snow hard under its boots.

The S-2 scout section, intact again with Frenchie, Herrick, and me, plodded behind the lead company. I had dimly wondered why we were behind the lead company but had no intention of asking anyone lest someone get the idea of sending scouts forward. I assumed that Company A had its scouts out, which, after all, was normal during an approach march. But why Lieutenant White, Jake, and the S-3 section were with the battalion commander in front of the company I had trouble understanding.

The regiment was generally moving north and east. We passed Flamierge (some five miles northwest of Bastogne) and went on until we struck the Ourthe River, where we turned to Houffalize and trudged east to the Our River with the bunkers of the Siegfried Line beyond its far bank. The total distance from the Bois de Fragette was between twenty-five and thirty miles. It took us about two and a half weeks to cover the distance. Neither the weather nor the occasional savage resistance of Germans determined to hamper our advance were of much help to us.

As usual we had no idea where we were going or why. We didn't know we were again on the attack. We had been told only that we were moving to a new position. I was not particularly interested in our location. It was nice back here behind Company A. The path was level and easy to walk. We had been told not to talk, so the only sounds were the soft chafing and clinking of our equipment and an occasional distant explosion, too distant for me to wonder what or where it was.

Suddenly the column stopped. When it did not move on immediately, the men began to sit down as though on order. First the men with heavy equipment, the mortar men and the machine gunners; then, one by one, the riflemen until only a few eccentrics were standing.

A murmur rippled back along the column: "Gabel, up forward." The scout section stood up. "Not you guys," I hissed; they instantly sat down again. I walked along the column until I passed the Third Platoon where someone said, "Better stay in close; we're in a minefield"; so I continued my walk in the center of the column, whispering, "Excuse me—pardon—sorry," as I stumbled over the outstretched legs of Company A. I couldn't understand why we should be in a minefield with Battalion Headquarters leading the column, but I didn't dwell on the problem.

The command group presented an odd tableau. All were standing around except for one figure lying in the snow and one, the battalion commander, Alton Taylor, walking in short, jerky steps back and forth. Four steps in one direction, four steps in another, like a nervous, caged hyena. I walked toward Jake, who was standing next to the man on the ground. It was Tony Mora and he was moaning softly. I looked at Jake and he said, "Stepped on a shoe mine. Go see Whitey."

I went to Lieutenant White, who was standing at one end of the colonel's eight-step cage. Next to White stood a German NCO and next to him two of Company A's riflemen. The German was a first sergeant, and I made an appreciative clucking sound to the riflemen. They winked in acknowledgment.

"We need to find out about this minefield and what else is out there," said Lieutenant White. "See what you can do."

I nodded and walked over to the prisoner but spoke to the Company A men first. "How'd you get him?"

The men were scouts who had been walking "point." "Popped out of that hole," one of them replied, pointing over his shoulder. "He leveled a Schmeisser at me but then dropped it." I marveled. The German could have cut him in half with a burst of that Schmeisser before our man could get off one shot, yet there he had stood with his M-1. As though he had read my mind, the Company A man added, "I was scared shitless and was about to drop my rifle when he dropped the Schmeisser. Don't tell nobody."

I grinned and could have hugged him. "Any more Krauts out there?"

"Not that we could see."

I turned toward the German. Taylor, who had reached the far end of his eight-step cage, wheeled around and ran at the prisoner. He grabbed the German by his overcoat lapels and screamed, "Talk. Talk, goddamn you!" As we stood frozen in shock, he slapped the German twice across the face, saying, "Goddamn it, goddamn it!" It was my first experience with panic in our regiment, panic not only on the part of an officer but on the part of my battalion commander. The fact was hard to assimilate, but there it was, stark and awful. Our commander was terrified beyond control.

A feeling of revulsion and contempt came over me. A crack had been made in my collective idol, the officer corps. It would never be wholly repaired.

Lieutenant White stepped between the colonel and the prisoner and grabbed the colonel's arms. "Sir," he hissed, "sir, take it easy. We'll take care of it." Then, turning to me, he said, "Get him away from here. Go to work."

We moved the German first sergeant aside and I told him to take his hands off his head. Then I apologized. He smiled wryly and shrugged his shoulders. Perhaps in his long Army career he had seen this kind of exhibition before; but I doubted it. "Has he been searched?" I asked the men from Company A.

"Yes. Nothing," was the answer.

"Unit?" I asked the German.

He shrugged politely and said, "I'm sorry, but I am not in a position to say . . . ." Very polite.

Equally polite, I answer, "Doch, eben gerade." That is one of those untranslatable phrases that only a German could use. In this case, it meant, "But that is precisely the position you're in." From one of the long folds of his overcoat sleeves there protruded a white sliver, just a fraction of a millimeter. How many times had we been told about those overcoats during our training sessions? I reached for that white sliver and pulled a piece of transparent paper out of the sleeve fold. The German paled, his smile gone. It took no genius to tell that I had a map overlay in my hands that was of some importance. There were company and battalion symbols, boundaries, "goose eggs," weapons emplacements, and other goodies. "Once more," I said, trying to look grave, as though I could tell at a brief glance exactly what that overlay meant, "what unit are you from?" He told me and I wrote it down. Then I walked over to White, who stood silently next to the colonel, now sitting in abject resignation on the ground.

I handed him the overlay and he said, "Hot damn. Where was it?" I told him. He shook his head, then called a runner. "Get this to regiment. Ask if you can wait for any word they might have for us because we can't handle this thing. Then shag ass back here." To me he said, "Settle down. I'll call you." He went to the radioman and I went to Jake and Tony.

Jake was standing in the same position over Tony in which I had found him. Tony was moaning louder, doubled over, his overcoat covering him like a blanket. "When he stepped on it, it jumped right up to his bellybutton," Jake whispered. The mine had gotten Tony the way it was intended to get a soldier. Tony's pain was so great that he could not scream. Doubled over and holding his stomach, he rolled from side to side.

I was furious. "Where's the doctor? Where's the medic?" I almost yelled at Jake.

"Doc looked at him, said to keep him comfortable."

I ran the few steps to Company A Headquarters where the company medic was sitting on his helmet. "Tony's got to have some morphine. Give him a shot," I said.

The medic looked up wearily. "Ain't no morphine in the whole battalion no more."

"Can't you do something?" I asked desperately.

"I wouldn't be sittin' here if I could," the medic replied; I was ashamed.

"Where's the doc?" I asked again.

"Tryin' to get back to regiment for some stuff. Now get the hell off my ass, Gabel." The medic was clearly suffering as much as we were, perhaps more. There had been others along the column he could not help. Not even a battalion aid station could do anything for this type of injury.

I went back to Jake and told him about the doc. Jake called White. "Sir, I'd like to go back along the line to see if I can get some morphine from the doc. He's at regiment and I can probably get it here faster than he can."

"OK, Jake. Don't you step on one of those goddamn things." Jake sprinted off and I took my place next to Tony.

"Gabel?" Tony moaned as he rolled a bit and looked up.

"Yeah, Tony. Take it easy, now. Jake is going after some morphine and then we'll fix you up for evacuation."

Tony rolled again. "Can't stand the pain," he whispered. I felt that whisper cutting into me, felt helpless, useless, weak.

Back and forth Tony rolled, doubled up, moaning. "No, no . . . God, please. I can't stand the pain," he whispered in that awful, spine-chilling whisper. He was on his back, looking up at me. I couldn't see his face clearly for some reason, only that it was waxen, like the dead faces I had looked into so many times. One of his hands clutched at my leg. "I can't stand any more," he whispered. "Shoot me, Gabel; oh, please, please shoot me." The words pounded like a huge, soft mallet, pounded the breath from me. I wanted to run, to disappear into thin air. "Please, please," Tony urged. It would be like a morphine shot . . . like a morphine shot, went through my mind. The only way to help . . . . Perhaps I only imagined it, perhaps it never happened; but my hand reached toward my holster and the .45 I had gotten from that wounded mortar man near Flamierge. Help Tony . . . help Tony . . someone do *something*. . . . But my hand never reached the weapon. Then Tony whispered, "Oh, God . . . thank you, God; thank you." He stopped rolling; he sank back as though on a soft bed, his face relaxed. I thought, "Oh, God, You finally stepped in. What kept You so long? Now, please . . . stay a while." I looked at Tony to watch God at work. Again Tony said, this time in his normal voice, "Thank you, God. Oh, thank you." This time I could see Tony's face clearly. He was smiling, asleep, the pain gone; God was doing a fine job.

"Gabel," Lieutenant White called. I looked around. White was standing next to the battalion executive officer, who seemed to have materialized shortly after the CO had been restrained by the S-2. I had only perceived him, felt that he was talking to the staff officers, but didn't know or care what went on there. I was still rooted to the ground next to Tony. Lieutenant White walked up to me and gently took my arm. "Come on, Kurt. He'll be all right." I was being led away, toward the people in the command group. I was still thinking of what else God was going to do for Tony, how He was going to get Tony back to the regimental clearing station. But anyway, He was really at work . . . .

"We're going to have to move the battalion," Lieutenant White said. "Do you think you can get that Kraut sergeant to show you where the mines are?"

"Sure," I said and walked over to the German. I was happy to be put to work, to be given a reprieve from the unspeakable horror that had rooted me, body and soul, to that damnable spot. Yes, Tony would be OK now.

"I need Herrick and Frenchie and some engineer tape," I said to White, who either had had the same idea at the same time or who understood instantly. I went back to the German. "You are going to show me where the mines are and how we can get through," I informed him.

He said, "I don't know where they are."

"In that case," I said, "you and I are in a lot of trouble because we're going to take a little walk." Herrick and Frenchie had appeared as though they had been stamped out of the ground. Both had rolls of white engineer tape.

"OK," I said to them, "the Kraut and I will start walking and you, Herrick, will lay the tape where we walk. If we run out, Frenchie will get some more."

Herrick looked dubious. "You know what you're doin'?"

"Hell, yes," I said, and Herrick shrugged.

"OK . . . ," he said, still doubtful. Though I was not conscious of it, for the first time someone was trusting me as I trusted Jake or Lieutenant White or the exec.

"Let's go," I said to the German. I handed my submachine gun to Lieutenant White, asking, "Would you hold this for me?" He nodded.

One of the Company A riflemen asked, "Want us to go along?"

"Nah, thanks anyway," I said. Then to the German, who had put his hands on top of his head again, "Take your hands down." I drew my pistol. "We're just going for a walk. Walk ahead of me and walk slow. Go ahead. Now."

We moved out of the little clearing we had been standing in, a U-shaped clearing that perhaps started the minefield along the lower bow of the U where the lead company was. Ahead lay a snow-covered field and then another woods. The sergeant stopped, looked, angled toward the right. I could see two small triangular flags with skull and crossbones on them. I knew now that we were safe. In fact, I never had the slightest doubt about our safety and felt very sheepish later when White made a to-do over a "heroic" act. If there was a hero, it was Herrick who did not know that we were perfectly safe, who stayed close behind me expecting to get blown apart just like Tony. "Did they forget to take the flags with them?" I asked the sergeant with laughter.

"That's what I was checking on," he replied. "They were in too much of a hurry to get out of here to get the markers."

We walked on, making a jog here and there between the flags. I was looking up now and began to get an overview as I followed the little yellow pennants. There were enough that had not been picked up to give a pretty clear indication of the breach, and I almost thought that I could do this job without the sergeant.

"Where are they supposed to be now?" I asked conversationally, hoping that, in disgust at the sloppiness of his unit, he would forget that I had pretended to study and understand his overlay.

"Outpost in those woods," he said, "but the unit is supposed to be in the next one after this. We were supposed to have been relieved, but now I don't know what's going to happen." What a way to interrogate, I thought with some pride. He was responding soldier to soldier. He was responding to my Hamburg dialect, and he was talking as though we were going back to his unit where he would chew out those sloppy recruits who failed to pick up all the little yellow pennants. It was just a walk, as I had known it would be. Not only that, but I felt that we could walk straight up to their OP without being fired upon—maybe even get that entire outpost to surrender. Later, when Herrick and I talked about it, he had said, "You goddamn son of a bitch, *now* you tell me!"

"Well, here we are," said the German, kicking at the last little pennant. "The whole thing is stupid, anyway."

I agreed, feeling a little sorry for him. "OK, Horseface," I yelled to Herrick, no longer feeling the need for talking softly; "let's go on back." We returned along the tape, and I told Lieutenant White of my conversation with the sergeant. White made some notes, sent the German and the Company A men back, and walked over to the exec. I told Frenchie to stand by in case one of us was needed to walk the tape, then Herrick and I went back to Tony. It was getting dark now. Jake had settled down on his helmet beside Tony.

"How is he?" Herrick asked cheerfully, happy to be back at the CP.

"He's dead," Jake said softly. Now I saw that the overcoat was drawn over Tony's head. So that's how it was, I thought. That's how Tony had been evacuated. We sat down next to Jake and said nothing.

Lieutenant White came over. "OK, you guys," he said, "we're going to settle in for the night and leave first thing in the morning. Get some sack time."

Jake pointed to where he wanted us and we dug in. I dug a shallow hole, both because it had become routine to scrape the ground whenever we came to a prolonged halt, and also to get rid of the snow. There was no need for a real foxhole because I was convinced there would be no mortar or artillery fire. I slept without dreams. Dreams would come much later.

Jake shook me. "We're moving out." It was still dark, but my watch said that it was morning. Everyone was up already, munching K-rations and drinking powdered coffee. Some men were moving around and a tactical column was taking shape.

"Why didn't you wake me?" I mumbled.

"You needed the sleep," Jake said.

"Where's the Horseface?"

"I sent him up with Frenchie. Come on, let's say goodbye to Tony." The column started to move. We stepped over to where Tony lay. I lifted the overcoat from his face. It was not really the Tony we had known, just a waxen stranger whose real self was elsewhere, safe, evacuated.

"Goodbye, Tony. See you somewhere . . . ," one of us said. Then up we walked to the command group and took our place in the column. Soon the battalion hit its stride; we were really stepping out, our feet occasionally tromping on the white tape.

Ahead I saw Company A enter the woods, two rifle platoons up, one back. No shots were fired. The battalion command group entered the woods. "Nothing," shouted one of the platoon leaders. Quickly, routinely, a perimeter was established and the CP dug in. Herrick got out the squad cooker and lit it. We filled our canteen cups and one after the other heated our second cup of coffee.

14

To Niederwiltz, Luxembourg

Digging in this mid-January evening on the way to the Our River was relatively easy, maybe because there were a lot of pine needles this time. Though we couldn't get to the engineer shovels, which were well guarded now, digging went smoothly and fast; our hole was almost as nice as the one we had dug at the edge of the Bois de Fragette.

Just before supper Jake and I were called over to Lieutenant White's hole at the CP. "Let's take a little walk," said our S-2; we went to the edge of the woods where the rifle companies were. "Get your glasses out," said White, and we took our binoculars from their cases. In front of us was a white field, turning gray in the dusk, and beyond that another wood. "Look out at the woods and as far right as that little protrusion," White directed. "Find the house?" We nodded. "Regiment says that's a Kraut battalion CP," White explained. "I think they're full of shit, but I want to know just what the hell it *is*. Check it tonight. Questions?"

We swept our glasses back and forth over the terrain in front of us. Jake said, "Do the companies know anything about that? Can they tell us anything?"

"Christ, Dalton! We just *got* here," answered Peter White, annoyed. "There's no contact out there and before we screw around with patrols I want to know what's in that house. Any more questions?"

"What makes 'em think it's a CP?"

"Spooks from G-Two. More questions?"

"No, sir."

"OK, when you guys get through here, have some chow and then get ready. And just for the record: I want Gabel and Frenchie to go. Maybe Herrick. You, Jake, stay home. Clear?"

"Clear, sir," mumbled Jake. Our S-2 nodded and walked away.

Jake mouthed an obscenity and looked through the glasses again. White was a mind reader. He was also a professional and a good S-2. For this type of reconnaissance mission he was using exactly the right tools: scout observers. That's what the scout observers were for. An S-2 section leader had no business out there unless no one else was available. White would go himself, as he often did; but this was a very specific, pinpointed mission, and there was simply no need for him or for Jake to go. Need determined what White did. Any unnecessary exposure, movement, work, or other expenditure of energy irritated him. In his way, he was like Captain Spears whose Company A, my good old Company A, was watching over this gray-white field. There was nothing that Company A could not do when the need was there. But John Spears was furiously intolerant of anything that expended valuable blood or energy to no purpose. Perhaps that is why I liked Peter White. He was the staff equivalent of John Spears.

There was nothing to indicate the presence of the enemy across the field or near the house. For a moment I thought that perhaps all they wanted to know was whether the field was mined, but I was instantly ashamed of the thought. White was incapable of any concealment or duplicity; had he suspected a mine field, he would probably have led the patrol himself. He certainly would have said, "I think there are mines out there. Good luck." Neither were there dark depressions indicating *Schützenlöcher* (German foxholes), or mounds, or anything else unusual. Although the Germans were good at camouflage, they weren't perfect. My own question was what was in those trees. But the house was in *front* of the trees, and there certainly was nothing in front of the house; so how could it be a battalion command post?

"Bet there's nothing out there," I said to Jake.

Jake kept on looking through his glasses. "Well, let's go eat," he finally said. We walked back to the CP area.

We had hot C-rations and hot water for coffee. Jake briefed Frenchie and Herrick while we ate. There were no questions and no discussion.

When it was dark, we headed out. Frenchie and I were armed only with pistols; Herrick had my submachine gun. The only real concessions we made to our "scouting and patroling" training were the wool knit caps we were wearing, and the only reason we wore no helmets was that we hated them. Here was an opportunity to leave them behind without getting chewed out, and so we did.

Although the S-2 had already told the company of our mission, we passworded and countersigned our way through the line company, told one of the squad leaders that we'd be back through in an hour or so, and started across the field. We were looking for track or tire marks as we went along, but it had just snowed and the field was as unruffled as a new bed sheet. Just before we got to the house, we came across a little copse that had looked like a part of the main forest from our lines. There were four or five empty holes in that little island of trees, and we became cautious. Frenchie picked up a German gas mask and dangled it in my direction. I nodded and Herrick nodded so Frenchie put it down again. He and I drew our pistols.

We were very close to the house now. It was of sturdy stone with a low stone wall around it. The gate was open. No sound could be heard. Only our boots made small crunching noises on the snow as we made our way forward. I went through the gate quickly and squatted up against the inside of the wall, looking left and right as I did so; then I waved to Frenchie, who took a seat next to me. Herrick followed immediately. The courtyard was empty.

A barn and a stable building stood with doors wide open. Frenchie and I checked them and Herrick waited, his head constantly going from left to right and back again. There was no sign of anyone or anything, not even another gas mask (which seemed to be a favorite German throw-away item, just like ours).

We walked around the house, involuntarily in Indian fashion. Nothing.

We found only one door and we tried it. It was unlocked and opened silently. We entered in the usual manner and remained still, our backs to the wall on either side of the door. We were in a square entry hall onto which several doors faced, and through the bottom crack of one of them shone a light. We strained to listen but could hear no sound. The three of us had the same feeling; there was no one in the house except in that room. I clicked off the safety of my .45 and heard Frenchie do the same.

I went to the door, pleased that I made no noise. Frenchie and Herrick followed. Now we could see that the door was not entirely closed. I looked at my companions and they nodded. I kicked the door open, jumped inside and to the left, and crouched down, back against the wall. Herrick burst in and sprinted to the far right corner of the room, the submachine gun level and rigid, its stock pressed to his right hip as he pointed into the center of the room. Frenchie followed and stood to the right of the door, pistol level and steady.

It was a school-approved entry. We had exploded into that room by the book, and our guns were now effectively covering a little old lady of perhaps eighty who was sitting in an easy chair and trying to read by the light of a kerosene lamp.

Her easy chair was before a tile stove. The back of the chair was turned so that I could see her left profile from where I was standing. More annoyed than startled, she turned her head toward the commotion behind her. Herrick tipped the barrel of his submachine gun straight up at the ceiling, like a little boy who has just been caught doing something unspeakably naughty. Frenchie clicked his safety back on, holstered his weapon, and stuttered an apology in French. I still held my pistol in my sagging hand as I stared stupidly at that annoyed, lovely little old lady in her long black dress and her knitted black shawl. I can think of only three other times in my life when I was as mortified as I was at that moment.

I holstered my gun and told Frenchie, "Say we're terribly sorry."

Frenchie said, "I already did that"; his voice sounded as if it were about to crack, like the voice of an adolescent. But he said something else in French, at which the lady slowly shook her head.

As though we all had the same idea at once, we assembled around our lady so that she didn't have to move her chair to see us. We must have been a sight because she laughed suddenly and again shook her head slowly as she looked at each of us in turn. At her laugh, charming and forgiving, we managed a grateful but still embarrassed smile.

"Frenchie," I said and noticed that I whispered, "tell her that we need to ask some questions and make sure that she knows we're just trying to do our job." As Frenchie translated, she turned toward him, lifting her head slightly and lowering her lids. She looked really regal.

"Are the Germans anywhere around here?"

"No. They were here, but they left."

"When did they leave?"

"Yesterday in the afternoon."

"Were they in this house?"

"Yes."

"Would it be all right if we looked through the rooms?"

"Certainly." I nodded to Herrick and he left.

"Please tell me about the kind of soldiers who were in this house and what equipment they had." Frenchie seemed to have trouble with the word for "equipment," but our lady knew just what kind of information we were after. There had been a captain and a lieutenant and several men with telephones and radios. The captain left in a car and the lieutenant left on a motorcycle with a sidecar. In the woods had been some half-tracks and soldiers, perhaps a hundred, and she had to say they were all trying to be very polite . . . she smiled a gentle rebuke that indicated, "Not like *some* people I know."

She said they were all in a hurry and pointed in the direction they had departed. She explained that the highway was out there.

Herrick came back. He had found only a German newspaper and a canteen in the house. They had been very neat. "Frenchie, tell the lady that we could not win the war without her," I said—and I meant it. Frenchie was delighted to oblige and, by the time it took him to translate that one sentence, I surmised that he conveyed the fraternal and respectful greetings of the president and the people of the United States as well as the degree of esteem in which they held Madame. He bowed. Madame was clearly delighted. "Is there anything we can do for the lady?" I asked.

Frenchie turned red at her answer and translated, "Yes. Knock the next time we call." We left, closing the door softly behind us.

Although there was no danger, we walked back the way we had come, spread out in the pattern that had become habitual. We walked in the glow of that lovely grandmother back there, and I was annoyed when our LP broke the spell with his challenge. We identified ourselves, continued on our way, and repeated the exercise when we reached the squad's position.

At the CP I gave Peter White a playback of our misadventure and verbatim dialogue with Madame, and he chuckled (I almost said "giggled") while making notes. We told him about the holes in the little copse, gave him the German newspaper, and showed him on a map what direction our little grandmother had indicated that the Germans had taken on the highway angling northeast. "Not bad," said Peter White with that almost giggle while Jake stood by with a broad grin. "Now you guys go to bed. You've got one helluva lot of work to do tomorrow." Peter White clearly liked his job.

Before breakfast the next morning, the S-2 briefed us that we had lost contact with the enemy, who were now withdrawing from the Ardennes to their previous positions within the German border, positions they had held along the Siegfried Line east of the Our River before their last desperate push of mid-December that resulted in the Bulge. Regiment was frantic to know where they were. This time regiment did not want the battalion to move from its position until reconnaissance pinpointed the still dangerous panzers. There would, now that the weather had cleared, be some air recon as soon as we could get it; but they wanted us to take a look right now without waiting. So we were to get ready to move generally astride the main road toward that little town—White pointed to his map—and come back as soon as the first German was sighted. Questions?

I asked if I couldn't go alone. "You a hero or something?" White asked. Very much to the contrary, I explained. Ahead was open country affording no cover. A patrol would be fired on. A single man would not be fired on; the Krauts would only be curious about a single man. And when I got to within talking distance, I would be OK. I would bring 'em back alive.

There was a long silence. Jake grinned his pixie grin. White said to him, "He's got a point. Once Gabel gets to within talking distance of his relatives out there—*if* he gets that close—they're goners." Everyone laughed. "OK. Except *don't* talk to anybody if you can help it. Just take a look and come back. Go eat, move out, and be back no later than ten. That gives you over three hours."

After breakfast Jake and Peter White walked me through the company and past its OP from where I knew they would be watching me as far as they could. I therefore acted like a scout, working my way forward as though I were being graded in training. When I was sure they could no longer see me, I quit snaking parallel to the road and got on it.

It was a beautiful morning. I started to whistle the title song from "Oklahoma." The road was straight and asphalt-paved, showing here and there a cave-in at the shoulders and track marks where a panzer had gone into the ditch. The asphalt was deeply rutted, but that can happen to any well-traveled road, I thought. Despite the panzer tracks, there was something decidedly civilian about the road, the landscape, the morning, and the whole oddball situation. Even though I was now almost a mile forward of our line, I was happy and felt safer than I had in a long time. I was absolutely certain that I was in no danger and that when I ran into the Germans I would get into a long, easy conversation with them and either get the information we needed from them or talk them into coming back with me—or both.

I was stepping out now, striding down the center of the road. I certainly wasn't marching. I was taking a brisk morning walk, and I was now whistling, "Oh, what a beautiful morning . . . ." With a touch of chagrin I thought of the concern on the faces of Jake and Peter White when I left them at our OP; but I had tried to tell them that I had not volunteered for a "dangerous mission." I was simply demonstrating what is known in Yiddish as *chuzpah*—audacity without danger of physical violence—and I knew I would feel like a big phony when I made my after-action report.

The road curved east. As I rounded the bend, I saw several trees felled across the road some two hundred yards ahead. In the center of the roadblock, two haphazardly placed barbed wire barriers that the Germans called *Spanische Reiter* (Spanish riders) framed an MG 39, its barrel peeking over a tree trunk, covering the shoulder of the road to my right. The gray helmets of the gunner and his two crew members shimmered darkly in the morning sun. I stopped whistling but took a few more steps before I halted so as not to make any sudden, startling moves. My heart pounded. I had not expected a roadblock.

I waved, raising my right arm high and semaphoring it above my head, the Thompson sub hanging from my right shoulder swaying back and forth with the motion. I wanted to be sure that they saw I was armed, alone, and not trying to surrender.

There was no response of any kind. No bullets, no words. I bent my tongue back and gave out with a shrill whistle, then shouted, *"Hey, Ihr da. Moment mal!"*

Nothing.

Slowly I walked toward the left shoulder of the road and watched the barrel of the machine gun. It did not move. Again in slow motion, I took my binoculars from the case and, like an interested tourist, put them to my eyes. The glasses showed me no more than I had seen with the naked eye, a roadblock covered by a German crew-served weapon. It was plain and simple; an MG 39 with a crew of three was before me.

As I returned the binoculars to the case, I shouted, *"Hey, Kinder! Schläft Ihr denn?"* And as I inquired whether they were asleep, I realized that they must be dead. I walked straight up to them, occasionally looking beyond down the road. There were houses in the distance, and left and right the woods were appearing once more. But nothing moved.

The dead Germans reminded me of the first batch I had seen before we entered the Bois de Fragette. There was no blood; there was not a mark to be seen on any of them. All three wore their helmets, and their equipment was intact. They were not yet frozen and moved relatively easily as I searched for their paybooks and other papers. Just when I had decided that, under the circumstances, it would not be prudent to take the pistol from the gunner because if I met other Germans I must be one-hundred percent American, I saw that his holster was empty. In fact, the K-98s with which the assistant gunner and the ammo bearer should have been armed were not there either. Puzzled, I looked for hand grenades and peered into ammunition pouches. There were no grenades and the pouches were empty. There was no belt in the machine gun, and the two gray ammo boxes supplying it were empty, too. The gun itself seemed to have been damaged, from the look of the twisted and empty linkage protruding from the receiver. I was totally mystified.

I checked my watch. It had been less than an hour since I'd left Jake and Peter White. What could anybody do with this screwy information. I wondered and decided to go ahead into the village. I had plenty of time. I returned to the road from the far side of the block.

When I looked up, I saw at a distance a dark figure on a bicycle pedaling along the road. As we approached each other, he took on the shape of something military but not German. He stopped beside me and dismounted.

He wore a dark blue, almost black uniform with gold buttons. By the blocked cap with its shiny bill, I recognized him as a gendarme. Slung across his back was a K-98 Mauser rifle; he was now tentatively fingering its leather sling. I waved and said, "Good morning," walking up to him.

He dropped his hand from the rifle sling and grinned. Then he said, "Ha, Haaaa!" almost like Frenchie. We shook hands.

"Do you speak English?" I asked.

He grinned some more and shook his head.

"Sprechen Sie Deutsch?"

"Etwas," he grinned. I suppose I was grinning, too. Both of us were now walking automatically toward the village, he pushing his bicycle, looking at me as though he were trying to figure out which of his long-lost brothers I was. The dumb radiance on his Gallic face was infectious. The Germans, he said before I asked, had just departed. They had been very much in a hurry and the locals helped them a little with packing and so on. Now I must come and have a glass of wine. I said that I must get back to my unit to make my report, but he wouldn't hear of it. He would not talk to me any further until we had settled down to a glass of wine. Then he would tell me whatever I wanted to know.

Well, Jake and Peter White had said I was supposed to find things out.

The little village seemed deserted, but it was intact and very clean. The gendarme, his face still beaming with that seraphic expression that was beginning to make me feel undeservedly proud, steered me toward a two-story brick tavern from which a sign showing a white prancing horse swung over the sidewalk. In the dining room of the Cheval Blanc, the entire male population of the village seemed to be assembled. They sat around the scrubbed wooden tables, talking softly and smoking foul-smelling cigars and cigarettes. As we entered, all talking stopped abruptly, as though on order. I took off my helmet and bowed my little German bow. We stood in the silence and then, again as if on order, a table near the long, simple bar was cleared and simultaneously one of its occupants came toward us, gravely extending his hand to me. "Résistance belgique," he said. We shook hands and he motioned us to the table.

"Parachutiste americain?" he asked.

I nodded. A bottle of red wine and glasses materialized. The man filled the glasses, sliding one of them gently toward me, not like the sliding of a glass in a western movie. Five men raised their glasses to me and I picked up mine to return the salute. We drank in silence. Only the gendarme smiled.

"Parle français?" the man asked.

"Regret," I said. "Je parle allemagne."

"Bon," he nodded, refilled my glass, and told me in German what unit had been here, in what strength and how armed, when they had left, and in what direction they were moving. If I could wait, there would be more information later in the day. Big frog that I was, I naturally said that I had no time to wait. I downed the third glass of wine proffered me.

I did manage the presence of mind to write down the information and map references, but I failed to ask for a knowledgeable Resistance man to accompany me back to my unit. A sad omission in our intelligence training was stress on the information potential of the civilian populace, particularly of members of the Underground, the police, and demobilized soldiers. To me, the Resistance men and the gendarme were merely civilians who, like my little old lady, might be able to tell me the "where—how many—what equipment," but that was about all. It would be some months before that misconception would be corrected. Meanwhile I was very happy with this solid bit of front-line information. Peter White would like it at battalion level, and so would regiment and division. My mission was accomplished.

Unsteadily I stood up and rendered an elegant "Merci bien et bonne chance, mon amis," discovering that, after my third glass of wine, I could speak French quite fluently. Due to a lack of vocabulary, much of it was German with a French accent; but neither I nor my new acquaintances seemed to be disturbed by that small technicality. Finally I bowed and waved my way out, graciously declining an escort, and reeled my way along the empty main street in the direction from whence I had come.

It was rough going. Though I had at home on certain festive occasions been given a partially filled glass of wine at dinner, I had never before had three full glasses in a row, in a few minutes, with or without dinner. Carefully I picked my way through the gently swaying village and onto the undulating asphalt highway. Suppose, I thought, just suppose the Germans changed their minds; suppose they decided they'd better screen their withdrawal and send a *Spähtrupp* on a couple of motorcycles with sidecars? It was an appealing idea and I grinned to myself. Not only would I have a nice group of prisoners, but I would get a ride home. Not only would I get a ride home, but I would get to ride one of those BMW motorcycles. I'd like to know how they compared with the Harley-Davidson. The hell with the Cushman I'd tested in England. I'd get to ride in a sidecar. Good thing it would have a sidecar because I would probably not quite manage a solo on this terribly unsteady road. I tried to whistle, "Oh, what a beautiful morning," but couldn't quite do it.

There was no way I could get lost. I knew that what I had to do was simply to stay on the road. But when the woods on the right of the road swam and spiraled into my view, the woods where the line companies of the 513th were, I remembered that I would have to get off the road and approach our OP like a battalion scout, the way I had left it. White would take a dim view of a scout who didn't have sense enough to creep and crawl and hide behind trees and slither through gullies and generally act the way a scout should. I'd been trained. And I knew White and Jake would be up there, waiting and watching.

I stopped to look around for the little gully I'd used as a "concealed" approach to the road. It was a mistake. The moment I stopped, the entire landscape started to revolve slowly around me. I sat down in the middle of the highway to continue my orientation in relative safety. It did no good. There was no gully. I would have to guess my way to the OP. I got up, lurched forward, and fell down. I tried propelling myself on my hands and knees and decided that that was a good, steady way to get to the point where the gully should be; but my submachine gun fell off my shoulder and clattered to the road. Why, I asked myself, had I taken the stupid thing in the first place? With some difficulty I got up and shoved the weapon back on my shoulder. I then resolutely stepped off the road, gully or no gully, to scout my way though the woods and up the hill. I fell into a depression and started to swear. I swore (in another sense) that as soon as I could regain a semblance of equilibrium, I would go home directly, without further concessions to my scouting and patroling training.

There I lay. I heard scraping and crunching in the underbrush ahead. Then I heard Jake's concerned voice saying, "You hurt, Gabe?" That did it. I nobly rolled over on my back and looked into his concerned face. I also looked into the concerned face of Lieutenant White. They were panting from their run through the brush down the hill, and their eyes went over me to find the wound with which I was so heroically making my painful way back to the friendly lines—like a one-hundred-twenty-pound John Wayne. I had great difficulty resisting the temptation to say, "Oh, it's nothing . . . ."

Gracefully relaxing on my back, I explained that I was only temporarily indisposed. I began my story with the meeting of the gendarme.

"You were in the *town*?" White asked, forgetting the dire condition I was in.

"Village," I corrected. "Just want you to understand I had three glasses of wine in three minutes in line of duty. Forced to do it." I'd used Jake's favorite expression and he turned his head away from me. "Got everything written down," I continued desperately. "Even map renefrenceses . . . refness . . . ref-er-en-ces." White busted out laughing and so did Jake.

"No one," he sputtered, "but *no* one will believe this."

"Good," I said and struggled to my feet.

We got back to the CP without anyone else asking whether I was hurt, and Peter White debriefed me. He studied my notes, made marks on his map overlay, and listened critically to my slurred account of the past hours. "Why," he asked when I mentioned the Belgian Resistance men in the tavern, "didn't you bring one of them back here with you?" I said that I thought it wasn't important and noticed that White did not care for that explanation. Except for that, though, he seemed satisfied. "Not bad," he said finally and put on his helmet. "Now hit the sack. And that's an order."

When I woke up, supper was already over; but Jake had fixed me a sandwich and be darned if I didn't sit up to eat it. "We move out after breakfast tomorrow," Jake said, and I had visions of settling down in the comfortable room of the Cheval Blanc until it was time to go back to the States. With my luck, though, I decided, one of the companies was probably already there, and I'd be digging an OP hole in the snow outside that delightful little place.

"Anything you want me to do?" I asked Jake after I had finished my sandwich, not really wanting to get out of the nice warm sleeping bag. "Nope," he said, and I immediately snuggled down into its recesses and slept very soundly indeed until Jake woke me up for breakfast the next morning.

Along the trail in the woods where our chow line was set up was a long line of trucks. They were parked close together as though we were all on maneuvers taking a tactical break. Their tailgates were down and so were their seats. They were facing the direction from where we had come, away from the village with the charming Cheval Blanc. I should have known.

"What's the transportation for?" I asked Jake as we got in the chow line.

"We're going to Luxembourg," Jake said.

It sounded nice; it sounded like rear echelon. My headache soared away. I forgot about the village and began imagining picturesque little towns waiting for us in the Duchy of Luxembourg. If I thought at all about the seeming anomaly of higher headquarters being frantic to maintain contact with the Germans one day and forgetting all about them the next, it didn't bother me. Perhaps the Krauts were too far off, and fast-moving armored would have to haul out after them. It did not, in any case, concern me. I was simply happy about the prospect of a nice truck ride to the rear. I hadn't the slightest notion about where we were in relation to what had become known as the "Bulge," had never seen an area map of a scale smaller than one over twenty-five thousand, and did not know that Luxembourg (its eastern border defined by the Our River and the Siegfried Line) was on the southern extremity of that Bulge, which, like an obscene bit of intestine that had popped out of the straining body of the Reich in its final effort to stem the *Götterdämmerung*, was being pushed back where it belonged. And the decimated 513th was to be a small suture down there.

Breakfast consisted only of C-rations because Baier and the other mess sergeants had to load up at the same time we did. We hoisted ourselves and our equipment aboard the deuce-and-a-halfs and the convoy moved out.

Slowly our vehicles made their way along the rutted, sloshy trail, the trucks whining in four-wheel drive, and I wondered if anyone would take over our holes or if this entire area had already become the rear. These truck drivers had been relaxed, in no hurry to leave; that was a sign of how far from the front line things had become here.

We rolled south—though I didn't know that—the trail to a dirt road and finally onto a highway. We entered Bastogne, apparently on its main street. We stared at the litter—abandoned vehicles and equipment, damaged buildings, rubble—attesting to what the 101st had experienced in holding the place. This is what Mande St. Etienne had been all about, I thought as I looked at the shells of houses on either side of the street. Slowly we made our way through the town, a busy place with heavy traffic of trucks and jeeps.

We left Bastogne and after a while turned east, though again I didn't know the direction we were traveling in. To the east was Germany and the retreating enemy, but you couldn't have proved it by me. The landscape was no longer interesting. No one talked, and the slow-moving convoy whined monotonously over the snow-covered secondary roads through the familiar pine forests. Like a good infantryman, I dozed off whether I needed to or not.

Frenchie's loud "Ah, oui!" wakened me. We were in a fairly well-battered town. Frenchie was waving at a couple of girls on the sidewalk carrying milk cans. The girls waved back, but did not return Frenchie's yellow smile. "What's this burg?" I asked, and someone said, "Wiltz. Luxembourg."

This, too, seemed a busy little town. I hoped it housed a QM depot or something equally close to civilization. I would like it here. But the damn convoy did not stop. We crested a hill and went sharply down. "Hey, driver! Stop at Powell and Market," someone from San Francisco shouted. The downhill ride continued at a gentler angle and we passed a sign marked "Niederwiltz." "What's it say, Gabel?" someone wanted to know.

"Lower Wiltz," I said. "Guess we just came through Oberwiltz," I added facetiously without knowing that I was right. I was making fun of my first German signs. Where there's a *nieder*, there's got to be an *ober*. I wondered briefly why I had never thought that was funny before.

Niederwiltz was less damaged than Oberwiltz, and the houses were smaller. They thinned out with larger gardens between them, and finally they became rural. Here and there a neat stone house would have a barn and a stable, all surrounded by its own fields and orchards. But still scattered about the countryside were suburban brick houses belonging to the well-to-do, who wanted to get away from town and pretend to be farmers.

At the edge of this rural suburb, with its head in another direction and its tail even with a small old farmhouse, the convoy finally came to a halt. The drivers kept their engines running, I noticed. "OK, you guys! Hit it! End o' the line!"

Tailgates slammed down and we spilled out of the trucks. Scarcely waiting until the last man got out, the drivers closed the tailgates and climbed back into their cabs, putting the vehicles in gear. By the time we were formed up, the convoy had expertly turned around in a frozen field and was smartly heading back toward Wiltz. Only our mess trucks and some jeeps were desultorily standing near the old farmhouse. Wherever we were, it was not to the liking of our truck drivers.

We were told to sit down in place, but we were not told to spread out; so things could not be as bad as the rapidly disappearing convoy would have us think. Officers and some NCOs, including Jake, walked forward into the woods, and before I dozed off again (good infantryman that I was), I supposed they were going to reconnoiter our new positions and relieve whoever was there now.

Jake nudged me and I opened my eyes. "Wait till you see your new home," he grinned; "OK, S-two and -three. Let's go." We walked toward the edge of the woods to a two-story red-brick house of the gentleman-farmer variety. Jake waved an introductory hand in its direction and said, "There it is." I couldn't believe my eyes. The house was completely intact. It even had its windows. When had I last seen a completely intact house?

"Oh, kind sir," wailed Horseface Herrick, "do not make fun of the peasantry."

"That's it, men. Don't ask me how or why," said Jake. Even he couldn't quite believe our extreme good fortune.

The house was surrounded by a fence in which several large gaps had been made by tracked vehicles, but that was the only evidence that the war had intruded into this corner of Luxembourg. An attractive entry with stone steps was just right of center. On the left of the house below street level was an oversized two-car garage to which a broad concrete driveway dipped down rather sharply. The garage had two large wooden doors. Jake pried one open just enough for us to squeeze in. I still didn't believe it.

That garage hadn't seen a car for a while. It was clean enough to serve as an operating room, and there were several straw mattresses along the two long walls. On a small wooden table in the center was an old-fashioned kerosene lamp. We had light. At the far end on the right, steps led up into the house. On the opposite end was a little iron stove. Ben Franklin? It was a lovely scene.

"What's upstairs?" Herrick wanted to know.

Jake scowled and said, "The gentry, you peasant." The officers were up there—the CP was up there, and the officers and first sergeant would sleep there. But, said Jake, raising a lecturing finger, at the first few mortar or 88 rounds, they would undoubtedly join us down here in our lovely garage. "So let's make ourselves comfortable while we can," Jake concluded. We each instantly picked a mattress and put our equipment on it.

"Get some wood for the stove, Horseface," Jake said, just as Herrick was about to make himself comfortable on his mattress.

"Right, chief," Herrick grumbled and sauntered out the garage door. Herrick, we knew, would in the middle of a desert unerringly go straight to the finest burning material. We could see the stove lit already. With a little cooperation from the Germans *and* from higher headquarters, this might well turn into a most satisfactory stay.

Herrick couldn't have been gone more than five minutes before he came back carrying some kindling wood and several fine briquettes wrapped in newspaper. No mere coal for Herrick. He acquired for our garage those expensive, long-burning briquettes that were almost impossible to come by. He blessedly busied himself at the little stove and soon a fire was crackling and snapping merrily, red flames licking through the kindling at the delicious briquettes. I decided for the millionth time that Herrick was indispensable.

That night I felt so utterly comfortable and safe on my straw mattress in that wonderful underground fortress of a garage that I tried not to go to sleep. But sleep I did until Jake woke me with the words, "Breakfast will be served on the patio, sir."

15
Niederwiltz

At breakfast Jake told me that our new position was west of the Our River with the front-line bunkers of the Siegfried Line sitting high on the wooded cliffs *on the other side*. This news made me feel even better than I already did. I was absolutely certain that we wouldn't be fighting. Over there were the Germans in their concrete bunkers, and over here were we, and that was that.

No one would send infantry across that river. The Germans would not leave their bunkers.

We would simply sit here in our luxurious garage and wait for the Air Corps to bomb those bunkers into rubble or for Corps Artillery to do its stuff. When later during the day Corps Artillery actually did fire on the German positions, the muffled impacts of the "vvvhroooms" of its eight-inch howitzers shaking our house and garage, my speculations concerning leisure weren't necessarily confirmed.

For a few days we were warm. The euphoric mood held. And the missions for the scout section were straight out of *Alice in Wonderland*.

It seemed the companies were short of bread. The mess sergeants had not been able to convince the QM ration breakdown people in Wiltz that we were all growing boys and needed plenty of the staff of life. So Peter White wanted the scout section to take a couple of duffel bags and go to Wiltz and get some.

Baier was deeply interested. He gave us two empty duffel bags and Frenchie, Herrick, and I started up the long hill to scout the rear echelon for bread. There was no time limit for our shopping trip, but we were requested to try to make it back before supper so that the bread could be served with our evening meal.

First came the gentle slope to and through Niederwiltz where we got a good look at the relatively undamaged and comfortable suburban houses. Then came the steep approach to Wiltz's main street with its slippery cobblestones under our boots. Artillery and bomb damage was considerably more noticeable on our walk than it had been from the trucks.

The ration breakdown point was easy to find; it was in a slightly damaged warehouse right on main street. We walked into its cobbled yard. A truck was backed to the loading dock and several GIs were hauling ration cartons onto it. "There's the bread," Herrick said, pointing to stacks of the stuff in the warehouse.

We watched and waited until the truck was loaded. Then we went into the warehouse toward the bread bins. "Hey, you guys!" one of the GIs shouted at us. "Where do you think you're goin'?"

It was understood that Herrick, as the official scrounger, was in charge of the shopping trip. "Gonna get me some of that there bread," Herrick drawled without so much as turning his head or slowing his pace.

As we stopped by the bread bins, the GI called, "Hey, *Sarge*!" and a staff sergeant appeared from somewhere deep in the interior of the warehouse.

"What's up??" the sergeant asked.

Before the GI had time to answer, Herrick drawled with a friendly smile, "You guys made a mistake with the bread. Our outfit didn't get its share. So we're gonna just fill up these here duffel bags is all."

"You guys nuts?" asked the sergeant.

Herrick turned to Frenchie. The sergeant was obviously no longer there; he was utterly ignored. "Hold the bag open," he said, and Frenchie spread his hand inside the bag's rim to make a beautiful wide opening. Herrick reached up, took two loaves of bread, put them in, and reached for two more.

The sergeant stepped up to Horseface, saying, "Just one goddamn minute . . . ," and it looked as if he was going to grab one of Herrick's arms.

Herrick turned slightly and dropped his arms at his sides. Frenchie put down his bag and made a small turn toward the sergeant and the GI. I stepped back slightly. We had made an almost innocent change in our position. Almost. It was enough for the sergeant to take stock. His three unwelcome shoppers, three paratroopers, were just standing there, but one with a .45 at his side, one with an M-1 slung crosswise on his back, one with a Thompson submachine gun hanging from his right shoulder; all they wanted was some bread.

"Hey, Sarge," Herrick drawled slowly. He was still smiling, but the smile was different now. I remembered having seen a smile like that in a western movie about a Mexican bandit with big white teeth holding up a gringo stage. "Sarge," he repeated softly, holding his hands, palm out, imploring. "We don't want no trouble, Sarge. Honest. Now, how about you and your buddy there holding these bags, and we'll fill 'em up and be on our way."

From where I stood with my Thompson, I could see the GIs who had loaded the truck slowly coming toward us. They decided to stop and watch. All we wanted was some bread; but we really wanted it, and we were obviously going to get it, one way or another.

The prudent sergeant and his helpers picked up the bags and held them open. Herrick filled one and Frenchie the other. I could feel myself grin. I also stood and watched the GIs watching us. When the duffel bags were full, Herrick said, "Thanks one hell of a lot, fellas. *Sure* hope we don't have to trouble you again. That's the 513th Parachute Infantry mess trucks that were short of bread." He slipped his left arm through the carrying strap of one duffel bag and waved with his right. Frenchie shouldered the other bag and the three of us strolled past the silent GIs and onto the street.

At supper time we were clearly heroes. But we had now also been designated as worthy helpers of Chief Scrounger Herrick. Neither Frenchie nor I minded very much. The job was certainly better than going on patrol, and we looked forward with pleasure to more local shopping excursions.

These excursions did materialize because the sector on the fringes of Niederwiltz stayed quiet. We heard rumors that division had ordered the Second Battalion on our flank to send patrols across the Our and that they raided deep into the bunkers of the Siegfried Line; and we heard and felt the efforts of our Corps Artillery. But none of this disturbed our almost domestic routine.

A very close second to the luxury of our garage was the chow. Cohen had outdone himself. The little farmhouse at the extreme edge of Niederwiltz where Cohen had set up his kitchen had almost immediately become a culinary Camelot that drew and held troopers, NCOs, and officers like a magnet. Regardless of the time of day, no one passed it without going in. The warmth of the field ranges reached every nook and cranny of the house, and the smell of mysteriously concocted stews, swiss steaks, chicken, and even doctored-up C-rations would have drawn the most satiated epicurean inside.

Since there was no practicable way to keep the strays out, Cohen had set up a huge steel can of steaming coffee in the entrance hall. Next to it on a small table he put loaves of white QM bread and jam. (There was now, the scout section noted with justifiable pride, an overabundance of bread in the entire battalion.) There was a constant coming and going in that entrance hall, and everyone was smart enough to recognize it as an inviolable barrier to the working part of the kitchen. They stood around with their canteen cups full of coffee, munching white bread and jam, and peered in to watch the cooks at their ranges and make really complimentary remarks. The remarks finally went to Cohen's head. Through Jake and finally Peter White, he placed an order for civilian pastries to replace the QM bread in the entrance hall. The order was duly passed on to us, and the next shopping expedition was launched. The very incongruity of procuring *pâtisserie*—the word Cohen used—intrigued us. No one believed it could be done, and it became an Arthurian quest for the glory of our Camelot in Luxembourg.

Again we were on the main street of Wiltz, and again Herrick knew exactly where he was leading us. He turned into a side street and stopped in the middle of the block as though he had lived in Wiltz for years. "Voilà," he said and pointed to the *Bäckerei* sign over the door of a half-demolished house. He opened the door, stood aside, and bowed me in. "Your move," he said.

The small white, immaculate German bakery was crowded with customers, all women. Most of them were dressed in warm, sturdy, almost prosperous clothing. They looked at us, it seemed to me, with some annoyance. This was, after all, a depot town, and there had been soldiers present since the war started—Belgian, French, German, and now American. These soldiers were strangers and seriously interfered with the lives of the civilians, including the way they managed to buy their food. But when they noted that we did not belong to the Comm-Z troops who inhabited their town, they softened somewhat. Two or three smiled tentatively, and we smiled back while we waited our turn at the counter.

Though it was strange for me to hear German spoken by civilians for the first time in my war experience, I was too absorbed in our "mission" to reflect on it. I was fascinated by the fact that the glass display case under the sales counter actually had, beside some delectable-looking rye bread, an assortment of pastries. An incredible victory seemed to be at hand.

The store had emptied and we stood before the display counter, facing the woman behind it. She looked elderly to me, though she was probably no more than forty years old. As we approached her, she stiffened; her features were cold and forbidding.

"May we buy some pastries, please?" I asked, using the very diffident German expression for that request which has no English equivalent and accompanying my request with what I thought to be a charming smile.

She stared at me and neither my delicate German nor my charming smile made the least impact. "No," she said coldly.

My aplomb gone, I could only mutter, "We will pay whatever you ask . . . ."

Even more sharply she repeated, "No!"

The three of us armed soldiers stood silent and helpless in the chill of her presence. Then I queried, "May I ask why not?" in gentle German.

During a long pause she looked at each of us, and there was the momentary recognition that we were different from the other soldiers in the town. But she gave no smile and the chill did not dissipate. "Why not?" she said, her eyes boring into mine again. "Come with me."

Herrick, Frenchie, and I looked at one another. Although they understood no German, they grasped the situation. It was like being on silent LP and having a sudden small noise sound out in front of us in the dark. But I went behind the counter, followed by my two buddies.

On the right in the passageway behind the counter, the grim owner of the bakery had fixed a sleeping corner. Near a door stood an old but neatly made up couch, a night table, and a small chest of drawers. On the left was another door. She led us toward it.

The house had been half demolished. When she opened the door we looked outside, or rather, we looked at the huge pile of rubble that had once been the living quarters of her bakery. Only a portion of the front wall remained standing. "You did this," she said, stretching her arm toward the rubble. Then she said, "My daughter is under that," and added, "My husband also will not come back." She turned her cold eyes on me and my politeness and said, "That's why not."

I had no answer. Futile to say, "We didn't do it. Not even our DivArty did this." Futile to say, "Not many of ours are coming back either." Futile to say that we'd rather be in California or Wisconsin or Oregon.

I was unutterably sad for her, but the pile of rubble with her daughter under it and her dead husband were the inevitable concomitants of the dreary necessity of war. I wanted *pâtisserie* for my unit. I was sad, but I was sad for all of us, not just for her. "We're sorry," I said. "All we wanted to do was to buy some pastries for the men *in our unit*." We walked back into the store and I said in gentle German, "Please excuse us," and made ready to leave.

She smiled suddenly, a slow, tired smile, and said, "There are only a few pieces left, but you can take those."

As she put the pastries in a bag and I struggled to get my wallet out of my pocket, a girl of perhaps seventeen came through the door on the right of the counter. The woman looked up and said, "My other daughter, Leni." It sounded like an introduction and I shook hands with her and introduced the other two of us. Then the mother gave us her hand

and, for Pete's sake, told us *her* name. Our encounter had suddenly and astonishingly turned into a friendly social occasion.

"How much may I give you for the pastries?" I asked as she handed me the bag.

"Nothing. They're priceless," she answered and then quickly said, "You're not from the garrison here, are you?"

"No. We're paratroopers. We just got here. But if we can't pay for them, we won't take them."

"Quatsch," she said; "Nonsense. It's the least we can do."

I could scarcely believe the complete change of attitude; but before I had a chance to answer, her daughter said, "Come in the kitchen and have a cup of coffee." She opened the kitchen door. I looked at Herrick and Frenchie, who were both grinning, just like me.

The kitchen was actually the bakery but had been rearranged so that the women could cook and eat there, too. We sat around a table and took our helmets off and propped our weapons against the chairbacks. "Much better," said the lady of the house.

I had an idea. As our coffee arrived, I said, "If you won't let us pay for the pastries with money, then let us bring you some coffee or C-rations or something."

"We have plenty to eat."

I pursued my thought. "That's not true. Besides, I'm really asking a great favor. If we can bring you flour, would you bake a few extra pastries for us?" I translated quickly to Herrick and Frenchie, and they liked the thought. After all, it was Herrick who would have to scrounge what she needed, and Herrick could see no problem. The bakery lady said that it was very difficult to get white flour and powdered sugar and in the end was delighted to accept our offer with the assurance that there would be ample pastries to go around.

Later in the afternoon, when Cohen got a look at what we brought him, we found that there would be no need for Herrick's procurement talents. Cohen gave us flour and sugar and other little ingredients we couldn't name, told us to take the stuff in his mess jeep and, for Christ's sake, go right back there *now*. Jake, who was having his afternoon coffee while waiting for us, gave his qualified consent. "Not you, Gabe," he said. "White needs you after dark."

Playtime was over.

Herrick didn't show up at the garage that night. He got hit by a stray mortar fragment while he was talking to a medic in front of the aid station, went straight to the clearing station in a fortunately waiting ambulance, and from there was sent back to France. Frenchie made the pastry run alone.

I reported to the CP.

Shortly before we climbed on the trucks in Belgium for our ride to Luxembourg, Lieutenant Colonel Alton Taylor had been relieved of command of our First Battalion; Major Kies took over and was promoted. The change of command showed; our CP now somehow reminded me of Ace Miller's forward CP.

Physically, of course, our command post in the quiet, stable sector of Wiltz could not be compared to that of the Second Battalion under German armored attack in Mande St. Etienne. Here we were in a large, undamaged house—a miracle. Each staff section had its own office. The S-3 actually had two offices set up in the living room and the adjoining dining room. S-1 and S-4 were also set up nicely in adjoining offices that had once been the *Herrenzimmer* and the library. Only our little S-2 section was cramped for space in a room off the kitchen that must have been the maid's room. Peter White had only half jokingly protested, and he had been told (with a grin) that space was allocated according to need and expected production.

It was the quiet, professional hum of the place that reminded me of Mande. Now there was no more need for the staff to counterbalance the CO. It was very clear even to the uninitiated like me that our new commander knew exactly what he was doing and that the staff smoothly complemented the command and control that emanated from a superior soldier.

There was, to be sure, the occasional cussing of company commanders when they were told of the latest operational acrobatics that regiment had imposed on battalion. One such gyration was still in the discussion (or cussing) stage when I reported to White. On the way to our maid's room I heard Captain Spears say, "That's the most stupidest goddamn thing I ever heard of," and there seemed to be no disagreement by his battalion commander.

Lieutenant White sat on a bed that was still in the little room. He clamped a map mounted on a board between elbows and knees. It was covered with the inevitable sheet of acetate and on the transparent material were the customary red grease-pencil markings representing the enemy position.

White returned my salute and put the map down. He waved me over where I could see it and said, "That's where they are, nice and snug in their bunkers. Corps can't dig 'em out. Air Corps can't dig 'em out. So guess what?"

"Oh, *no!*" I moaned.

"Oh, *yes*," said Peter White disgustedly. "They're getting boats from the engineers and want the battalions to put troops across the Our. Companies have already tried it without boats; but that river is swollen and fast, so we quit it. Now they say division wants us to cross in force."

Believe it or not, I had never seen the river. I had not been interested in it because I had thought of it as a wall separating us from the Germans, in effect permanently blocking our movement and for us representing the end of the war. I suppose that, in their own way, the company commanders had thought of it like that, too. Most of the company commanders were replacements for the original ones. What was left of the companies was totally exhausted—used up. Further expenditure of this blood, which to the officers was as precious as that of their own children, seemed almost criminal. Nothing was to be gained here except a promotion or a headline for some general. And so Peter White finally showed his disgust; he was unable to disguise it from one of his men.

"Our battalion commander wants a thorough recon first," White continued. "Can't wait for the boats, though. We don't want to attract that kind of attention, anyway. Now, there's no way to get across the damn river except maybe one. You and I and a bazooka team are gonna try it."

White had obviously spent some time at the river, although he had kept us uninvolved so far. It was typical of him. But now battalion had gotten a warning order, and like it or not, battalion would have to prepare to execute an ensuing crossing order. White would have to get enemy information, and the best way to do that is to take a prisoner or two. Maybe we could even get a look at the bunkers and their approaches. But for the life of me, I couldn't figure out what a bazooka team had to do with crossing the river.

Three of us walked the trail twisting through the woods and meandering across the company positions down to the river a quarter of a mile away. Jake had pestered and cajoled our lieutenant to the point where White had let him go along just so he wouldn't have to listen to him any more. "If you get hurt," White had said to Jake, "you'd better damn well keep out of my sight." Jake had cheerfully promised to do just that. He kept his promise.

The path was narrow and steep, strewn with small, slippery pebbles. Thorny, obstinate underbrush encroached on both sides and clawed our uniforms and weapons. The dense brush and woods made the afternoon seem like evening. Walking was difficult; I lost my footing and fell several times.

White chuckled each time I fell. Finally he remarked, "They want the companies to carry engineer boats down this path at night."

At the bottom of the hill we came out of the woods and White held up his hand. A bazooka team and a couple of men with submachine guns sitting at the edge of the woods started to get up, but White waved them back down.

The Our River, which I had never heard of, is supposed to be a small, insignificant, easily fordable stream. But now it was in roaring flood, boiling over its banks in many spots and carrying dangerous debris on its fast-moving trip past the Siegfried Line. To step into it meant to be swept away.

"See that little bank over there?" White said to us and to the bazooka team. He had to raise his voice over the noise of the river. A longish, sandy portion of the river bank on our side looked like a little dark beach. But from it protruded a sandbank shaped like an arrowhead. It hadn't been washed away, and it remained exposed to German fire. "From there we'll conduct our little experiment," said Peter White.

He began to explain. Coming from anyone but him, I'd have branded the plan as totally harebrained, downright idiotic. On his instruction the bazooka team had brought along a coil of thin rope. One end of the rope was to be tied to a bazooka round. That's what I said. It would be fired into a certain tree across the river. White would go upstream, swim across (it was still January), and secure the rope. The two troopers with the submachine guns, Jake, and I would cross by way of the rope. The bazooka team would cover us. We would go up the opposite bank as far as we could on any approaches we would find, look for stray Germans, and take them back with us. If we found the position across the river soft enough—without too many pillboxes between the river and the bunkers of the Siegfried Line—we would leave the rope where it was and we'd put a combat patrol across to act as a bridgehead for the troops crossing later. Any questions?

Was Peter White furious enough at orders from higher headquarters to satirize them? Probably. We had all heard fantastic schemes before in this outfit, but this one took the cake. I refrained with difficulty from asking if White thought he was Spencer Tracy in "Northwest Passage." We all skipped the questions. They would have lasted the afternoon.

"Let's go," said White, and our little group walked to the sandbank, in full view of the Germans. "Fire a test round across to that tree first," White told the astonished trooper with the rocket launcher. And there we stood, as though we were on the range at Fort Bragg trying out new tactical airborne tricks at leisure.

The gunner's astonishment left his face as he looked at the cliff with bunkers on top, the launcher on his shoulder. Of course he could demolish it. The ammo bearer inserted a round, wired it, and tapped his gunner on the shoulder as he stepped away from the tube. Almost instantly the gunner fired. The three worked as though they were one. I could see the round arch across the river and into the branches of the tree. I heard no explosion other than the back blast of the fired round; but the projectile was right where Spencer Tracy White wanted it.

The gunner turned his head toward White without changing his position. "Not bad," said White. "One more, then we'll do it with the rope."

Ammo bearer and gunner repeated the smooth, flowing operation of loading, aiming, and firing; again the round went home to White's satisfaction.

By now I had completely forgotten the Germans and was totally engrossed in our experiment. As so often in the past, after one of these wild schemes was actually initiated, I was convinced that it would work against all odds, no matter what I had thought in the beginning. Peter White might very well be playing games for Battalion. I was nevertheless convinced of the infallibility of our officers in spite of the jarring revelation of panic under fire with which Lieutenant Colonel Alton R. Taylor, erstwhile commander of the First Battalion, had terminated my military virginity. His replacement had made things well again. Taylor was all but forgotten, as if there never had been a crack in the officer corps of the 513th.

So there I stood, looking across the foaming, roaring Our River at the Siegfried Line. The utterly puzzled Germans had finally been stung into action by one of their very nervous officers. On our side was the problem of the rope. At best, it would be burned by the back blast. At worst, it would foul the tube and hurt the gunner. But White would make his plan work, if only through sheer will power. I *knew* that. Our lieutenant would walk on water, reconnoiter the bunkers, take his prisoners, and let Battalion know that it could establish its bridgehead. I stood there and believed.

Just as the ammo bearer finished tying the end of the rope coil to a projectile, something close to us exploded dully. It was a new sound; I thought I'd heard them all. There were more. They were some soft kind of explosions with the mere suggestion of a puff of concussion. None of us went down. No one took cover.

"Hand grenades," explained White.

Then came the motorcycle rattle of an MG 42. "Forget it," said White. "They can't hit a goddamn thing from where they are."

And so we stood there except for Jake who was down on one knee, his rifle propped on his hip ready for use, and he was grinning at me.

"All right, get that rope across," said White; then two mortar rounds crashed into the water too close to us. This time we took cover—except for the bazooka team. There was more machine gun fire and, although we couldn't see where it was coming from, the three of us with submachine guns fired in the general direction of the German bunkers.

"Save it," White shouted. "You're way out of range, anyway; and so are they." The rocket launcher fired at last. The projectile with the rope lazily spun out of the tube and splashed limply, dispiritedly, into the water almost as it left the tube.

"Oh, shit!" said White, and two more mortar rounds crashed near us. The Krauts' aim was improving. "Break it off," said White. "Back into the woods!"

Spencer Tracy White's experiment for the sake of the lives of his troops had come to its unfortunately inglorious conclusion.

It was growing dark when we got back, and Jake and I went straight to the kitchen to get chow while Peter White reported to battalion that the Krauts were throwing hand grenades down to the river and were also using some rather respectable mortars. And a rope stretched across the river by means of a rocket launcher would, after all, not work, thank you very much.

That night we were about to hit the sack at our garage when Peter White stuck his head in at the top of the stairs and told Jake, "Captain Rockett needs one man from your section to replace a machine gunner." I shuddered. Things had got so bad that at Wiltz they were using scouts to fight now. I braced myself. The choice lay between me and Frenchie. The only reason I thought I might have a chance of staying in my nice warm sack was that I had just come off "the experiment" and that White would want me for more of the same. I could talk German.

"OK, Frenchie, you're next," said Jake, and to White, "When do we get him back?"

"Don't know. Should have replacements any time now," White answered and pulled his head back into the CP at the top of the stairs.

Frenchie put on his webb equipment and called me several dirty names in French, grinning all the while. I said, "TS," and zipped up my sleeping bag; but I wasn't as happy as I should have been. Frenchie's bunch would be at the river and maybe they'd have to cross it in combat patrol strength after all. The higher-ups didn't call for a machine gunner replacement for nothing.

I couldn't sleep. What the hell did Frenchie know about a caliber 30 light machine gun that I didn't know? Neither of us had fired one since

Benning. I didn't even remember how to adjust head space, so why should Frenchie?

Nothing much happened until after midnight. Then we heard explosions, soft ones and hard ones. Then the whiplashes from a Schmeisser or two, and the stuttering of a caliber 30 light machine gun. My stomach was uneasy. Rifle fire, machine gun fire, Schmeisser fire, and the short bursts of an MG 42. The bastard knew exactly what he was firing at. I sweated. "God *damn*," I said, and Jake answered, annoyed, "All right, all right . . . ." He wasn't sleeping either.

Frenchie's 30-caliber answered in longer bursts. It sounded awkward in comparison with the 42. More explosions, and more short bursts from the 42 were delivered in vicious, rapid sequence. That Kraut gunner wasn't playing the game from the top of the cliff. He was down below somewhere, and he knew exactly what he was doing. And he didn't need to adjust head space.

Jake and I got out of our sleeping bags at the same time. I wasn't sure just what we were going to do, but we were going to do something. We couldn't stay quiet. I was putting my equipment on when the 30-caliber stuttered again. At the same time the German machine gun cut into the chatter with the rest of the belt in two agonizingly long bursts. There were some explosions, some rifle fire, and a ridiculous sounding M-1; but the 30-caliber was silent.

I dropped my webbing and lay down on top of my sleeping bag, and Jake lay down on his. I didn't listen any more to the sounds coming from the river. Neither Jake nor I spoke.

In the morning White told us that Frenchie had died behind his machine gun. There were, he said, quite a few dead Germans in front of the gun. We did not ask and he did not say where the combat patrol was, what had happened to it, or even what company it was from. He did say that the engineer boats had arrived and that we would be going down to the river after dark.

We walked to chow, Jake and I. We had almost made it through to the end of this Bulge business; now, here in the quietest sector we'd been to, Herrick gets out and Frenchie is gone for good.

"What's the matter with you?" I said to Jake.

"Nothing. Why?"

"You're limping."

"Oh. Must have sprained my ankle last night."

The boats were actually here. They were on trucks parked halfway between the CP and the kitchen, and we stopped to look at them. Jake moaned softly and sat down by one of the trucks. I commanded, "Take off your right boot."

"What for?" he asked querulously.

"I want to see your foot." The heel of his right boot was gone and the leather was gashed.

"Oh, for Christ's sakes, mind your own goddamn business . . . ." It didn't really sound like Jake.

A medic passed on his way to the mess hall and I stopped him. "Dalton can't walk and he won't take off his boot," I told the medic. Jake started cussing.

"Take it off," said the medic, putting his mess kit down. Jake cussed some more. "Take it off or I'll cut it off," said the medic and drew his knife from the scabbard strapped to his right boot.

"You go take a flying . . . ," Jake shouted just as Major Morris Anderson, commanding the Third Battalion, walked by.

Anderson stopped and said, "What's goin' on?"

I explained. "I think Jake Dalton got hit in the foot last night by the river, but he's giving the medic a hard time."

"I sprained my ankle. Big deal, sir," Jake said, grimacing up at his interrogator.

"Take off the boot," said Anderson, and Jake did. His foot was a bloody mess. The medic peeled off the bloody sock.

"Tag him and get him out of here," said Anderson to the medic. And to me, "If he gives you guys any trouble, I want to know."

"Yes sir," I grinned.

"You miserable rat," Jake said to me while the medic bandaged him. Anderson shook his head and went on to the kitchen.

"OK, up on your *left* foot and let's go," the medic commanded and put Jake's arm around his shoulder. He said to me, "I'll take this nut to the aid station. You go ahead and eat."

"Have fun," I said to Jake.

Jake said, "You and I are through for good."

Walking back from a lonely chow, I saw a field ambulance pulling away from the aid station. Suddenly its rear double door slammed open and Jake—who else?—jumped out, landing on his left foot and falling in the slush. "Hold it!" a medic yelled at the driver, and the vehicle stopped.

It just so happened that Major Anderson, too, was returning from the kitchen. I yelled to him, "Major Anderson, look . . . ." He had already seen. This time he was genuinely angry. He jumped the few steps toward Jake and hauled him up before Jake could try to get on his feet by himself, and Anderson was none too gentle.

"Look, Dalton," he growled at the chagrined, injured Jake, "You get your ass on that ambulance and you stay there and you go wherever they send you. I've got enough problems with this crazy outfit without having goddamn cripples around, do you understand me? You pull this shit once more and I'll throw the book at you!"

Jake hoisted himself to the position of attention minus the right foot on the ground, saluted, and said, "Yes, sir!"

He scrambled back into the ambulance and Morris Anderson stalked away mumbling, ". . . like running a goddamn nut house . . . ." I waved at the departing vehicle and Jake gave me the finger out the window of the double door.

Late in the afternoon White came into the garage and said, "Let's go, Kurt." We walked back to the boats the troopers were offloading from the trucks. Each squad handled one boat and carried it back past the CP to an assembly point. There they placed automatic weapons, rocket launchers, mortars, and ammunition in the boats and waited for the order to move out. White and I simply followed them around. I felt totally useless. I don't know what White felt, but I can imagine.

When it was dark, the column was ordered to move out. They were to go in silence so as not to lose the tactical element of surprise.

I hefted my submachine gun, told White what party I was going with, and squeezed into one of the details carrying the blessed engineer-supplied boats. The troopers with the heavy loads on their shoulders made remarkably little noise until they came to the long downward slope in the woods. From then on the column crashed, rumbled, and banged down the treacherous path amid the curses of the men. A trumpeting herd of pregnant elephants, as Anderson said later, would have seemed silent in comparison.

None of the boats in our sector ever got into the water. We came under mortar, artillery, and automatic weapons fire, and the whole operation was suddenly called off. In total disgust, Anderson, who had agreed to the bazooka tactic earlier, pulled his troops back up the hill and left the boats where they were. When one of the unit commanders asked whether the boats shouldn't go back, he said, "Screw those goddamn engineer people."

After this fiasco we settled down to doing what we should have been doing all along—we waited to be relieved.

16

Châlons-sur-Marne, February 1945

It was before the middle of February 1945 at our R and R camp outside Châlons-sur-Marne. Our duffel bags had been stacked in three huge piles, one for each battalion, by the men from the service company that had trucked them in from the old regimental base camp at Mourmelon-le-Grand. Not many were picked up from these piles. After I found Jake's and mine, I manhandled them to our tent and threw them on the bunks I had reserved for us.

There were five canvas bunks in the tent assigned our section, but I was alone in the tent. Jake would be the only other to come back after the hospital released him; meanwhile I was the S-2 section leader without a section.

Peter White had told me that I had been promoted to sergeant. That surprised me, particularly since I hadn't even known that somewhere along the line I had made corporal; but I had not been able to muster the energy for much interest in my new status. Even when White told me that the regimental S-2 had informed him I was to be transferred to the Counterintelligence Corps (CIC) for operations in Germany—no doubt after first going to their exotic school with plush quarters in a fancy Paris hotel—it seemed not to matter much. In fact, the news, though expected, disturbed me because I could not imagine being apart from Jake or, although he was an officer, from Peter White. That the transfer meant being out of the 513th did not even register. Such a contingency was simply unthinkable. So there I sat in the empty tent, a sergeant and section leader and a potential CIC agent, strangely melancholy in the face of extraordinarily good news, trying to get used to the unearthly quiet without trying to think about anything else. The empty bunks made the task exceedingly difficult.

The 513th Parachute Infantry Regiment we had joined as our first and only unit essentially was no more. We had sustained an incredible 80 percent casualties while never once failing to achieve our mission. [*Editor's Note:* Gabel's view of the ferocity of the fighting was later confirmed by the eminent BBC correspondent Chester Wilmot:

"Throughout January 3rd and 4th the American positions around Bastogne were subjected to a succession of heavy and well-coordinated attacks by elements of eight divisions. The battle that developed was the fiercest of the entire Ardennes campaign, and most costly, especially for the new and untried American divisions which Patton was obliged to commit west of Bastogne in order to relieve the pressure on the town. Although bad weather denied them air support, the defenders held fast . . . and none made any serious penetration" (*The Struggle for Europe* [London: Fontana Books, 1952], pp. 697–98). I might add that total American casualties during the January fighting exceeded those incurred during December.] Those of us left were now noncommissioned officers, and most of the remaining cadre NCOs had either become officers or were waiting to be commissioned. Replacements were arriving in the companies and we would start all over. What would that be like?

Some of the replacements had already settled into their new units. They looked the way we must have looked at one time, and they were very shy and quiet when one of us was nearby. I resented them as intruders but then forced myself to regard them as the replacements for our men that they really were. After all, they were like us. They simply had not been in combat; that was the only difference. The same selection criteria applied to us had been applied to them. The same training we had undergone, they had undergone. They were young, intelligent, highly disciplined, motivated, honorable, in the best physical condition, and superbly trained. Among them quietly walked the potential Herrick, Frenchie, and those magnificent riflemen who had assaulted Royal Tiger tanks. They were as much 513th as anyone. As it turned out, they proved it when the division in Operation Varsity crossed the Rhine in the most successful parachute and glider operation in history. And they proved that America could create and maintain elite units equal to or exceeding the caliber of the finest and oldest traditional European regiments.

The NCOs of the 513th had been given permanent passes, and after 5:00 P.M. we were allowed to go to town. Shuttle buses (in the form of deuce-and-a-halfs with benches down) were to take us from the tent area to Châlons. But we had to be in Class A uniform.

It was a strange sensation to unpack my duffel bag and put the rumpled winter uniform on the bunk. I had packed that bag in England, in an entirely different world, as an entirely different man. Or had I really changed so radically? And why the melancholy now that I was unpacking my things in relative peace? I was going to get my Class A uniform pressed; I was going to take another of those showers in hot water at the shower unit; and I was going to town to have a beer and dinner. No one would shoot at me; the town would be completely intact without so much as one bombed-out building; and there would not even be an air raid because the Luftwaffe had just about had it. So why the melancholy?

The melancholy persisted while I stood in line at a tent transformed into a tailor shop waiting for my uniform to be pressed. It persisted while I stood under the hot shower for the second time since Wiltz, and it was still there when I was finally sitting in the deuce-and-a-half on my way to Châlons.

The wonder of that truck ride along the dark, quiet *chaussée*—a paved, smooth road that made our ride as comfortable as any luxury tour bus ever would—inhibited us and imposed a nearly reverential silence. Here and there a car would pass, its headlights on and blinking a high-beam caution to our driver. Headlights on! Like the smooth asphalt road, a signal of peace. And as we approached the town, there were more lights. Châlons was in partial blackout, but it looked bright as day to us.

Slowly our truck rolled through the town. We peered at the houses, all intact, with soft lights behind closed curtains. There would be real civilians behind those curtains, and they would pursue their lives without artillery interruption and without grimy infantry throwing hand grenades into the windows and kicking open their doors. Not even bombers would ever again disturb their sleep at night.

The truck came to a gentle stop. The driver turned around to us and said, "This is the main square and I guess most of you guys want to get out. I'm going on to Seventeenth Headquarters barracks. There'll be a truck here to go back to the tents every hour until midnight." He talked softly, sensing the mood of his passengers. We mumbled our thanks and jumped off.

For a long moment we stood quietly on the pavement as our truck pulled away. Old buildings, a church not quite a cathedral, streetcar tracks gleaming in the dim light from the one street lantern allowed to burn under the reduced blackout—to our night-accustomed eyes the square was civilization bathed in light and we took it in as a man takes in air after having been under water for too long a time.

Slowly the group drifted apart, quietly, carefully, lest this peaceful mirage be shattered by a rude noise or a tromping boot.

Another sergeant and I walked along one of the streets radiating from the square. I did not know the sergeant. We had simply picked the same direction at random. "This is really something . . . ," he said softly. Without looking at him I recognized the indefinable melancholy. I nodded. We walked slowly, savoring the silence.

Suddenly there was a rumble behind us followed by a high screech. We sprinted apart and dove into the gutter, flattening ourselves close to the curbstone for maximum protection against whatever it was that announced its coming with a rumble first and a screech after.

A partially lighted streetcar came around the corner, its wheels biting into the curving tracks with the peculiar noise that sets teeth on edge. The people on the streetcar looked out of their windows at us. We got up and stood, heads down, brushing each other off. I felt strangely ashamed, as though I had just done something rude, just demonstrated ungratefulness to the people of Châlons. The streetcar passed, the people on it quickly averting their eyes; in that fraction of a second, when we the soldiers and they the people of France had looked at each other and looked away, we seemed to be fused in our shame. We had shattered the peace they were trying to share with us, and they had witnessed the infinitely sad and very intimate act of obeisance to the God of War rendered within the particular shadows of death that are impenetrable to those who are not combat infantry. For a fraction of a second, we and they had been touched and made one by the shame of war.

"Cheez . . . ," said the young sergeant softly and squared his cap. Without ever having looked into each other's faces we waved a tired wave and walked apart from one another, on our separate ways.

There was a restaurant at street level in an apartment house of the Edwardian era, an architectural type that seemed to dominate this part of the town. More accurately, it was a pub—a neighborhood pub—found in practically every European community with only slight local variations in character. The lines of lambency left by a possibly deliberate carelessness in the drawing of blackout curtains added to the special glow of the evening and reminded me that I had come for food and drink in a place of warmth and comfort. I decided to try peace once more and walked in.

I parted another carelessly hung blackout curtain and stepped into the light of the restaurant, which momentarily hurt my eyes. It was a large pub, but its low ceiling and half paneling gave it a special ambience. Most of the tables were taken, and I was surprised to see quite a few American soldiers scattered throughout the "regular" clientele. I could tell at one fast sweep that there were no 513th or 507th troopers among the GIs. The *publicain* came over to me and shrugged apologetically; but I pointed to a small unwanted table in the far corner where a large tile stove took up most of the space, and my host guided me toward it.

It was a snug little table nestled between the corner of the stove and the wall where a door to the kitchen constantly swung to and fro for two very busy waiters. I half turned toward the stove and stroked its smooth tile flank with my left hand, enjoying its warmth and thinking of the stove by which that little old lady had sat and tried to read her book when three American paratroopers crashed into her gentle presence, looking for Germans who had already fled.

The warmth of the room, its friendly lights glowing softly from several greenish tiffany ceiling lamps, blue cigar and pipe smoke curling toward them, the soft murmur of the patrons, the smell of French cooking, of wine and beer—the sights and smells and sounds of peace—settled over me like a blanket and I tried to snuggle into it, to give myself to its comfort and safety.

Slowly, shyly, and a little guiltily, I felt happiness sweep up next to melancholy and crowd my soul. Its incipient overflow was beginning to moisten the corners of my eyes and in terror of a deluge I concentrated on the GIs in the room.

They were not troopers, I thought. They were GIs. There was no derision in that classification. According to the newspapers, magazines, books, and movies, the GI was winning World War II. He walked a mile for a Camel. He had Hitler, Mussolini, and Tojo speared on his bloody bayonet. In back of him stood Rosie the Riveter. To him came Bob Hope and Francis Langford, Marlene Dietrich and Ingrid Bergman, Bing Crosby and Frank Sinatra. He was loved, admired, and respected by all the allies he came in contact with, mostly loved, though. He was feared by the enemy as an individual, as resourceful, as inventive. According to Ernie Pyle, the regimented German, disciplined from birth, blindly carrying out orders, was no match for the imaginative, innovative, scrounging, good-humored, compassionate GI, who, with his native irreverence toward authority, could outsmart and outfight any of those products of authoritarian militarism. And then the GI could go home to his just reward, to his mom and her apple pie, to his girl and his old job.

I believed a good deal of this. There was nothing wrong with our propaganda machine. And the GI had been here longer than we had. He had been in Africa and Sicily, in Normandy and on the German border before we came on the scene. He was all right!

It was just that we weren't GIs. We had never thought of ourselves as GIs. We were paratroopers. We were not competing with GIs or anyone else. We were not comparable. We were paratroopers!

Most of the GIs in the pub seemed to be from Comm-Z, support elements belonging to the rear-echelon command known as the Communications Zone. Here and there soldiers wore the same shoulder insignia I was wearing, the yellow eagle's talon of the Seventeenth Airborne Division; but that was all we had in common. They belonged to Division Headquarters and were as far removed from the 513th and the other line regiments as the Bois de Boulogne from the Bois de Fragette. For a short while, before the regiments had arrived, they had been "airborne" to the local Comm-Z men; I was not a welcome sight to them.

For a moment I tried to imagine what it would be like to be at Division Headquarters. I had never even been to regimental headquarters, had never known where it was throughout our moves in Belgium and Luxembourg; so I had certainly not thought about Division Headquarters. It was such a foreign environment that there were not even any stories about it. But the division commander surely would be in a warm place, and so would the staff and the other people. And they would be able to sit in a warm place to eat. And I wouldn't be surprised if they slept in a bed and could take their uniforms and boots off—they might even have a shower unit somewhere. Beyond that improbable luxury my imagination did not go. So would I trade with them?

My melancholy and my happiness had made themselves comfortable. Like two disparate but equal creatures, they had settled in, not to be put out soon. But they were quietly lying side by side, snoozing peacefully for the moment. No, I would not trade with the men from division! I would not trade with anyone, including General Eisenhower or President Roosevelt! And, thank God, it was too late now anyway. Even if Peter White's story about my transfer to CIC came true, the order would arrive too late. I would simply be a 513th trooper disguised as a CIC agent.

And now my happiness stirred, stretched lazily, and yawned contentedly before it put its head back between its paws to resume its snoozing.

When the waiter finally brought a menu, I ordered the most expensive thing on it and a large glass of beer.

Epilogue
One Last Great Jump: Operation Varsity

WILLIAM C. MITCHELL

Bernard Montgomery's strategy to cross northern Germany in the fall of 1944 by first opening a narrow but extended corridor through Holland was highly imaginative and certainly spectacular, but also militarily uncharacteristic of the flamboyant field marshal. So was the haste with which this potentially war-ending feat was planned and implemented. Although the two American airborne divisions, the 82d and 101st, were highly experienced and the British 1st Airborne somewhat less so, they were provided little notice and no practice for such a difficult and audacious operation. Operation Market-Garden had no precedent. Thus no one was surprised when it failed.

And, so, in the Allied defeat at Arnhem was born Operation Varsity, the airborne phase of Operation Plunder, names given the attempt to cross the Rhine River and end the war in the spring of 1945. Operation Varsity, or the "Rhine jump," on March 24, 1945, at Wesel, Germany, was to become the last and most spectacular but perhaps least known great airborne feat of the war—in fact, of all subsequent wars. Never again would entire divisions be committed in airborne warfare; never again would gliders be employed; and never again would the ill-fated C-46 be used to ferry paratroopers.

As if to prevent a repetition of all the errors committed during Market-Garden, Montgomery's plan to both encircle the Ruhr industrial area and unleash an armored advance across the northern German plains was a model of thorough preparation and near flawless execution. So successful was the operation that, in retrospect, some military thinkers and historians have deemed it unnecessary and, therefore, far too costly. Whether necessary or not cannot be finally determined. I argue that all objectives of Varsity were realized; but critics are partially correct in maintaining that it was far more costly than its planners expected. Whatever the strategic debates, Kurt Gabel's 513th Parachute Infantry Regiment (PIR) participated in the jump, and he had every reason to be proud of his 1st Battalion and the regiment because each of the three battalions was awarded the Presidential or Distinguished Unit Citation for their actions on the drop zones.

The Overall Situation

Having closed out the Bulge from December through February, the Allies had by mid-March 1945 reached the Rhine River. Because the Rhine, especially the lower portion flowing through northern Germany and the Netherlands, is a formidable military obstacle, ways had to be found for crossing and preferably in more than one place. Montgomery's front was the most strategically located, the most strongly defended, and where the river was at its broadest, therefore his was the most challenging task facing the Allied commanders. Montgomery's response was to open a 30-mile front stretching south from Emmerich to Wesel, Germany. Wesel, only 40 miles southeast of Arnhem was, like Bastogne, an important crossroads for communication and transportation (see Map 1). If a crossing could be established and maintained, it would enable a firm base from which to encircle the Ruhr Valley as well as permit an armoured dash straight to Berlin. (The selection of Wesel as the site for the operation is interesting in that Montgomery had in early September 1944 seriously considered it in place of Arnhem for Operation Market-Garden, but finally decided against it because the Allied air forces had warned him that a jump on Wesel would entail heavy casualties because of the thick antiflak defenses over the Ruhr. Six months later, the flak was still in place.)

The German Defenses

Although Germany was clearly exhausted and unable to mount further offensives, it had shown an extraordinary capacity to prolong the war and make victory more costly for the Allies. As subsequent research was to show, German production of many important tools, weapons, and supplies of war actually increased during the later war years and German resolve and ability to fight were only beginning to be questioned.

Across the Rhine, Montgomery confronted a mixed bag of potential opposition ranging from remnants of some superb parachute formations to the *Volksturn* consisting of elderly men and young boys. One did not know which of these opponents one might encounter even

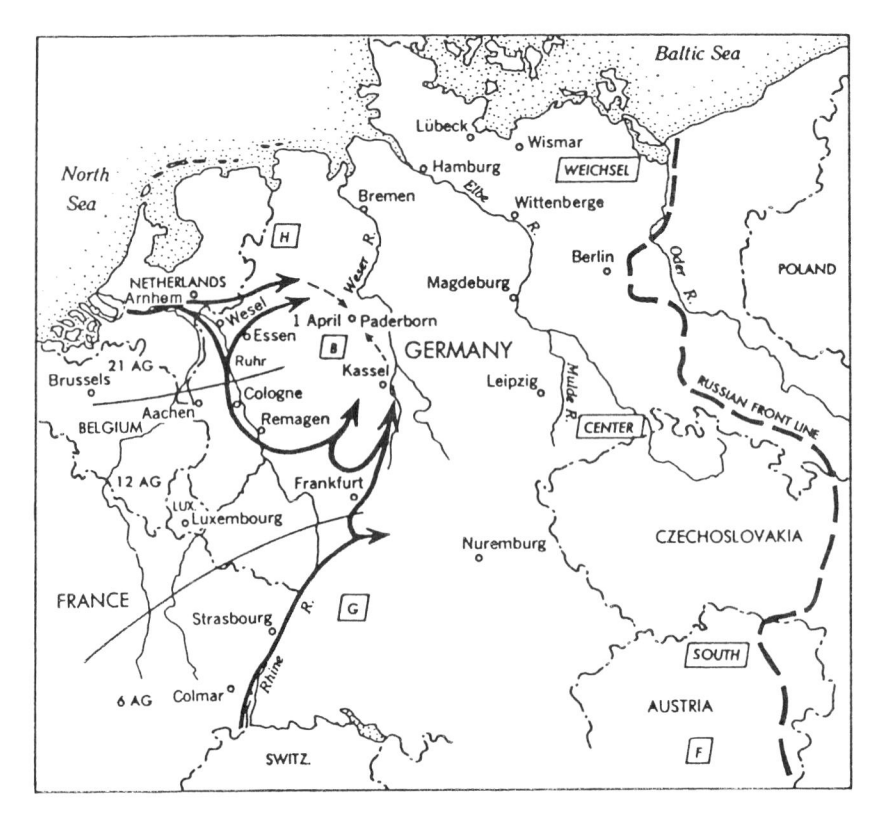

Map 1. Situation, March 28, 1945 (from John D. Eisenhower, The Bitter Woods *[New York: G. P. Putnam's Sons, 1969], p. 444)*

within a company front. In any case, the defenses faced by Montgomery exceeded by far those anywhere along the Rhine. For example, defense of the northern sector was entrusted to General Alfred Schlemm and his 1st Parachute Army. Schlemm had led paratroops in Crete, Russia, Italy, and the Reichwald; he was, to say the least, an able, experienced commander of elite troops. Although he had three parachute divisions (6th, 7th, and 8th), all had been tired by continuous fighting and were down to 3,000 to 4,000 men apiece. There was a shortage of heavy weapons, ammunition, and so on, but each division was supported by around 200 artillery pieces. To the south of these troops was the decidedly inferior 84th Infantry Division, which was also exhausted from fighting during the previous two months. At the northernmost flank of German defenses were some armored units without much armor.

Supporting these defenses were a considerable number—nearly a thousand—artillery and antiaircraft guns, many of which had been used to defend the industrial Ruhr just to the south of Wesel. Their easy shift to the north was hardly unexpected. The German Command had long anticipated an airborne operation somewhere in the 40 miles between Arnhem and Wesel for the simple reason that airborne thrusts in that area made considerable sense. The Rhine had to be crossed and the only places where large airborne formations could be dropped were in the flat lands of the lower Rhine. The one thing the Germans did not know was the actual day of the invasion. As matters turned out, the Germans had installed approximately 114 heavy guns and countless ground defenses in the actual areas of the parachute drop and glider landing zones. This was a heavy concentration because the projected assault area measured only 4 by 6 miles. One can gain a better appreciation of the density of this fire power by examining Map 2, a rare map that shows the exact positions of 90 of the German guns. Allied aerial photos did not do a good job of disclosing the defensive arrangements nor did the seemingly overwhelming artillery and air force bombardment preceding the jump seriously damage the opposition.

Operation Varsity: The Tactical Plan

Having learned a number of lessons from Market-Garden, Montgomery and the planners from the 18th Allied Airborne Command decided that the operation had to be made during daylight, that the entire operation had to be confined to a small area, and that all troops had to be brought in simultaneously and not dribbled out over several days as was the practice in both Market-Garden and Normandy. The idea was to simply overpower the defenses by dropping directly upon them. And to ensure that there would be no prolonged isolation of the troops at the end of a 50-mile-long corridor as in the case of Arnhem, these paratroops would be only a few miles from the Rhine boat crossings. And, further, to surprise the Germans it was decided not to drop the airborne first and then conduct the river crossings but to initiate the water crossings first, the night before the drop. In short, the army and airborne were still learning on the job.

Although some consideration was given the possibility of using three divisions, limited transport prevented that option and in the end it was decided to use one British division, the 6th Airborne of Normandy fame, and the American 17th Airborne, which had had much training and, as we have seen, a brief but highly intensive and bloody battle experience in the Ardennes and Rhineland campaigns. The British division would fly in from bases in Britain while the 17th would take off from numerous airfields around Paris (see Map 3).

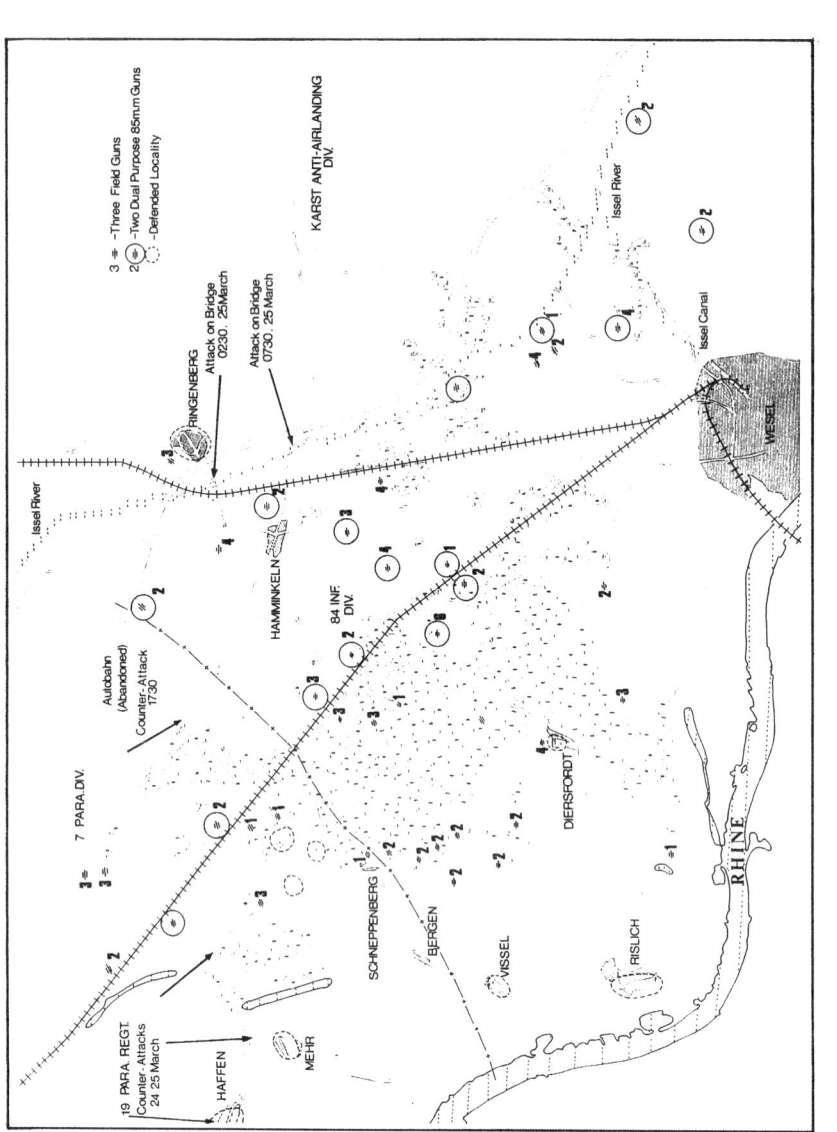

Map 2. *German Defensive Localities and Gun Positions, March 24, 1945 (from Napier Crookenden, Airborne at War [New York: Charles Scribner's Sons, 1978], p. 89)*

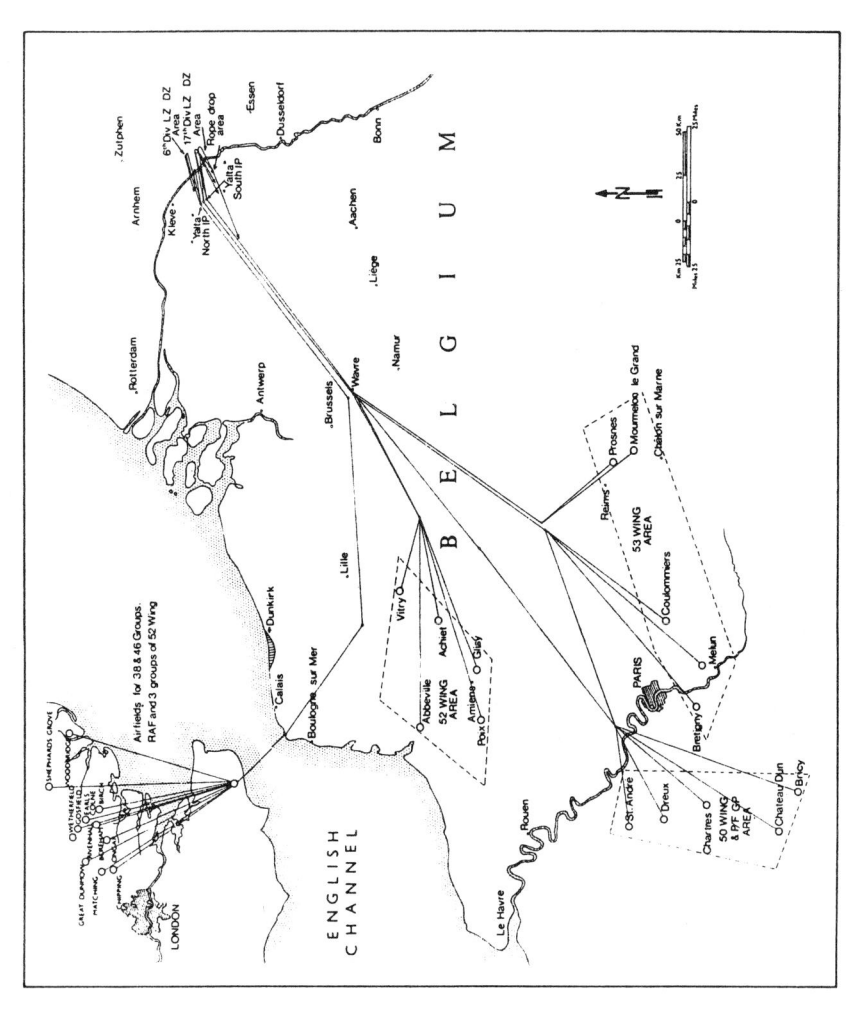

Map 3. Operation Varsity Routes (from Napier Crookenden, Airborne at War [New York: Charles Scribner's Sons, 1978], p. 90)

The British would land on the left flank, or northern side, of the battlefield and the 17th on the right, or southern, flank. Both divisions would be smaller than those employed in Normandy and Holland, with the 17th bringing in two instead of three parachute regiments—the 507th, which had fought in Normandy and lost 800 men, and the 513th, making its first combat jump. Each American regiment would consist of 2,100 paratroopers and be accompanied by 375 men of a parachute artillery battalion. These 5,000 paratroopers would also be accompanied by the 194th Glider Regiment and its support groups, a total of 4,850 men for a grand total of 9,777 airborne troops.

The British contingent was smaller still, consisting of some 3,800 parachutists and 3,400 gliderists. The grand Allied total was barely 17,000 as contrasted with the nearly 21,000 who participated in the initial D-Day operations in Normandy and Holland. Total airborne personnel involved a week after the D-Day landings in Normandy and Holland numbered at least 30,000. The missions of each division, regiment, and its component units were established, and landing and drop zones assigned (see Map 4).

Varsity called for the invading river-crossing forces to link up to the airborne within a day or so to avoid the severe problems confronted by the British 1st Airborne Division at Arnhem and to a lesser extent by the American airborne, who were positioned much closer to the British line of departure in the Holland operation. Once the link-up occurred, the two forces could then mount a combined infantry-armored thrust to the northeast and across the plains of northern Germany as well as encircle the Ruhr with its industrial might and substantial military forces prepared to defend the stronghold. The plan was implemented but not without some glitches; some were typical of airborne experiences, whereas others were the fates of war.

"Here Come the Airborne"

March 24, 1945, was a mild, lovely spring day of the sort one would not normally associate with war and dying. After an early morning breakfast and rousing cheering sessions led by officers, the troopers donned their bulky equipment at numerous airfields in Britain and around Paris to begin their two- to three-hour flights to the drop zones. The gliderists clambered into their wood and canvas chariots to be towed, for the first time in pairs, by single transport planes (C-47s), a very hazardous undertaking. This beautiful morning was marred for the gliderists by ex-

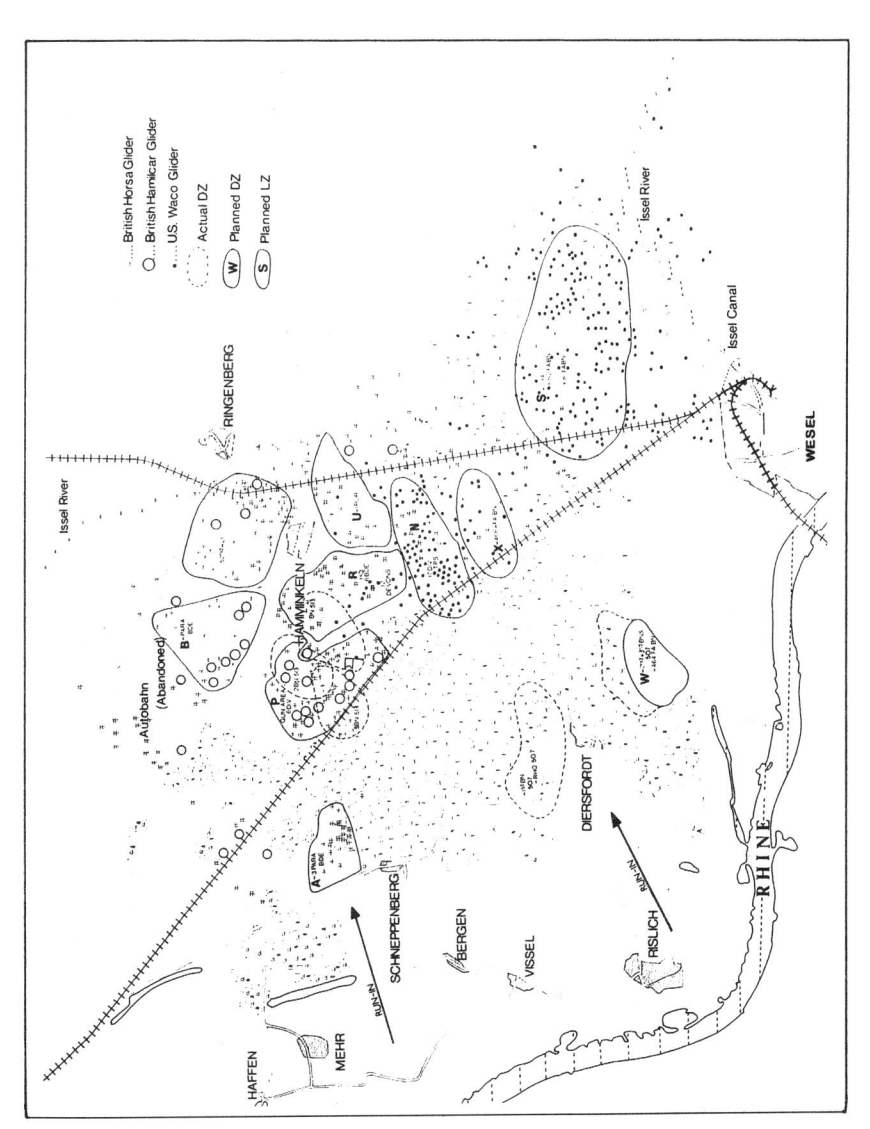

Map 4. Operation Varsity—British and American Dropping and Landing Zones (from Napier Crookenden, Airborne at War [New York: Charles Scribner's Sons, 1978], p. 96).

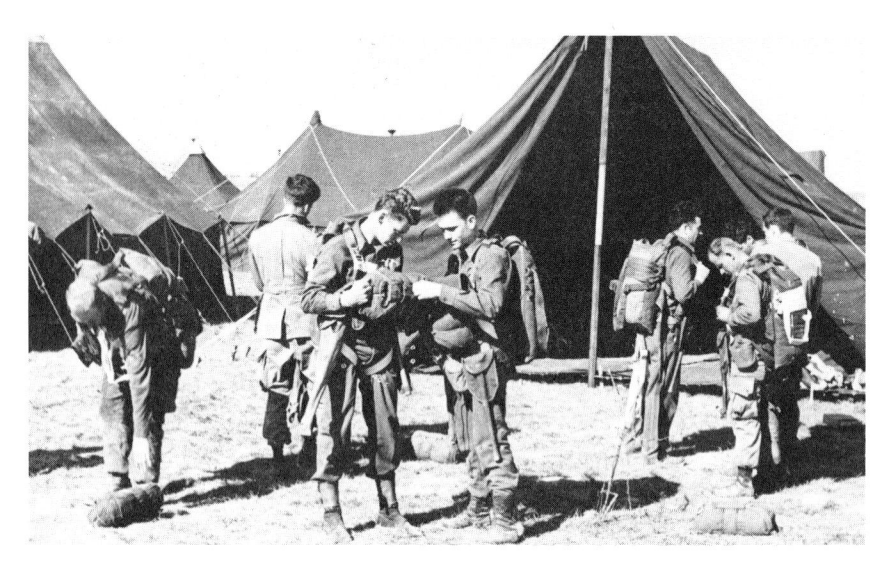

Getting ready for the jump across the Rhine River, March 24, 1945

ceedingly rough air currents that aborted 18 flights for the Americans and 35 for the British.

The gigantic and majestic procession was protected by 543 fighter planes and observed by hundreds of thousands of spectators, including Winston Churchill, Dwight Eisenhower, and virtually everyone living or stationed along the lines of flight. As the planes approached the Rhine River, the 3,500 artillery pieces Montgomery used to soften defenses stopped firing and the planes descended and reduced their speed to enable the jumpers and glider pilots to complete their tasks. But the balmy spring day—it was then 10:00 A.M.—rapidly turned into a day of intense warfare. The saturation bombing of the previous week and the artillery barrage and smoke screen set off by the ground forces shrouded the approach and the drop zones. As in past operations, some flights went off course, and although none approached the dispersions of Sicily and Normandy where troops were scattered over 40 miles, an entire regiment (513th) was dropped 2 to 3 miles north of their assigned zones amid the glider landing fields of the British 6th Airborne. This error had highly beneficial consequences for the 6th Airborne but disastrous ones for the American 466th Artillery Battalion, whose zone was to have been secured by the 513th before they arrived. As Map 4 shows, the 513th landed to the south and west of Hamminkeln instead of on DZX. There it joined forces with the British gliderists in securing the area.

But during the few miles from the Rhine to the drop zones and back, the C-47s and C-46s encountered the heaviest flak of the entire airborne war. Of the 72 new and untried C-46s that ferried the 513th, 22 were shot down, with the jumpers of all but one plane managing to get out but not the plane crews. Because the C-46 was being used for the first time it was not known that its fuel system was highly vulnerable to enemy fire and that it did not have the staying power and endurance of the reliable C-47. Its great advantages consisted in its size—it could carry up to 30 jumpers as compared to 18 for the older C-47—and its having two doors, one on each side, which enabled much more rapid exit and, therefore, less dispersion on the ground. With less dispersion, assembly time is reduced and the units made more cohesive. The weakest link in an airborne operation is its assembly time upon landing. One must remember that assembly is bad enough in a training jump let alone under intense enemy fire.

The flak and ground fire were the most intense of any airborne operation of the war. One experienced American officer who had also participated in Normandy said there "was no comparison," while an equally experienced British officer observed that "this daylight drop was to make Arnhem look like a Sunday picnic." The German artillery and antiaircraft gunners had years of experience in fighting off the air raids over the Ruhr Valley. The knocking down of 80 aircraft was done in a matter of minutes. Those who jumped or rode gliders down through the fire compared it to the Fourth of July fireworks they knew as children. The losses during the first two hours were not only far beyond predictions but the highest of the airborne war. Air force crews plus glider pilot losses included 91 killed in action, 280 wounded or injured, and another 414 missing in action. Of the 405 British gliders, 10 were shot down and another 284 riddled by fire as they made their approach. Half of them landed in what one historian termed "terrifying crash landings." Only 80 of the big Horsas and Hamilcars landed untouched or damaged. Of the 878 much smaller American Waco gliders, only 13 were shot down, but 300 of these came in two hours after the initial landings and so fared better. Still, over half of the gliders were hard hit by flak and ground fire and nearly all made crash landings amid heavy small-arms fire.

From the perspectives of the individual paratrooper and gliderist, the flight to the drop zone was hardly a majestic one. In fact, most of us remained seated in our bulky equipment and parachutes and could not see much of a flight pattern. Our time was spent in silent prayer and a lot of singing, joking, and smoking. For the new men of the 513th, the greatest anxiety concerned their own courage, whether they would be afraid and, worse, fail their comrades. Every experience since they entered jump school was designed to ensure that they would not fail and they did not.

Most ground forces enter combat gradually as they move toward the front and hear and see increasing signs and sounds of violence. First the thunder of artillery, then the rumble of the tanks and the terrifying sounds of the mortars and machine guns, and finally the bodies of the dead. Unlike infantry, the airborne drop from the skies and in this particular operation right into the midst of enemy defenses. Such dramatic and drastic immersion has its effects, effects that cannot be easily prepared for in training. Because parachute jumping is exhilarating even for the most experienced of skydivers, the excitement of jumping into combat is compounded enormously. Varsity had more of this excitement than any other airborne operation because the battlefield below provided an extraordinary scene and reception. The Germans were actually shooting at us and it was not a casual response. Every weapon was being fired as rapidly as its crews could fire them. The smoke and smell of the battle were everywhere and the jumpers could see and hear the tracers from machine guns and the puffs and flak bursts of the antiaircraft batteries. Others saw bullets and shrapnel enter the planes and kill and wound some of the jumpers and crew. Still others saw planes on fire or going down in flames.

Leaving the plane safely at 500 to 600 feet and having one's chute open is hardly the end of personal concern. Although brief, the drop seems like an eternity. Not being hit, not breaking a leg, and not landing helplessly in a tree or on a farm building become paramount considerations. And once on the ground the trooper must get out of harness and organize his equipment so he can begin fighting as well as locating his squad or at least platoon and company. Few paratroopers who have jumped in combat have had the wonderful experience of immediately recognizing landmarks and those who landed alongside them. Some 800 men of the 17th Airborne were listed as missing in action after the first day of Varsity. Luckily, most who were not injured, wounded, or killed did turn up within the next twelve to twenty-four hours. A familiar face, especially of one's leaders, is most reassuring even to experienced men.

Like all men in combat, the 513th learned once more that nothing serves to concentrate the mind as having a determined enemy firing at you. Fear subsides as one must deal with the source of the problem. Unfortunately, inexperienced paratroopers sometimes forgot a major lesson presumably learned in training: not to bunch up. Many of the new men sought the alluring but false security of nearness and ended up paying the price.

Both the officers and the men of the 513th found the terrain and

A few hours after the jump across the Rhine River

landmarks baffling because they did not resemble the mock-ups, maps, and photos memorized during the week before the jump. As the British paratroopers and gliderists landed in their huge Horsa gliders, it became clear that either the Americans or the British were in the wrong place. It was the Americans. Instead of being dropped approximately half the distance between Wesel and Hamminkeln (see Map 4), the 513th was dropped in the vicinity of the latter town, some 2 or more miles to the north. Hamminkeln was a strongly defended position manned by German paratroopers and SS troops. The 1st Battalion was dropped in the immediate vicinity of two batteries of 88 mm all-purpose guns and two batteries of 20 mm weapons, causing an intense battle and heavy losses for both sides. The most important consequence of the misdrop of the 513th was the salvation of the British glider regiment. In the opinions of Lewis H. Brereton, commander of the 1st Allied Airborne Army, and General Eric Bols, commanding general of the British 6th Airborne Division, had not the American paratroopers landed first to silence the enemy guns the British losses would have been catastrophic; indeed, the entire glider brigade might well have been destroyed.[1] As it was, they suffered losses of 40 percent.

Three hours after the landings, the 17th troopers who were not busy locating their squads, platoons, and companies and/or fighting Germans were suddenly jolted by the incredible noise of 240 B-24s flying in at 100 to 500 feet to drop supplies. Although the Germans must have been surprised and startled, they managed to keep their wits; they shot down 15 and badly damaged another 104 of these big but slow bombers. To make things worse, the supply drops to the 17th Airborne were off target, and only 50 percent of the bundles were retrieved immediately. But in contrast to the several Holland and Normandy resupply missions, all of Varsity's bundles ended up in the hands of Allied forces.

Despite the bad drop of the 513th, the partially misdropped 507th, and the hostile reception staged by the Germans, the two divisions were able to assemble most of their men in their own units before the day was out and most were to move to their designated areas (see Map 5). During the next two to three days, the airborne completed its link-up with those who had crossed the river by boat and bridge. Then came the combined dash across the plains and through the cities and towns toward Münster. The 513th had the good fortune to work for the next ten days with the highly experienced and elite British armored force known as the 6th Guard Armoured Brigade, which consisted of the Coldstream, Scots, and Grenadier Guards battalions who used the superb Churchill tank. During the next ten days they led the Allied advance into northern Germany. After taking Münster, the 17th Airborne joined the American encirclement of the Ruhr while the Guardsmen accompanied by the British 6 Airborne went all the way to Bremen.

The fighting from Wesel to Münster was sporadic and ranged from several highly intensive, costly encounters to almost unopposed dashes down major highways and roads. The 513th paratroopers rode the British Churchill tanks until opposition arose to halt the tanks, at which time the paratroopers were called upon to subdue the Germans. Some of the combined attacks took place at night, not an easy task when units are from different armies. But the cooperation was extraordinary. It had to be in order to overcome the Germans, who staged costly defenses at Dorsten, Haltern, Dülmen, and especially Buldern. The fighting at each of these junctures was usually brief, only a few hours, but violent, with both sides suffering heavy casualties. Many of the British tankers and American paratroopers distinguished themselves beyond comparison. Neither the Germans nor the Allies treated the war as all but over. At the end of most wars, shirking becomes a problem because few soldiers want to die or be maimed when the end is near, but that was not the case with these paratroopers and tankers; they fought as though the war had just begun and the outcome was still doubtful.

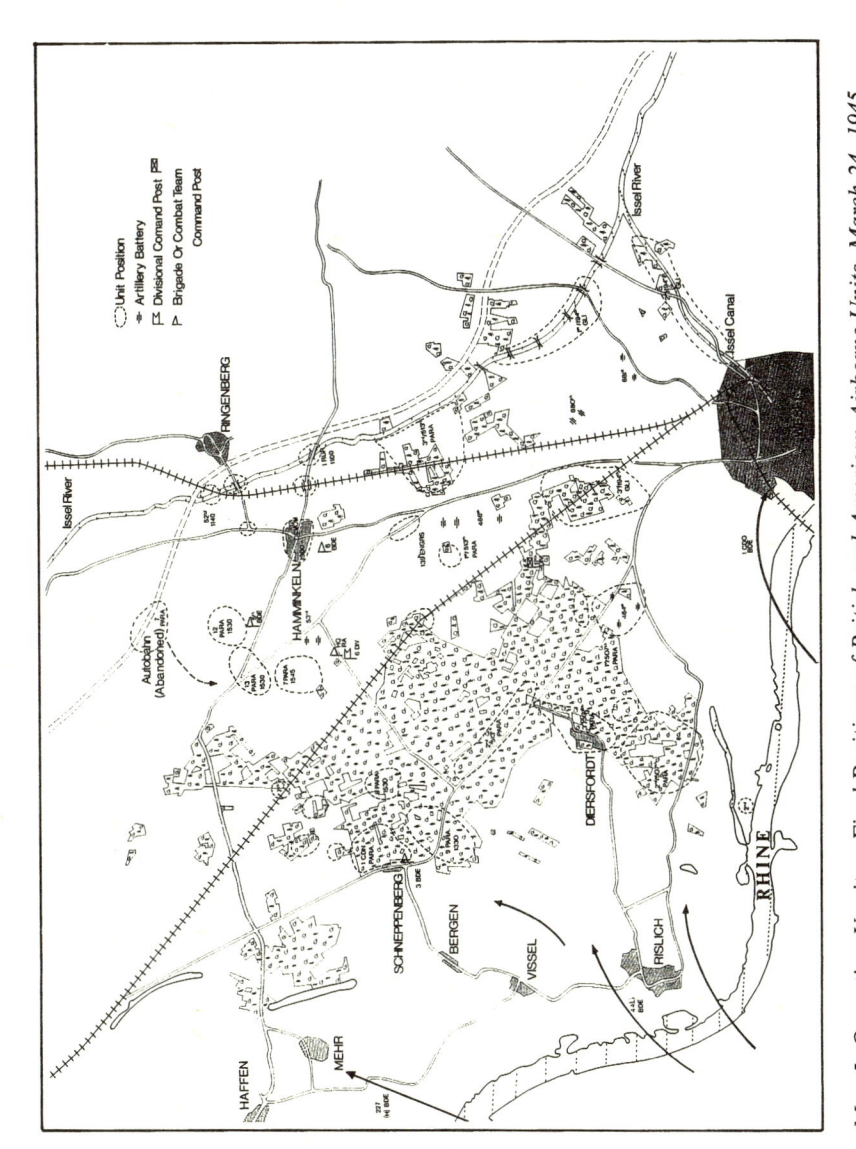

Map 5. Operation Varsity—Final Positions of British and American Airborne Units, March 24, 1945 (from Napier Crookenden, Airborne at War [New York: Charles Scribner's Sons, 1978], p. 107)

The Cost of "One More Great Jump"

By the war's end, most of the Allied brass were convinced airborne advocates and some, including General Marshall and Winston Churchill, favored daring mass jumps far to the rear of the front lines. And even Eisenhower, who shared a skepticism about the airborne with Omar Bradley, was thrilled by these vast airborne armadas and searched for more ways to use them. At least three dozen plans, including jumps on Rome and Berlin, were hastily devised but were canceled during 1943/45. Airborne envelopment, although spectacular and often highly effective, was costly in equipment and casualties among elite fighting men. The airborne divisions had the highest casualty rates among Allied forces, exceeding by far those of conventional units. Approximately one third of all airborne personnel became casualties of one kind or another as contrasted with the 10 percent among regular infantry divisions. The airborne rate was often higher than that suffered by marine divisions in the Pacific.

During the first forty-eight hours of this last great drop of World War II, the 17th Airborne Division lost 393 killed in action and another 834 wounded. Two hundred more names would be added to the KIA list during the next three weeks. And the 513th would eventually lose 190 killed in action. During those forty-eight hours the British 6th Airborne lost 347 men killed in action and 731 wounded. These losses when added to those already cited among aircrews and glider pilots totaled 831 killed in action and 1,615 wounded during the two days of March 24–25. Eventually the British 6th Airborne Division lost 700 men killed in action (about 100 fewer than they lost in Normandy) and another 750 wounded in action.

In addition to these human losses, few of the gliders were considered salvageable, some eighty planes had been shot down, and hundreds of others left in bad need of repair. The British gliderists of the Royal Ulster Rifles and Devonshire Battalions, among whom the 513th dropped, were particularly hard hit during the first day of the operation, with both units suffering more than 50 percent casualties. One fourth of the Ulsters were killed and many of them before they could leave the gliders. The Devons had even more killed, but a greater number managed to get out of their gliders and engage the Germans. The carnage would have been far worse had not the 513th been misdropped before the British arrived. British gliderist losses during Varsity were much higher than those suffered by the same units in Normandy. Paratroopers of the 6th Airborne fared better, although they lost one of their most able and colorful battalion commanders, Jeff Nicklin, a Canadian whose body was

A fate that befell many British gliderists and Horsa gliders

found hanging from a tree, still in his parachute harness, right over a German slit trench. The same fate was to befall Lt. Stanley Galicki, the fabled jump school instructor of whom Kurt Gabel wrote.

Gabel's pride in the 513th and in its performance during the Wesel jump was shared by the officers and men of the 17th Airborne Division and the army because all three battalions of the regiment were awarded the Distinguished Unit Citation for their efforts. But the gallantry displayed by the paratroopers was best and most movingly described by an officer of the British Guards Brigade whose Churchill tanks carried the troopers into battle after their three days on the drop zones. That officer was none other than Michael Howard, later to become a distinguished military historian as well as historian of the Guards Brigade. Of the initial contact with the 513th, he wrote: "The Coldstream [Guards] were to work with the Third Battalion of the 513th Para. Regt. commanded by Lt. Col. Kent, and the two battalions made contact immediately. The Guardsmen quickly found that they were to carry some of the finest troops in the American Army. They were alert and enthusiastic and their friendliness was irresistible. Their equipment was superb; after three days of severe fighting they were still cheerful and anxious for more."[2]

During subsequent days Michael Howard was to repeat his and his men's admiration for the 513th paratroopers. He wrote of them "leaping from their tanks to rush the Lippe bridges."[3] And on another occasion he noted that "a troop of tanks and a patrol led by Lt. Col. Kent returned to eliminate the Germans, which they did very thoroughly."[4] On still another occasion he spoke of the willingness of his own men to aid the American paratroopers who always fought with "all the vigour and determination that the Guardsmen had come to expect of them."[5]

And, in reflecting upon his experiences, Michael Howard paid the supreme compliment, one not often conferred by our reticent and often critical British colleagues:

> But without doubt the most memorable feature of the advance on Münster had been the harmony with which the Guardsmen and the American paratroops had worked together. In such an advance tank crews and infantry are completely interdependent; each rely for their very lives on the courage and comradeship of the other. Even when both are of the same nationality there are countless opportunities for misunderstanding and bitterness. Between Guardsmen and the Americans there was complete mutual confidence, and only perfect co-operation could have achieved such remarkable results. It was with real regret that the battalion learned at Münster that it would have to part company with its American friends. This comradeship between the Fourth Battalion and the 513 U.S. Airborne Regt. must rank with the partnership between the Third Battalion and the South Africans as one of the happiest episodes in the history of the Regiment and of the war.[6]

Still another historian of the Scots Guards Brigade observed

> that Troops about to go into action together for the first time always scrutinize each other carefully and this is particularly true when they are of different nationalities. They like to know what to expect of each other in the stress of battle. In a very few minutes both officers and Guardsmen had decided that these Americans would make fine partners in action. They looked tough and alive

and clean; their equipment from jeeps to wireless sets looked well cared for. There was nothing to show that less than three days before they had been fighting desperately on their landing zones and that it had not been easy for them ever since. They looked their part as the elite of the American Army.[7]

After ten days of joint combat in which they led Allied forces across Germany, this same historian and officer of the Scots Guards wrote: "The fighting qualities of the Americans had to be seen to be believed. Whatever the odds against them . . . they took on any task with the greatest enthusiasm, and loved getting into close quarters with what they called the 'filthy Krauts.' The phrase by which they will always be remembered is: 'Come on boys, let's go.' "[8]

The War Ends

After the 6th Guard Brigade departed for Bremen, the 17th Airborne was redeployed to participate in the capture of the Ruhr Valley. The Ruhr was taken by American forces with relative ease. The 513th participated in the capture of the industrial city of Essen, a city that was largely leveled by Allied bombing. After the surrender of German forces on May 6, 1945, the 17th Airborne Division became a part of the occupying army to the northwest and west of Essen and remained in that role until June when they were sent back to France. There they rested and some, including me, were awarded R and R in such fabulous places as the Riviera and Paris. During June and July the division was reorganized with its "high-point" men shipped home to be discharged and its relatively high-point men reassigned to guard duty with the 82d Airborne in Berlin. Men with low points were sent to embarkation ports to be reassigned to the 11th Airborne Division in the Pacific and eventual participation in the invasion of Japan, which was planned for early November 1945. These paratroopers never got to the Pacific because enroute the H-bomb ended the war, and they, too, were discharged. The 17th Airborne Division was used as a paper organization for the shipment home of high-point paratroopers from all airborne divisions. Thus the 17th sailed for the United States in August 1945 and was officially disbanded that same month. The 82d Airborne Division served on as the Honor Guards of occupied Berlin; the 101st Airborne performed the same service in Berchtesgaden. In Tokyo the 11th Airborne served General Douglas MacArthur in the same role. Like the 17th, the 13th Airborne Division, the only one not to see action in Europe, was disbanded to become a part of history. The 82d continues to serve the country from its traditional base, Fort Bragg, North Carolina; the 101st is based at Camp Campbell, Kentucky, and is now an air mobile division using helicopters rather than parachutes and gliders.

Notes

1. Lewis H. Brereton, *The Brereton Diaries* (New York: William Morrow and Company, 1946), p. 407.
2. Michael Howard, *The Coldstream Guards* (Oxford: Oxford University Press, 1951), p. 331.
3. Ibid., p. 332.
4. Ibid., p. 334.
5. Ibid.
6. Ibid., p. 337.
7. Patrick Forbes, *6th Guards Tank Brigade* (London: Sampson Low, Marston & Co., 1946), p. 125.
8. Ibid., p. 143.

Appendix A
The Honors of War

Military awards are given to individuals and to units, usually smaller than a division. The three battalions making up the 513th, the 466th Artillery Battalion (attached to the 513th during the Rhine jump), and the 224th Airborne Medical Company were awarded the Distinguished Unit Citation for Operation Varsity. A Distinguished Unit Citation was also awarded the 507th Parachute Infantry Regiment (PIR) for its achievements during the Normandy jump of June 6, 1944, when it was attached to the 82d Airborne Division.

Four members of the 17th Airborne Division were posthumously awarded our nation's highest medal, the Congressional Medal of Honor. Two members of the 513th—Sgt. Isadore S. Jackman of B Company and Pvt. Stuart S. Stryker of E Company—earned them, respectively, in the Battle of the Bulge and the Rhine jump. Both performed their heroic actions and died within the first few hours of combat. The other recipients were Pvt. George Peters of the 507th PIR and Sgt. Clinton M. Hendrick of I Company, 194th Glider Regiment. Both men earned their medals during the Rhine operation.

Although no single authoritative list of other awards to individuals can be found, various divisional and unit records suggest that the following medals had been awarded: Distinguished Service Medal, 3; Legion of Merit, 1; Silver Star, 43; Bronze Star, 120; Certificate of Merit, 7; Purple Heart, 6,298 (data compiled from *History of the 513th Parachute Infantry—11 January 1943-6 September 1945* [Washington, D.C.: National Military Archives, 1946], section 9; William E. Miller and Nat H. Youngblood, eds., *The Talon: With the 17th in Ardennes* [Paris: Imprimerie E. Desfossés, 1945] and Frank Langston and Justin P. Buckridge, eds., *The Talon Crosses the Rhine* [Paris: Imprimerie E. Desfossés, 1945].

Appendix B
Some Costs of War

Organized in August 1943, the 17th Airborne Division arrived in the European Theater of Operations in August 1944, but was not committed to combat until Christmas Day, nine days after the German counteroffensive began on December 16, 1944. After approximately forty-five days of official combat in the Battle of the Bulge and the Rhineland campaign and another twenty-one in Operation Varsity, the division's casualties were as follows: killed in action, 1,191; died of wounds, 191; wounded or injured in action, 4,713; missing in action, 426; total casualties, 6,521 (data compiled from *Army Battle Casualties and Non-Battle Deaths in World War II: Final Report* [Washington, D.C.: Statistical and Accounting Branch, Office of the Adjutant General, 1953], pp. 80–81.

In approximately sixty-six days of combat, the division lost an average of 102 men per day, one of the highest averages incurred by any division, including the other airborne, during the entire war. Because approximately 20,000 men served at sometime or another in the 17th Airborne, the overall rate was 34 percent, or about 2 to 3 percent higher than that sustained by the 82d and 101st Airborne divisions and three times the rates incurred by the regular infantry divisions serving in the European campaigns. The 17th Airborne division's rates are actually understated because hundreds of those on the roster of the division did not actually serve abroad or did not participate in combat or in all of the battles in which the division fought. In any case, the casualty rate was among the highest sustained by any division; that experienced by the 513th PIR was still higher.

With a total of 2,567 casualties of all kinds, or approximately 39 percent of the division's losses, Gabel's 513th PIR was the hardest hit of the division's units. It should be noted that the 513th constituted only 18 percent of the division. During the Battle of the Bulge, the regiment sustained 46 percent of divisional losses; during the Rhine jump, it incurred 50 percent of the division's casualties. In the Ardennes fighting, 62 percent of the regiment became casualties of one sort or another, a rate far beyond that of any other parachute regiment. Although the casualties suffered during the Rhine operation were lower, they were still in the neighborhood of 46 percent, and about two thirds were sustained during the first twenty-four hours of the jump. Total casualties of the 513th PIR can be summarized as follows: killed in action or died of wounds, 453; wounded or injured in action, 1,531; missing in action (includes captured), 577; total, 2,561 (data compiled from *History of the 513th Parachute Infantry—11 January 1943-6 September, 1945* [Washington, D.C.: National Military Archives, 1946], Section 8).

Of these losses, 247 were killed during the Ardennes; 190 in the Wesel jump; and 16 in Rhineland combat. Some 930 were wounded and/or injured during the Bulge, and another 79 or so were lost during late January and early February 1945. The Rhine jump left 521 wounded or injured in action. As to be expected, some troopers were wounded on more than one occasion during the same or different campaigns. Although official data on the incidence of multiple wounds and injuries is not readily available, we may assume that the number of such wounded is not small. And because of the higher risks entailed in parachute jumping—in both training and combat—one should expect a fairly high rate of injuries. Glider infantry units sustained a particularly high level of equipment loss and injuries during the Rhine jump.

We may justifiably but proudly conclude that the honors of war came at a very high price to the members of the 17th Airborne Division and in particular to the 513th Parachute Infantry regiment. Perhaps, the Regiment tempted Fate a bit too much when it adopted the black cat with black chute and boots as its insignia.

Index

A-bomb, 271
Air raids, London, 145-46
Allen, Wade, 80, 137
Allgemeine SS, 14
All Quiet on the Western Front (Remarque), 154
American Expeditionary Force, 153
American forces. *See specific armies, battalions, regiments, services*
Anderson, Morris, 211, 246-47
Andover (England), 142, 144, 145
"Approach and dispatch," 106
Ardennes campaign, xiii, 223, 249, 257; casualties of, 274, 275
Arlington Reception Center (Calif.), 16, 18
Army Battle Casualties and Non-Battle Deaths in World War II: Final Report, 274
Army General Classification Test, 29-30
Arnhem fighting, 257, 263; defeat in, 254, 255; units involved in, 148
Artillery: experience of German, 263; in Operation Varsity, 262. *See also specific campaigns, units*
Assault platoon, 170
Atlanta, Ga., 33
Attack techniques, 106
Aussies, 137
Awards, 273. *See also specific awards*

B-24s, in Operation Varsity, 266
Baier, Norman, 135, 140, 153, 155, 162, 167, 203
Basic Training, description of, 37-38. *See also* Parachute Basic Training
Bastogne, 160, 169-88, 212, 230, 249
Bastogne perimeter, 154-55
Bastogne Road, 173, 174, 206
Battle of the Bulge, 150, 223, 273; casualties in, 274, 275
Battle: The Story of the Bulge (Toland), xiii
Bayonet charge (Bastogne), 173-76
Bazookas, 48, 171

Beaulieu, Leo ("Frenchie"), 93-94, 107, 108, 138, 167, 204, 244-45
Belgium, 153-68
Berchtesgaden (Germany), 271
Berets, origin of, 148
Berlin, 255, 271
"Blood on the Risers," lyrics to, 126-28
Boats, Our River and, 245, 247
Bodies, search for, 206-10
Bois de Fragette (Belgium), 155, 171, 189-201, 212, 225
Bols, Eric, 265
"Boogie Woogie," jukebox and, 52, 55, 56
Boots, shining of, 97
Boston, Mass., 134, 135
Boy Scouts of America, 7
Bremen (Germany), 266
Brereton, Lewis H., 265
British forces. *See specific units*
British Museum, visit to, 145
British Royal Ulster Rifles gliderists, 268
Bronze Star, 273
Brotbeutel (knapsacks), 156
Brown, John Sloan, xii
Browning, F. A. M., 148
Browning automatic rifles, 47
Buckridge, Justin P., 273
"Buddies," importance of, 142-43
Bugle call, 59-60
Bugs Bunny, 96
Buldern (Germany), 266
Bunks, making up, 21-22

C-46s, in Operation Varsity, 263
C-47s, 46, 83, 87, 110, 112, 263; learning to exit, 114; in Operation Varsity, 260
Calhoun, Samuel, 174
California Bank (Los Angeles), job with, 4-7, 8-9
Calloway (driver), 182-85, 186, 191, 193
Camouflage, 193-95
Camp Barton-Stacey (England), 144
Campbell, John D., xii
Camp Campbell, Ky., 272

277

278 Index

Camp Forrest, Tenn., 134, 135
Camp Mackall, N.C., 134, 146; practice jump at, 117
Canteens, British, 144
Carbines, 47
Carter, Joe, 139
Casualties, 156–57, 161–62, 206–10, 225. *See also specific operations*
Cemetery, digging foxholes in, 153–54
Certificate of Merit, 273
Châlons-sur-Marne, 205, 248–53
Chattahoochee ferry, 46–47
Chattahoochee River, 37, 44, 125
Chattanooga, Tenn., 135
Chilboton airfield (England), 150
Christmas Day (1944), 153
Churchill, Winston, 262
Churchill tank, 266
Church services, 108–109, 144
Citizenship papers, getting, 135–36
Classification, 29
Classification and assignment (C&A), 32
Clausewitz, Karl, 211
Columbus, Ga., 33–34
"Combat in towns and cities," training for, 71, 146, 147
Command post: breaking down, 189–90; description of, 185; in foxhole, 201; in Wiltz, 240
Commands. *See* Jump commands
Congressional Medal of Honor, 273
Cooley, Joe, 141–42, 143
Counterintelligence Corps (CIC), 248
Cushman motorscooter, 149

Dalton, J. C. ("Jake"), 138–41, 153–56, 159, 163–65, 199, 204, 205, 245–47
De Haven, Gloria, 158
Der Schwarze Korps (newspaper), 14
Der Steuermer (newspaper), 140
Deuce-and-a-halfs, 155, 190
Devonshire Battalion gliderists, 268
Distinguished Unit Citation, 269, 273
Dog KPs, 38, 107, 120, 123–24
Dorsey, Tommy, 52
Dorsten (Germany), 266
Draftee Division: A Study of the 88th Infantry Division, First All-Selective Service Division into Combat in World War II (Brown), xii
Dulmen (Germany), 266
Du Maurier, Daphne, 148

Edwards, Irwin, 186, 188, 191, 211
EE8 telephones, 185
Egyptian Theater (Hollywood), 7, 95
Eighteenth Allied Airborne Command, 148, 257

Eighth Parachute Division, 256
Eighty-fourth Infantry Division, 256
Eighty-second Airborne Division (American), 148, 254, 271; awards to, 273
Eindhoven (Holland), 148
Eisenhower, Dwight, 262
Eleventh Airborne Division, 271
Eleventh Armored Division, 155
Emmerich (Germany), 255
England, 71; training in, 136–50
Essen (Germany), capture of, 271
Exercises: physical/mental screening, 40–45; presentation of wings, 132–33; Southhampton training, 147–48

Falkenberg, Bob, 9
Falkenberg, Tom, 9
Farmers Market (Los Angeles), 5, 6
First Airborne Division (British), 148, 254, 260
First Allied Airborne Army, 265
First Parachute Army, 256
First Parachute Training Regiment, 110; introduction to, 80–82; orientation for, 82–83
509th Battalion, 148
507th Parachute Infantry Regiment, 44, 96, 200, 201, 266; awards to, 273; in Normandy jump, 273. *See also* Seventeenth Airborne Division
513th Parachute Infantry Regiment, xix, xx, xxii, 44, 45, 82, 127, 248–49, 262; awards to, 273; casualties in Operation Varsity, 268; casualties in war, 274–75; description of performance of, 269–71; first battalion of, 265; first combat jump of, 263–65; mass practice jump of, 130; in Operation Varsity, 254; second battalion of, 170, 174, 182, 200, 201; stability of, xiii–xiv. *See also* Seventeenth Airborne Division
Flamierge (Belgium), 173, 206, 212
"Flash Gordon," 98, 107
Food, 90, 124, 203, 236–37; for Christmas dinner, 153; description of, 94; on frontline, 163; importance of, 66–67; K-rations as, 183; scouting for, scouting for, 234–39; and "tactical feeding," 66
Footlockers, 22
Formations, 54, 60
Fortan (England), 144
Fort Benning, Ga., 35–45, 79, 108, 146; description of, 35–36, 125
Fort Bragg, N.C., 72, 134, 146, 272
Fort Campbell, Ky., 72
Fort Warren, Wyo., 32
466th Artillery Battalion, 262, 273
Fourth Battalion (British), 270
Fourth of July, 72

Foxholes, 162-63, 201; description of, 167; digging, 153-54, 165-66; German, 220
France, action in, 153-68. *See also place names, names of battles*
Frederick the Great, 35
"Frenchie." *See* Beaulieu, Leo
Frying Pan. *See* Fort Benning, Ga.
Fuhlsbüttel concentration camp, 23-24

Galicki, Stanley A., 98-103, 105-6, 204, 269
Gas masks, 70, 220, 221
Geneva Conventions, 178-79, 180
German guns: MG-42s, 174, 177, 178, 180, 196-99; MG-39s, 175, 199; Schmeisser, 197, 245; 88-mm, 265; 20-mm, 263
German prisoners, interrogation of, 160-61
Germans, finding dead bodies of, 156-57, 225
Germany, description of house in, 185
Gliderists, British, 268
Gliders, 254, 265, 269; losses of, 269; losses of in Operation Varsity, 263, 268
Good, Peter B., 10
Good family. *See* Guttmann
Goodman, Benny, 9
Graves, registration of, 206
Green Berets, xxi
Green Books, xii
Greenfield, Kent Roberts, xii
Greenland, 136
Grenades. *See* Hand grenades
Grid-magnetic angle, finding the, 57-59
Guard duty, first, 31
Guards Brigade (British), 269-70, 271
Guidon bearer, selection of, 56-57
Guttmann, John (*Pappi*), 10-12
Guttmann, Leni, 5, 6, 10-12

Hager, Otto, 86, 93, 99, 107, 112-16, 120-30, 204
Haltern (Germany), 266
Hamburg, 23
Hamilcar glider, 263
Hamminkeln (Germany), 262, 265
Hand grenades: description of fragmentation MK 2, 68; qualification training for use of, 68-70
Harness manipulation, 89, 90
Helmets, description of, 81
Hendrick, Clinton M., 273
Herrenzimmer, childhood memories of, 11-12
Herrick, "Horseface," 138, 155, 167, 212, 216-17, 239
History of the 513th Parachute Infantry—11 January 1943-6 September 1945, 273, 275
Hitler, Adolph, 13-14, 150, 154
Hitler Youth, 7, 8, 14

Holland, 260
Hollywood, Calif., 3-17, 168
Hollywood Canteen, 17
Hollywood High School, 3-4, 7, 9, 16
Hors de combat, definition of, 105-6
Horsa gliders, 263, 265, 269
Houffalize (Belgium), 190, 212
Howard, Michael, 269-70
Howitzers, 105, 166, 200, 265

Iceland, 136
"I Got Sixpence," 60, 61
Im Westen Nichts Neues (Remarque), 154
Induction, 16
Italy, 137
"I've Been Working on the Railroad," 60, 62, 127

Jackman, Isadore S., 273
Jaeckel, Richard, 9
"Jake." *See* Dalton, J. C.
Japan, planned invasion of, 271
Jump commands, 87-89
Jumps, 120-23, 125-31, 137; first, 115-17; Operation Varsity, 254-71
Jump tower, 84, 90
Jump training: B stage, 79-97; C stage, 84-85, 98-109; D stage, 85, 110-33
Jump uniforms, issue of, 81
Jungvolk Fähnlein, 14

Keast, William R., xii
Kensington (England), 146
Kent, Lt. Col., 270
Kies, Maj., 159, 240
K-98 Mauser rifles, 156, 225, 226
Korean War, xx, 49
K-rations, 183

Labrador, 136
Lamarr, Hedy, 10
Lamour, Dorothy, 93
Langston, Frank, 273
Lawson Field, Ga., 80, 110, 115, 122, 127
Legion of Merit, 273
Leinbaugh, William P., xii
Leverson, Mark, 93, 107, 108, 131, 160
Line of departure (LD), definition of, 73
Listening post (LP), 187
Live fire training, 71
Liverpool, arrival in, 136-37
London, visit to, 144-46
Longparish (England), 144
Lorre, Peter, 10
Los Angeles Armed Forces Induction Station No. 2, 16
Luftwaffe, 250
Luxembourg, 199, 219-33, 234-47

Index

M-1 rifles, 47, 52–54, 130, 213; jumping with, 122
M-2 rifles, 166, 199
MacArthur, Douglas, 271
Machine guns, 47, 194, 245. *See also* German guns; *specific types*
Madame Tussaud's Wax Museum, 145
Mande St. Etienne (Bastogne), 169–88, 230
Maps, learning to read, 57–59
Marches, 71; description of, 60–62
Marshall, S. L. A., xiii
Meals. *See* Food
Medics, firing on, 178
Men against Fire (Marshall), xiii
The Men of Company K (Campbell), xii
Mess sergeant, importance of, 140
Mess supervision, 94
Meuse River, 153, 155
Miley, William ("Bud"), 134
Miller, A. C. ("Ace"), 182, 183, 184, 186–88, 211
Miller, William E., 273
Mines, scouting, 216–17
Mission, importance of, 77
Mitchell, William C., xiii, 254–72
Moir, William, 148
Monterey County, Calif., xix
Montgomery, Bernard, 254, 255, 257, 262
Mora, Tony, 141, 160, 213, 214–15, 217, 218
Mortars, 48; 60-mm, 190, 200; 81-mm, 160, 190
Motorscooters, 149
Mourmelon-le-Grand (France), 153, 248
Movies, 67, 94–97
Münster (Germany), 266; advance on, 270

Naturalization, getting certificate of, 135–36
Nazi movement, 13
Nebelwerfer (fog thrower) rockets, 172, 177
Neufchateau (Belgium), 158, 163
Nicklin, Jeff, 268–69
Niederwiltz (Luxembourg), 219–31, 234–47
Nijmegen (Holland), 148
Normandy invasion, 137, 257, 263
North Africa, 148

"Oakie," 22, 24, 26
Oberwiltz (Luxembourg), 231
Obley, William, 160, 165, 170
Obstacle course, 70–71
"Oklahoma," 224
187th Airborne Regimental Combat Team, xx, xxi
101st Airborne Division, 148, 155, 271, 272
194th Glider Regiment, 260, 273
Operation Market Garden, 254, 255, 357
Operation Plunder, 254
Operation Varsity, xxii, 249, 254–71; casualties in, 268; description of, 260–71; German defenses in, 255–57; losses in, 263, 268–69; number of troops in, 260, 261; positions of units in, 266, 267; situation before, 255, 256; supply drops for, 266; tactical plan for, 257–60, 261
Order to Report for Induction, 16
The Organization of Ground Combat Troops, xii
Our River, 202–18, 223, 230, 234, 236, 241; attempt to cross, 242–44; description of, 242
Outer Hebrides, 136

Palladium (Hollywood), 10, 13, 14
Palmer, Robert R., xii
Panzergrenadiere, 199, 201
Parachute basic training I, 49–62
Parachute basic training II, 63–78
Parachute landing fall (PLF), 84, 90, 100
Parachutes, 85–86, 100–101
Paratrooper song, lyrics to, 126–28
Paris, as takeoff point, 257, 259
Patch, arm, 124, 125, 134
Patton, George, 206, 249
"Peanut patch" drop zone, 125
Peters, George, 273
Photographs, aerial, 59
Physical examination, 12
Piccadilly, 146
"Pinocchio," 103
Pistols, 48
PRC-300 radio, 180
Prisoners, interrogation of, 177, 213–16
The Procurement and Training of Ground Combat Troops (Palmer, Wiley, and Keast), xii
Promotion to sergeant, 248
Purple Heart, 273

Quadrangle (Fort Benning), 35
"Quit slip," 38, 54, 55

Radios: AN/PRC-300, 186; PRC-300, 180
RAF Coastal Command, 136
Regimental review, 78
Reichswehr, 7
Remarque, Erich Maria, 154
Resistance, 226–27
Retreat, 195–99; German, 223
Reveille, 59–60
Rheims (France), 153
"Rhine jump," 254, 273, 274, 275. *See also* Operation Varsity
Rhineland campaign, 257
Rhine River, 249, 254; Allied advance on, 255; jump across, 262
Ridgeway, Matthew B., 148
Rifle qualification, 63–67

Rifles: care and cleaning of, 52–54, 65; German, 156. *See also specific types*
"Rifle squad in the attack," 72–75
Rigging, for first jump, 111–12
Rockett, Capt., 137, 160, 205, 244
Roosevelt, Franklin D., 74
Rope climbing, 70
Rosen, David, 202
Royal Tiger tank, 192–93
Ruhr Valley, 254, 255

S-2, assignment to, 137–39
S-2, training for, 144–50
Saint-Mihiel (France), 153
Salisbury Plain (England), 136
Sandhills area (N.C.), 130
Savoy (London), 145
Schlemm, Alfred, 256
Schmeisser, 197, 245
"School of the soldier," 29
Schützenlöcher (German foxholes), 220
Scouting enemy command post, 219–23
Scots Guard Brigade, 270
"Screaming meemies," 172
Sequitis bastatii, 107
Seventeenth Airborne Division (American), xxii, 134, 252, 257, 260, 266; awards to, 273; casualties of, 264, 268, 274–75; in occupied Germany, 271. *See also* 507th Parachute Infantry Regiment; 513th Parachute Infantry Regiment
Seventh Army, in occupied Germany, xx, xxii
Seventh Parachute Division, 256
Sharpshooter, qualifying for, 63–65, 67
Shetland Islands, 136
Siegfried Line, 212, 230, 234, 236, 242, 243
Silver Star, 273
Sinatra, Frank, 94
Sixth Airborne Division (British), 256, 257, 262, 265, 266; casualties of in Operation Varsity, 268
Sixth Guard Armored Brigade, 266, 271
Snipers, 165, 175
Songs, marching: "I Got Sixpence," 60, 61; "I've Been Working on the Railroad," 60, 62, 127
Southhampton (England), 71; devastation in, 146; tactical exercises in, 147–48
Spanische Reiter (Spanish riders), 224
Spears, John H., 49, 60, 110, 202, 211, 240
Squad: becoming leader of, 75–78; importance of, 77
SS panzer division, 177
Stenay (France), 153
Streicher, Julius, 140
The Struggle for Europe, 249
Stryker, Stuart S., 273

Sturmgewehre, 199
Submachine guns. *See* German guns; Thompson submachine gun; *specific types*

"Tactical feeding," 66, 164
The Talon: With the 17th in Ardennes (Miller and Youngblood, eds.), 273
Tanks, 192, 193
Taunton Staging Area, 135, 136
Taylor, Alton, 184, 212, 240, 243
Telephones, EE8, 185, 187
Texas (battleship), 136
Third Army, 206
Third Battalion (British), 270
Thirteenth Airborne Division, 271
Thompson submachine gun, 47, 54, 141, 158, 171, 182
Tidworth (England), scouting in, 144
Tidworth Barracks, 136, 137
Toland, John, xiii
Towers, description of control, 99
Training, S-2, 144, 146–47, 148, 149–50. *See also* Jump training; Parachute basic training
Treppendahl, Lt., 163
Trocadero, 158
Tug of war, 70
224th Airborne Medical Company, awards to, 273

Ulsters, casualties of in Operation Varsity, 268
Uniforms, 95–96; issue of, 28–29. *See also* Jump uniforms
U.S.S. *Washington*, 136

Van Creveld, Martin, xii
Veidt, Conrad, 10
Verdun, 153
Viet Nam, 49
Volksturn, 255
Volunteering, 3–4

Waco gliders, 263
WACs, 135
Walton, Ruth, 7–9, 12–17, 95, 168
Weapons, 47–48; German positions in Operation Varsity, 257, 258; issue of, 52–54. *See also* German guns; *specific weapons*
Wehrmacht, 7
Wesel (Germany), 254, 255, 256, 257, 265, 266
Wesel jump, casualties in, 275
White, Peter, 137–38, 156, 157, 160, 184, 190, 199, 202, 211, 213, 240, 241, 242–44, 248
Whitelaw, John L., 210–11
Wiley, Bell I., xii
Wilmot, Chester, 248–49

Wiltz (Luxembourg), 231, 240
Winchester (England), 144
Wind machine, 90
"Windmill Hill" (England), 136, 144
Wings, presentation of, 132–33

World War I, 153

Young, Farrin, 95
Youngblood, Nat H., 273